HALL

ANTON**MARKS**

The **X** Press

Published in United Kingdom by
The X Press
6 Hoxton Square, London N1 6NU
Tel: 0171 729 1199
Fax: 0171 729 1771

Printed by Caledonian International Book Manufacturing Ltd, Glasgow, UK.

Distributed in UK by Turnaround Distribution, Unit 3, Olympia Trading Estate,
Coburg Road, London N22 6TZ
Tel: 0181 829 3000
Fax: 0181 881 5088

ISBN 1-874509-19-0

ACKNOWLEDGMENTS

This work of fiction would not have been possible if not for a number of people and organisations who have given me their time, enthusiasm and most of all provided me with inspiration.

My appreciation goes out to all of you.

The X-Press publishing team.

Dotun Adebayo, Steve Pope.

Victor Headley, for taking the first steps, no one else dared.

The 'community stations' massive (Dem ah call us 'pirates'): Ragga FM, Powerjam FM, Vibes FM, Elite FM, Frontline and Unityfresh (Manchester). And all the others (too numerous to mention), up and down the country, who keep the music flowing and without whom, many of us would not be able to survive another day ah foreign…Before I forget my manners: to all unuh deejays (too black too strong!) who risk personal freedom to play the people's music…what can I say but EXCESS amount of RESPECT in every ASPECT.

Ranking Miss P: For always being at the end of my dial from way back when, and for still being there every Friday night with your Friday Night Jam and Sunday Best on 94.9FM (London)

Choice FM, Daddy Ernie and Commander B. For the vibes.

Kiss FM, David Rodigan for providing me with a mere taste of his encyclopedic knowledge of the music of kings, Reggae.

Addie's Intl. Sound System (NYC): Selector Baby Face.

Fifth Avenue, Dalston Junction: Thanks Debbie for providing the outfits for the models on the cover and for having the best collection of Dancehall couture in London. Wicked!

Barber Plaza and **Avant Garde** in Harlesden.

To the Teacher, Daddy U-Roy. We shook hands and spoke briefly but I knew that in the dawn of Dancehall, without the innovative toasting skills of yourself and King Stitt, Reggae Dancehall as we know it would not exist.

Fads (II) Boutiques: Rudy, for being an inspirational friend.

Clay Maclean. Me breddah. For sharing your insightful and unique philosophy of life, boss. Especially when I needed it. Big Up!

And last but not least to my family, who never lost faith.

Inspirations for writing this novel came from
the pioneering work of Shabba Ranks
and the other great deejays
Respect!

Reggae Dancehall? It ah spread like wildfire man, bruk wide.
Shabba Ranks, New Kingston

Me give a warnin' to de big man dem, me warn dem to stop
pressure de youth dem. Too much pressure 'pon the youth, that's
why de youth them a war an' a rob and a shoot, poverty, it a
build up crime, and that is not a lie.
Cutty Ranks, Penthouse Studios

Dung inna de ghetto when de gun harbour t'ing,
An de politician wid de gun dem a bring,
An' de crack an' de coke it a promote de killing,
Me check it out, de whole ah dem, ah de same t'ing
Bounty Killa, lyrics from single 'Dung Inna De Ghetto'

ONE

Gimme de gal wid de wickedest slam
De kinda gal who know how fe love up she man
An' if yuh waan fe get de medal
Yuh haffe get a slam, from a real ghetto gal
Lyrics from Beenie Man's hit single 'Slam'

"You can bubble, eh Ranking," she whispered in his ear.

"How you mean, baby? 'Champion Bubbler' dem call me, yuh nevah know?" Simba Ranking smiled, whining expertly to the slow groove, Sonia tight against him. The lovers' rock music vibrated loudly from the battered speakers, its rough edges annoying to a digital stereo ear, but posed no problem for the ghetto people who were there to dance and enjoy themselves. This was no uptown 'cool profile' establishment. This was a dancehall in its rawest form, the sound reflected the feel of the people — rugged and uncompromising. Tonight Simba felt mellow, easy.

The woman in his arms snuggled even closer, her head on his chest, totally relaxed. She moved with him as if they were seasoned dance partners. No clumsy stepping on toes, she knew all the moves and much more.

Dis fit t'ing yah definitely have potential, Simba thought, but as always he kept his options open and scoped the venue from pillar to post. He was glad he had made the right move at the right time. The girl was not only 'fit', but also fresh on the scene, a new face to the jaded dancehall circuit.

From the moment he prepped her entering the dance, he figured that here was a woman who knew what she had and

1

knew what to do with it. Shaped like a Coca-Cola bottle, she drew the hungry stares of the sharks in the place and with good reason. She had a small waistline, a big batty and a sweet little face. Like a lobster she had all 'de meat inna de tail' and the Ranking loved that. He couldn't resist such a combination at the best of times, but under his sensi she was positively irresistible. What finally made up his mind about being with this woman tonight was how she danced to herself. Doing the 'tatty' in her corner without any backative, confident enough to go to a dance without a posse in toe.

Tonight was her lucky night.

Simba casually looked around, still held close to his new woman and clocked the familiar faces — the good, the bad and the ugly, all situated about a 'lawn' bustling with activity. He spied Big Breast Patsy from Twelfth Street leaning on the bar, Bow-Legged Sharon from Portmore stood to her right, deep in conversation, and Cherry Lips Barbara, 'the whining machine' over by the turntables.

Tonight Simba wasn't in the mood for the old faces. He needed a new vibe and he felt only Sonia could give it to him. There was no disrespect to the ghetto girls that he knew and loved, but for a 'cocks man' that was just the runnings.

And so two smiles and a Heineken later it was as if Simba and Sonia had known each other for years.

She gripped him tighter still, her lips moving silently to the words of the song as she pressed herself closer to him. Simba felt the softness of her breasts and smelt her perfume. He kept his thoughts of slackness in control for the real thing that he knew would come later. He pulled her even closer so that their lips were touching, albeit lightly, and their crotches rubbing against each other, their waists rotating in perfect sync, as only true 'bubblers' could.

The girl was sexy, no doubt about that, and she knew it. Simba's hardness made his point of view crystal clear, but he was in no rush to get away and neither was she. When it came to romancing the women he regarded himself as a connoisseur amongst Yard man. He believed his reputation must precede him at all times, even if it meant a few well-placed lies. Because women talked, and when they talked about him he wanted them to say he was the best. He liked to give the impression of cool detachment, a man who didn't care one way or another what happened because women were no problem for him.

The Ranking had to rush, 'no gal'.

His hand slipped down to her backside cautiously and caressed it in full. Sonia cooed with pleasure, a signal in Simba's ears to continue, and he did. He gripped more firmly, pulling her closer to him, the pleasure showing in his eyes.

Sonia was de lick, fe real.

Skate City was packed to the rafters with the excited faces of ghetto people as they cast off the worries and problems of political violence and day to day living and let full volume rub-a-dub music touch them to their souls. Congregated for the first time and celebrating a tentative cease fire between the warring political factions, were the people most affected by the madness from both parties, the sufferah's.

Dis dance yah ah go hot! thought Simba as he caressed the nape of Sonia's neck. Even the open air venue of the concrete skating ring could not cool it down. The music was hot and the ravers generated more heat, but it was also one of those warm Jamaican evenings, clear skies and an atmosphere filled with the scent of good sensimilla. Normally the Ranking would stay away from any dance that had a political agenda attached to it. The politics 't'ing' had corrupted and destroyed too many people's lives…many of them people he personally knew. And in his own way he had helped to spread their warped cause but he had learned since.

This unity dance was worth him breaking his promise. He had seen too much blood shed in his nineteen years, especially in the ghetto. If he could do anything to help heal the wounds and give peace a try, he would do it without a murmur. Simba sighed, releasing those thoughts and focused instead on the merriment. He blew out a gush of hot air as if that could somehow cool him down, but it only reminded him of the ever-expanding crush of people still trickling inside and more body heat. Everybody was sweating. Even the Ranking felt a bead of sweat trickle down his armpit and winced as his string vest absorbed it. On a night like this, the last thing he wanted was his crisp shirt to be damp with perspiration. His starched brown African linen shirt and matching baggy trousers had withstood the friction sparked with Sonia's whining, but streaks of sweat would not do. He needed to look and feel fresh when he held the microphone. His mind couldn't be focused on how he looked, but on delivering 'intelligent' lyrics in a style which 'no bwoy' could imitate. No matter, there was still time to cool down. Right now he wasn't about to let go of Sonia before this song was done.

The lovers' rock took its time, with Bishop, the operator eventually, barking the 'whine an' grine t'ing' to an end, making the Cool Ruler eventually fade out. It was as if Sonia hadn't even noticed, for she continued dancing seductively, with Simba tight against her. She was in no mood to let go yet. So in the few moments of silence that it took the operator to select another record, Simba took the opportunity to whisper in Sonia's ears a brief run-down of what he would like to do to her body if she gave him the chance. Sonia giggled and Simba mentally scratched one more notch on his soon-to-be-smoking gun.

"Well a'right! Unuh ah hear me, crowd ah people." Bishop's voice boomed through the speakers. "Right yah now, t'ings ah come up to bump, man." The operator's manic laughter resonated over the hum of human excitement, followed by a few bars of the theme from the movie *The Good, The Bad & The Ugly*.

"Wid no further hitch or stick, gal pickney, ah some raw-chaw dancehall business we deh 'pon man...Calling Simba Ranking! Simba Ranking, you're wanted at the I-trol tower...Ranking! Come hol' de mike, my yout'. A long time

4

you deh 'bout, boss. Step up man."

The Ranking took a deep breath and eased himself out of Sonia's tight embrace.

"Me soon come baby," he said, turning in the direction of the set. "Just keep it warm, seen."

"Nuh fret Missa Rankin, me nah go nowhere."

Sonia smiled sweetly, her hips still swinging to the tune as the young deejay disappeared through the swaying wall of ravers.

Simba made his way steadily and confidently up to the turntable. The stragglers were in their positions. The young hopefuls waiting for a bly from the selector so they could be blessed with the opportunity to chat on the mike. Simba saw himself in many of them but that was then, now he was everyone's focus. The sound was set up in the middle of the stage, an array of tape recorders of every size and form surrounding every speaker. The largest, yet invariably cheapest recorders belonged to private individuals who wanted their personal recordings of this session. The smaller, 'hi-tech' recorders belonged to unscrupulous vendors who would have the tapes duplicated several hundred times before the night was out for sale at the markets in the morning.

A true sound man didn't mind this unauthorised duplication, for they knew that it was a way of promoting their set throughout Jamaica and even internationally. Simba was a true sound man, and he considered the plethora of recording equipment to be a 'big up' rather than a diss. To him it was an achievement that tapes of Nubian Hi-Power, the sound he chatted for, had now reached as far afield as Flatbush in New York and Brixton in London.

Simba got the dancehall bug early, he had long forgotten how but he couldn't have been more than five or six years old. He remembered how, even that young, he would steal away at night to listen to the different sounds in the area, sometimes by himself and sometimes with other pubescent 'runaways', and he always got in without paying. At first, he was so small he could sneak in without the gate man seeing him. As he grew older he took to talking his way in. The only obstacle to his passion were the severe beatings with a gineppe switch which his father or Mama Christy used to dish out when he came home. But all the beatings in the world couldn't stop him. He was already hooked, and it was an addiction he had no intention of kicking.

He didn't know it at the time, but those early sessions were to be his education, because the cream of deejays passed through the sounds he followed. Reggae legends: Big Youth, U-Roy, Tapper Zukie, I-Roy, Prince Far I, Doctor Alimantado, Trinity, Brigadier Jerry...the list went on and on. These artists, some of them already stars, never forgot their roots and regularly held dances in the ghetto at ghetto rates. They inspired a whole generation of ghetto youth to make something constructive with their lives.

One such youth was the Ranking himself.

As he grew older Simba got into writing lyrics and shadowed the control towers every Saturday night for a chance at holding the coveted 'mike' to drop his new lick. The race, however, is not for the swift, but for he who endureth to the end. With only a Red Stripe beer to quench his growling hunger, Simba would sometimes wait through an entire session for his opportunity.

It was worth the wait, the music was in his blood.

Eventually his persistence paid off. Operators like Bishop and Mikey D finally decided that the young Simba was ready and started passing him the mike on a regular basis. Simba soon repaid their confidence in him by tearing up their dances week after week with his own particular mix of 'gun an' gal' lyrics. By the time he was in his teens, Simba had built up a reputation amongst the massive for being an 'up and coming' youth with 'nuff potential', and a born showman and entertainer.

If you can make it in reggae music, you can make it in any music. For the dancehall audience is as merciless as it is merciful; the hand that will big you up is the same hand that will use you as target practice. If you perform well, you won't find a more loyal crowd to boost you, but if you don't have the lyrics, the riddims, the sweet tone of voice or just as importantly a rep, you stand little chance of surviving.

Despite his street level support, Simba hadn't reached nowhere near the potential he knew he had. After all this time, he was making little money from his PAs around town. Some nights he would leave a session without enough money for a box dinner at Mr Chin's. It had got better, but nowhere near his expectations. But in time he knew things would be different, and the dance would bring him fame. Then he would proudly take his mother away from the tenement yard to a dream home in the new Portmore housing scheme, where hardship would be nothing more than a bad memory. No guns, no violence. Just music. First, though, certain things had to be worked out correctly. Particularly on the business side of things. What he really needed was a hit record to carry his voice all the way across the world. That would be it. *De big time!* His dreams of fame remained with him always, he hadn't been idle and had clapped a few tunes for a couple of producers, but nothing had been released yet.

Ah jus' time.

As Simba mounted the stage and took the microphone from Bishop, he felt the butterflies flutter in his stomach as they always did. Even after all this time, it still gave him an adrenaline rush to stand in front of a crowd with a mike in his hand. There was something breathlessly sexy about the power it gave him and at the same time it chilled him to realise that one slip would result in public humiliation, not just in Kingston, or Jamaica, but outernationally. It was too late for second thoughts. His natural talent would take over as it always did, and the lyrics would flow. This was his ultimate calling in life, and it deserved nothing but his best.

"I waan big up all de girls dem," Simba's hoarse voice growled through the speakers. "Cah Simba love unuh bad, man. Sonia, hol' it tight, seen?"

He paused momentarily, then exploded into the

microphone:

"OPERATOR, COME DUNG!"

The operator did, and a wicked riddim followed.

Like a veteran, Simba 'rode' it with ease. He seemed to know just the right combination of words to thrill or amuse the audience. As the rhymes shot from his mouth like bullets, the crowd swayed with him. He lifted their spirits with his brand of reality lyrics, and dramatised every line like a seasoned actor. The crowd responded with unrestrained enthusiasm. Simba Ranking was a deejay who spoke to their hearts and to their feet:

Oh yes!
Me done know, nobody haffe fe tell me
Dunkirk gal dem have de whinry
Me done know, wid a matic ah mi brain,
Ghetto living is pure hardship an' pain
So all bad man, de Ranking a show dem
PACKAM! PACKAM! *Is not de solution*

The Ranking hit them with a mixed set of cultural and bad bwoy lyrics to show his lyrical dexterity. And when he called confidently for the downtown posse to "flash unuh lighta," his request was met instantly as lighter flames lit up the lawn. The boisterous shouts of his name above the din of special sound effects from Bishop was evidence enough that he had pleased them.

"Live good inna yuh neighbourhood."

He finished on a high.

"Rule!!!""

His set over, Simba passed the mike to the next deejay in line, a Greenwich Farm youth called Woodpecker, who arrogantly strode on stage with a look that could only be described as sheer contempt for everyone and everything. He held the mike close with both hands, lips twisted in a screw just as the tune burst from the speakers. And just like his bad attitude a flow of lyrics came from his mouth filled with obscenities and threats directed at the rival opposition party. His intentions were made even clearer. As the tune continued he stepped up his torrent of abuse, intent on upsetting the peaceful vibes. The fact that the session was being held in opposition party territory didn't seem to perturb him, he just continued to cuss them, relentlessly.

A fearless but suicidal move.

The crowd, which consisted of mainly opposition party supporters, started to show signs of a mood swing. The feelings of 'one love' were transforming to agitation and hostility. People began cursing openly. A bottle arced out of the audience, shattering to Woodpecker's left, warning enough for him to stop what he was doing and exit the stage...quickly. But instead he simply threatened the anonymous culprit and persisted to the very end of his set. When he'd finished, Woodpecker came off the stage with a sardonic grin on his face.

He was aware that he had upset many people who had come to Skate city to forget, but he didn't care, and simply stepped into the midst of his posse who circled him in a protective shield. They were not intimidated by the vicious stares in their direction, but simply kept their hands very close to their waists.

The vibe had changed for the worst. Simba, feeling edgy, led Sonia towards the exit at the far end of the rink. He'd been going to dances long enough to spot the signs of trouble. He saw the expressions of anger caused by Woodpecker's insults, spread through the ravers like ripples through a pool of water.

Suddenly he recognised a man out in the middle of the crowd, and the sight sent a cold shiver down his spine. It was Tony Hewitt, a local gunman for the opposition party. His cap was pulled low over his eyes, but Simba could still recognise his unsmiling face.

"Bloodclaat, de don deh on yah."

Simba's stomach tightened at the implications. *What was he doing here, tonight of all nights?*

Tony Hewitt and his men protected the opposition party's interests in his neighbourhood. Depending on who was making the assessment, Hewitt was either a cold-blooded murderer or a Robin Hood of the sufferah. Either way, he was a ruthless legend. Everybody knew the story of how he had survived an ambush in the night by a rival posse outside a dance when he was shot eight times, taking two in the head and one in the groin.

Hewitt went after the men who ambushed him and put exactly eight bullets, including two in the head and one in the groin, into each one. None of them survived.

Simba knew that Tony Hewitt didn't take to people 'dissing' his party. He had a bad feeling about this. The gunman's sudden appearance could only mean one thing.

Trouble inna de dance.

The Ranking watched keenly as the gunman disappeared and reappeared amongst the revellers near Woodpecker. Hewitt stood glaring through the crowds at the deejay who had dissed not just his party but him personally.The young DJ was too preoccupied with his spars to have noticed anything out of the ordinary.

Simba grimaced. It was as if he was the only person in the dance who had seen what was going down. He sized up the situation and imagined the carnage that was about to unfold. As bad as Tony Hewitt was, he was on his own, while Woodpecker had a posse of five or six ruffnecks around him. Simba figured that at least one of them must be strapped for them to be so bold in the first place.

If more than one of them had a gun, it would be a bloodbath. He had to think fast. It was about to go down, but there was nothing he could do to warn anybody else. Maybe he was imagining the whole thing. Still, he decided, *see an' blind hear an' deaf*, the unspoken code of the street.

"What you seh we leave dis place yah, now baby," said Simba with a wink of his eye, trying to play down the urgency of his request.

"You horny, eh man. Mek we wait lickle first nuh," she teased him smiling.

But Simba was no longer in any mood for games. He took Sonia's hand and led her towards the exit. Sonia protested a first, but only halfheartedly, looking forward to what the lover man had to offer.

10

Simba couldn't help feeling a twinge of cowardice as they stepped through the gate into the cool night air. He would have previously hung around to watch the altercation between the gunman and Woodpecker, but his days of guns and badness were over. He left that to the young bloods who could not be reasoned with.

Too many of his friends had died for the sake of politics or survival, his name wasn't going to be added to the list. As long as neither he nor his family were being threatened directly, he didn't want to know.

Simba skipped across the road with Sonia beside him. There was virtually no traffic on the Constant Spring Road even though the 'state of emergency' had recently been lifted by the government. As he led the way towards his parked Honda 90, Sonia laughed aloud.

"Ah you dis, Ranking?" she burst out, pointing to the rusty motorbike. "You sure it can manage two people?"

The Ranking shrugged his shoulders. "Yuh see *my* wheels, me nuh want no gal diss it, seen. When me change it fe a Ninja next week, you same one ah go want fe spread out 'pon it…so if yuh ah come, just hitch 'pon de back."

Sonia was hesitant at first, but decided that a Honda 90 was better than no transport at all, but only just. She climbed on, lapping her skirt under her, and held onto Simba from behind. She wasn't convinced in the slightest by Simba's boast but that didn't matter, she would enjoy the 'ride' in any form it came.

As he cranked the engine to life the sound of gunshots rang out from across the road.

"Jesas Christ!" Sonia squealed, as screams of panic pierced the night air. As he revved up the 90 another volley of gun fire erupted from Skate City.

Simba didn't even flinch; to him the outcome was obvious. Unconcerned, he simply eased the bike away from the kerb, looking forward to a night of serious 'bed wuk'. He would read about the carnage in the *Daily Gleaner* tomorrow.

No problem.

TWO

A very attractive woman in her late twenties, Monique St. John stood at the window in her brown Escada business suit, looking down at the traffic on Knutsford Boulevard, taking in the activity of the lunch-time rush with a vacant stare.

The sun was at its height, and although she felt relieved that her office was comfortably cool she still yearned to be out on a beach, away from the mundane work regime.

But these were dangerous times, and even though this part of Kingston was relatively unaffected by the civil war that threatened to engulf the so-called garrison constituencies, you could never be too careful.

She walked back to her desk and cast a critical eye over the front page of the morning's *Daily Gleaner*. *'Deejay shot dead at dance'* screamed the headline.

It was just another painful statistic amidst the mounting paranoia everyone felt. What could you believe as the papers continued to fuel the speculation and confusion? *'CIA dirty tricks campaign destabilises nation'* or *'KGB funded terrorists seek to derail fair elections'*...

Monique sighed. *These were crazy times.* Gun law was not a part of her world, but she could not help imagining how the families and especially the children downtown survived amidst the guns and death.

She was the typical uptown girl, fair-skinned with long coffee-coloured hair, a lithe body and smooth features which could have been carved by a master sculptor. She carried herself well, leaving no one in doubt that she was from the very finest breeding that Jamaican high society could offer; but in actual fact she wasn't.

Her family and background were much more modest than that. She had subsequently married into wealth, power and social status, but as a young girl she had known meagre times; now she identified more with the rougher areas of town, even though she was originally from the country. They understood real hardship, and she could relate with that. It was more than could be said for her peer group, who had only heard about suffering and the ghetto in the songs of Bob Marley.

But sufferation was a distant memory. Now she was the toast of every social gala, the envy of many of her female counterparts, and admired by several of the richest and most powerful men in the Caribbean. For she was Monique St. John, business executive and wife of Hugh Bartholomew St. John, known to his associates and enemies alike as the Saint. Hugh was one of the handful of men who could claim to 'own' Jamaica, or at least have a firm down payment on the mortgage.

It would have been easy for Monique to fall victim to the 'hype' associated with her wealth, but she had her feet firmly on the ground. She was under no illusions about her position in life, or the reason influential men regularly showered her with gifts. They may very well have found her charming, as they claimed, but their enthusiasm was spurred on by other desires.

They practically clambered over each other in their attempts to lure her into bed, but with no success. They ignored the fact that she was married…or was it so obvious that she was miserable and unhappy?

Since she said 'I do' to her 'dream man' three years ago, many of Monique's illusions about marriage had been shattered. She had known that Hugh was a shrewd businessman and a cunning politician when they first met, and that made him even more attractive to her.

But she had never expected such a drastic change from suave rascal to a pure raas.

There was no other word to describe the man she had married, the man who treated her like she was an appendage to his power politics, the man who had grown so accustomed to getting his own way in everything that married bliss became a living nightmare. Monique discovered too late that all the money in the world couldn't give her what she wanted the most, to be loved and to give love in return.

It might have been bearable if they had started a family. That would have at least been some small consolation for an unfulfilled marriage. With two or three kids around she would have concentrated on being a mother and wouldn't have cared less if her husband came home drunk after three whole days of womanising.

But a family wasn't to be. From the first night of their honeymoon her husband had rejected the idea of children outright, with no explanation. No manner of pleading and scheming from her would make Hugh change his mind.

At the time she had tried to put on a brave face, to give Hugh time, because she truly wanted her marriage to work. But she couldn't keep that up for long. Why was Hugh being so obstinate? What was wrong with having children? Several times he had dismissed the question as if Monique was making a big deal over nothing, but she didn't let up. Arguing with him had alleviated some of her anguish, but she viewed a marriage without children as untenable. Things had been further compounded by Hugh's behaviour over the last six months. The Saint had threatened to slap her on numerous occasions, and even tried to a few times. In reply Monique had threatened to kill him, and given out all the signs of a desperate woman who would take desperate measures. It had kept him at bay, but she didn't know for how long.

What little affection she had left for him had disappeared over time and now there was nothing left. His ego seemed to have grown to the point where he seriously believed that he could disrespect his wife and then rub shoulders with his colleagues as a respectable politician. What she missed the most, though, was how interesting he was to her in the beginning of their relationship. She wanted to know everything about his work life as the CEO and owner of Tuff Construction.

In those days the stories he would tell her about his travels and the people he met as Member of Parliament in Western Kingston were always a high point for her when they met in the evening. But she should have realised how selfish he was, as he never once asked Monique how her day went.

Gone was the sparklingly clever man she had married. Hugh now reserved his wit and intelligence for his string of women. The only thing outside of sex that seemed to interest him now was power.

Monique, on the other hand, longed for some adventure in her life, something more than her responsibilities as Director of Tourism and Promotions could provide. More than anything she needed a bigger challenge in her life than Hugh St. John.

But could she really simply walk out of her marriage? It wouldn't be easy to give up everything she had built up for an uncertain future, but more importantly she didn't know whether she had the energy or resources to protect herself in the inevitable fight with Hugh.

She knew her husband didn't allow anybody to walk out on him, and she had been married to him long enough to know what he did to those who dared. Her intuition had told her long ago that the rumours about the Saint had more truth in them than she would like to admit.

An uncontrolled sigh of frustration left her lips as she considered her options. *Maybe it's better not to rock the boat and just carry on the way things are.* Her thoughts were interrupted by a knock on the door.

She turned around to see just the plump bespectacled face of Debbie, her new personal secretary, peering around the door at her. The older woman smiled.

"The meeting with the Japanese tourist delegation has been set for six o'clock this evening, Mrs St. John."

She entered.

"Your brief is on your desk."

Debbie wondered if she was getting through. Her boss' thoughts seemed to be thousands of miles away.

"It will give you a good idea of who you'll be talking to and give you the opportunity to practice pronouncing some ah dem name deh."

She grinned at her own humour, Monique simply nodded. Debbie looked up at the wall clock, surprised that it read 12.15 already; she didn't want to miss her lunch date.

"I'll be leaving for lunch now, Mrs St. John," she said, raising her voice to make sure that it registered clearly with her boss. "Was there anything else you wanted me to do?"

"You go ahead, Debbie," Monique said, her attention shifting back to work. "I won't be back in the office today anyway, so I'll make preparations for this evening's meeting from home. If you need me I'll be there." She paused thoughtfully. "And if you want to leave early today, you can. You deserve it."

"Thanks Mrs St. John," Debbie beamed. "And I'll see you in the morning."

She walked through the door and closed it silently behind her.

Monique eased her white BMW through the traffic, wondering whether to have lunch at a Chinese restaurant or have her cook prepare a meal. She decided to head for home, and cruised east through the sunny streets to the hills, pumping the pedals in her stockinged feet. Barry Gordon's midday show thumped out the sound of Lt. Stitchie's *Young Gal Wear Yuh Size*. Monique nodded in time to the rhythms, her thoughts tracing the long journey she had taken from her roots in Westmoreland. She was born in the bushes of Cornwall Mountain to an American father she never knew and a Jamaican mother who worked in hotels in

Negril, to support her daughter through the Common Entrance exam and Immaculate Conception High School in Kingston, where Monique graduated as head girl with the best 'A' level passes in her year. Then she studied for a degree in Mass Communications at the University of the West Indies, which she received with honours.

Now she had money, power and influence too. But she had learned the hard way that the best things in life are free. It costs nothing to retain your pride or your roots.

She stopped the BMW at the traffic lights on Old Hope Road; home was not far away now. She started to edge the car up the moderate incline at the foot of Beverly Hills, past the extravagant homes of the rich and famous. She'd often thought that the 'Hill' was like a reflection of society. On the way up, every level was occupied by someone with more power and influence than the level below. At the peak, where she was heading, were the movers and shakers of Jamaican high society; the crème de la crème. An enviable position in most people's books, but her appreciation of her status had died along with her appetite for married life.

She slowed the BMW to a standstill in front of the ominous-looking electric gates of her home. Marshall, the new security guard, came out of his tiny cabin yawning.

What's wrong with this jackass? she asked herself as she waited for him to open the gates. How this dimwit had ever been licensed to carry a gun was beyond her.

"Is there a problem, Marshall...or is it that I have to be waiting in the hot sun until you decide to let me through?"

Her sarcastic tone was edged with irritation.

The guard stopped suddenly and seemed flustered.

"S-s-s-so...sorry Missus St John. Me nevah certain ah you, Ma'am," he called out, waving the car forward quickly to hide his embarrassment. Monique kissed her teeth and drove through with a screech of tyres. She could not believe that he was not familiar with her car after a week on the job.

Monique parked the car, slipped her high heels back on and hurried up the steps to the heavy mahogany front door. In the hallway she called out to Maude the cook, but there

17

was no answer. She sighed and made her way to the kitchen.

It was spotless, with no sign of the cook. Monique remembered it was Maude's day off. She slipped off her shoes and rubbed her slender feet. *Might as well get out of this suit for a start*, she thought, and padded off down the long corridor to the master bedroom. Nearing her bedroom door she noticed a cheap blue blouse, certainly not one of hers, on the polished wooden floor, then realised there was a trail of discarded clothes on the floor leading to her room.

As Monique stepped closer to the bedroom door, she heard the sound of muffled moans from inside. Her heart sank and her anger flared. How could the bastard do this to her in her own home? She eased the bedroom door open, and her anger turned rapidly to craziness.

Pepy, the maid, was on the bed, on her back, legs parted wide, groaning with pleasure. Hugh St. John was between her legs, fondling her large breasts in time with his thrusting hips, sucking her ear lobes ravenously, a low moan escaping his lips. They rocked together like ebony and ivory, him white-skinned and she a dark coffee brown.

Monique spun away from the spectacle and headed for the utility room. From the top shelf in the tool cupboard she pulled out a 9mm Browning automatic wrapped in chamois cloth. She unwrapped it and headed back down the hall. How ironic, her husband had given her the gun to protect herself but she'd never needed to use it before. Now, it seemed, she'd be using it on him.

The fucking dog and this slut haven't even noticed, she thought as she entered the bedroom. The maid lifted her backside off the bed to meet him with increased speed, and wrapped her legs around his waist, then the excitement overcame her. Her ecstatic wail as she came in multiple shudders, sent a shiver down Monique's back.

She clicked the safety catch off and aimed the gun at the couple on the bed...

Monique had always loved the good life. Her mother had

18

said it was her American blood. Free enterprise and the American way. It was funny how her mother really believed that.

Monique had always had a head for business. She had sugar daddies even at school, rich benefactors who were willing to do almost anything for this 'fit young t'ing'. These boopsies were often frustrated when they realised too late that they would never 'pick de cherry', and that she was getting more from them than she was giving in return.

"Yuh will make some powerful man de ideal wife."

Her mother had made predictions about her future all through her life, but that one actually became true.

After school, her beauty and charm opened doors for her all the way to the top of society. And then she met the 'powerful man', self-made millionaire politician Hugh St. John, and they married. The *Daily Gleaner* described it as a 'story book union'.

St. John was on the verge of orgasm. At the edge of his awareness, he heard the safety catch click. He blinked, then opened his eyes and saw his wife.

In shock he swallowed his groan of sexual release. The dark image of Monique standing in the doorway with the gun held in both hands, made his cock go limp in a second, the prospect of being shot chilling him to the core.

"I hope you had an enjoyable fuck."

Monique's voice wavered slightly, as did the gun.

"Monique! Wha...what you t'ink you doing, woman?" he blustered, leaping up in the bed. Beside him, the maid crawled up to the bedhead in abject horror, her eyes like saucers and mouth stupidly open.

"What am I doing? You dutty dog, is what the fuck you *t'ink* I'm doing?" she said, close to tears.

"Monique, fe God sake, *please* put the gun down. Someone might get hurt..."

Hugh tried not to let his fear show on his face.

She had never heard her husband use the word 'please'

in all the years she'd known him. Maybe a gun to his head could clear up his ego problems after all.

Monique pointed the gun at the woman sobbing on the bed. Pepy was trying to cover her nudity with both hands, but with breasts that size, it was an impossible task.

"Miss Monique," she cowered as her mistress approached, "me nevah mean fe do it, please nuh shoot me ma'am. Ah Missa St. John, him nevah stop bother me an' feel me up an' ah put argument to me. Him promise fe gi' me money an' me did waan buy a frock fe go ah dance…"

Pepy's pleas were abruptly silenced as St. John sprang towards her with his hand raised.

"Shut yuh fucking mouth, you lying bitch!"

The back of his hand lashed across her face, knocking her off the bed.

"Stop!" Monique screamed.

She pointed the gun at the maid, who was wailing as she struggled to pick herself up. "Come outta me fucking house, and I never want to see your ugly ass again. You got that?"

"Eh-heh! Eh-heh!" Pepy garbled, nodding her head frantically with relief at the reprieve. She hesitated for a moment, as it crossed her mind that this might be a ploy by Monique to shoot her in the back, then grabbed what she could find of her clothes and headed for the open door.

"Get the fuck out of my sight," Monique screamed.

The maid disappeared.

"So wha' you ah go do now, Miss Monique?" asked St. John. He had his fear under control now and was sneering at her. He moved closer.

"I swear to God, Hugh, if you come any closer I will castrate you with a bullet."

He stopped in his tracks.

"How could you do this to me, Hugh? In my *home*, in my *bed*, with the fucking *maid*? I knew you were scum and you couldn't be trusted, but seeing it with my own eyes…"

"Don't bother with it," Hugh sighed. "Don't even think about getting into the jealous wife routine, woman. You trying to tell me that you've been faithful to me all this time?

Don't try an' take me fe no poppy show."

A smug smile returned to his face as his comment seemed to fluster his wife slightly. He stepped closer, but Monique waved him back.

"I'm not on trial here. I've been faithful throughout our marriage. You were the one fucking around in *our* home, *my* bed. Couldn't you have shown some respect and taken her to a whore house or something?"

"The heart was willing, but the flesh is weak…"

His smile broadened and he inched closer to her.

"You think this is funny, you bastard?"

She aimed between her husband's eyes, but the Saint maintained his cool.

"All this over-reacting serves no purpose."

He was three steps away from her, his voice a whisper.

"We all make mistakes, nuh true?"

"Don't even try…" Monique warned, but Hugh was too quick. He leapt forward, grabbed the gun and wrenched it from her grip.

"You were just in an enviable position, Mrs St. John, and you wasted it," he smirked. "You realise how many man would like to do that as well as pull the trigger, woman. Plenty." He laughed out loud. "You're a lucky woman because you're mine but don't push yuh raas luck. Now come out yah before I really lose my temper."

He pushed her through the door.

"Two can play at your game," Monique warned.

"No Monique, get it right. *I* can play, but nobody else." His smile slowly soured into an impassive scowl. "You know exactly which side yuh bread butter woman…you're not in a state to talk sensible right now. So until you are you'd better leave before you do something silly again."

He turned his back on her and kicked the bedroom door shut. Monique knew that meant the end of the discussion as far as her husband was concerned.

For her it wasn't the end, not by a long shot. It was just the beginning.

THREE

Monique squirmed uncomfortably in her seat as the meeting at the Kingston Chamber of Commerce droned on into its third hour. Her mind had been wandering in and out of the proceedings.

Try as she might to think about other things, she couldn't stop remembering Hugh screwing the maid in her bed. She had never really thought about how something like that might affect her.

Now she knew. If any of her past feelings for him had remained, now there was nothing. The single tenuous thread which had held them together, the respect for their home and their memories was broken. There was nothing left.

That hurt. But what hurt her even more was a comment Hugh had made, one of his stinging but insightful observations about their relationship: *I need you and you need my money*. The truth of it made her resent herself for the attachment she had to the trappings of wealth. Now the stark reality faced her: she had to choose either luxury and misery, or independence and happiness.

The waters became murky.

It wasn't that she was naive about the ways of the world: she'd always had a feeling that Hugh had other women outside. As unacceptable as that proposition was, in her mind she took the stance that, as long as the 'woman ah yard' was shown respect, it was a bearable evil.

Until this happened.

Now she was again questioning their three years of marriage. She had put her emotional needs a sorry second to Hugh's grand aspirations. But now she was counting the damage done by boosting his already inflated ego. Their marriage had become a war of wills, and she was losing.

Hugh was still upset at her for pulling a gun on him and treated her like a stranger in her own home. He had taken to referring to her friends as 'high class whores' and let it be known that he did not want his wife associating with any of them. They stopped visiting.

Now some of the men at work, who previously enjoyed harmless flirting with her, had heard the rumours. They kept their distance, unwilling to test the reputation of her obsessive husband.

Why didn't she just walk out and leave it all. Why?

Because she was afraid. Afraid of Hugh and what he could do to her. He had threatened to reduce her to a pauper begging on the street and destroy her name if she tried. And God knows he could do it.

She was trapped until she could find a way out, but refused to let the pressure get to her. Life went on, and she would survive, making the best of a bad situation. She tried to see it with optimistic eyes but no matter how she viewed it her future seemed dim.

Monique was relieved to hear the Minister for Tourism adjourning the meeting. She shook hands with the gentlemen and ladies from the American trade mission and departed for home. She wasn't usually this eager to get away to the Beverly Hills mansion , but the Honourable Hugh St. John was away and the house would be tension-free for the weekend.

The thought of three days of peace thrilled her, and her outlook became brighter. Overhead, large white clouds blocked the hot sun, providing a minute's relief for sunburnt Kingstonians.

Monique's BMW crawled along Knutsford Boulevard. Her blouse was unbuttoned at the neck, her hair untied and

23

bundled at her shoulders. The breeze through the window was refreshing. She stopped at a red light and, in an instant, bedraggled little boys in khaki suits descended on the car with buckets of water and squidgy sticks. They started cleaning the windscreen, their little faces serious, wiping away the soapy water with quick swipes, proud of their workmanship.

"Dat alright fe yuh lady?" one youth asked her, his two front teeth missing. "Not a mark."

"Not bad," she commented. "Here."

She stretched out her hand and deposited two ten dollar notes in his hand.

"Make sure you share it, okay?"

But before she could hear his answer the light had turned green and the BMW was away.

In a rash mood, Monique drove the short route home through areas she normally avoided. As she thundered along Mountain View Avenue she was picturing herself under the shower, and then relaxing with a bottle of wine. By the kerbside, youths stood around in cut-off trousers and string vests, idly 'reasoning' in groups about their various exploits and boasting about which girl had succumbed to their irresistible charms the night before. Inquisitive eyes followed the BMW's progress as it turned left and rocked over an open sewer stretched across the road.

Monique braked sharply as a little boy crossed over with a stick and tyre, oblivious to her approach. The car stalled. She turned the ignition hurriedly. The engine struggled for a moment, spluttered, coughed and died.

"Shit!"

Monique tried the ignition again, with no luck. This was the last place she wanted to break down, especially in a car like this. She sat back for a moment, plucking up her courage, the youths on the corner watching impassively. Monique wasn't looking forward to this one bit.

Simba Ranking throttled his Honda 90 as he waited at the

half-demolished traffic light. He'd come up to Mountain View to check a t'ing, two streets up from where he was now, having already been home to 'hold a fresh' after finishing his Tae-Kwan-Do classes at St. Anne's. He noticed the BMW come to a halt not far from him, and tried to figure out who it could be. For one thing it didn't look like no area drugs man. Even though he didn't live in this neighbourhood, he knew most of the Kingston 'dons' and this was not one of them. Whoever it was, this was definitely no place for a top car to break down. He pushed his Joe 90 'mafia' up the ridge of his nose, his attention focused on the silhouette inside the 'crissas BM'. He watched carefully as the driver tried to start the car again. The engine produced a groan and a puff of black smoke from the exhaust, but nothing more. The angry driver shook the steering wheel in frustration.

He released the brake and let the Honda roll forward. No, this was not the place for no topanaris 'inna criss car' to break down, Simba reflected. He felt hot and his silk shirt clung to his back. It would be so easy to ride on past, but if he stopped to help he could form a contact that would be helpful in the future. *Yuh nevah can tell.*

Smiling to himself, he pulled alongside the stranded car. The small 325i was like a white spaceship, the tinted glass showing only a silhouette of the person inside. Simba knocked on the window.

For a moment he thought the driver was going to blank him. Then the door opened and a long pair of stockinged legs in high heels swung out onto the gritty road. A small group of young men had gathered, recognising the Ranking and hailing him up. But Simba's concentrated gaze was on *de healthy body t'ing* standing somewhat nervously before him.

"You alright, miss?"

His voice was coarse but reassuring.

"I...I don't know what happened," she stammered. "One minute I'm driving along and the next, this...it's the first time it's done anything like that."

She tensed back her shoulders unconsciously. On guard. Unlike many members of Jamaican high society, Monique wasn't afraid of the ghetto streets. But her BMW was a conspicuous sign of 'uptown', and getting killed or robbed in areas like this had nothing to do with whether you were afraid or not. Crime and political violence had no rhyme or reason in present day Jamaica.

Dem up desso, an' de sufferah dung yah so. The lyrics from the song rang true here. Then why didn't she feel threatened by this youth talking to her?

"My name is Delroy, miss. You buck up 'pon de right man, t'ings ah go a'right, seen?"

Simba spoke quietly and warmly.

"Are you a mechanic?"

Monique was suspicious.

"No, but me know enough fe help a situation unless you waan stay yah until someone else come to yuh rescue."

She shook her head.

"If ah nuh not'n serious, me can solve de problem right yah so. Jus' cool."

He motioned to her to sit down but Monique chose to stand, positioning herself so she could see what he was about to do. Simba shrugged and turned to face one of the smaller youths looking on.

"Yout', come go ah Missa Colin shop an' hol a D&G fe de nice lady nuh."

He paused and handed the boy thirty dollars.

"An' tek the change fe you an' yuh massive."

"Yeah, boss."

The boy scurried away with his friends, boasting loudly:

"Ah Simba Rankin' dat, y'know."

Monique stood watching him keenly. Her initial trepidation had lessened, and she was slowly forming a thin strand of attraction for her rough-cut saviour. She studied Simba carefully as the excited youth handed her a cool ginger beer. She wiped the mouth of the bottle.

"Simba Ranking," Monique repeated to herself quietly. "So ruffnecks can be gentlemen after all."

She had heard of him, maybe from the music charts or from one of the girls in the office who followed the dancehall scene. He was a deejay…and handsome too.

As Simba flew the bonnet of the car Monique kept her eyes on him, trying to figure out his age. He looked in his late twenties, dressed as he was in the typical 'dung town' fashion — a flowing silk shirt with a white vest underneath, and trousers of terylene and wool. His slender build was misleading. He was solid and compact with his dark face and piercing dark brown eyes, as sharp and defined as his high cheekbones, and thick but small lips.

"You waan start her up, miss?" Simba's muffled voice came from under the bonnet, interrupting her thoughts.

"Oh…I'm sorry. Okay, I'll give it a spin."

She felt like a schoolgirl again. Something about this guy was causing her heart to pound. She climbed in the driver's seat, turned the ignition and, as the engine turned, revved it.

"Ah you dat!" Simba cried triumphantly, coming over to the driver's door. "Jus' mek sure it see a mechanic soon, an' it will be safe."

He paused as he rubbed his greasy hands together.

"What's a nice lady like you doing, inna dem area yah?"

"Call it adventure."

She allowed herself a friendly smile.

"Next time try an' be careful whe' you drive."

He studied her carefully.

"Due to politics dem area yah ah hot up daily. Jus' mek sure yuh 'adventure' dem tek you to a safer place."

"I appreciate the advice…"

Monique was about to search in her handbag for some money to pay him, but thought better of it. Because you lived in the ghetto didn't mean you had no pride. She was afraid that he would take a token of her appreciation as an insult, she did not want to risk that.

"I just don't know how to thank you for the help. I don't know what I would have done if you didn't turn up."

"You woulda find a way out, miss."

"I'm not so sure." She paused. "And call me Monique."

"Monique," Simba replied blandly.

She revved up her engine some more.

"That's better." She smiled at Simba again. "You know what you were saying about a good mechanic to sort out my problem…do you know of any good workmen?"

The question seemed innocent enough, but it was loaded. Monique wasn't about to let Simba go. He interested her, and she wanted him to know that.

"Wid a car like dis you must know a mechanic from uptown," Simba queried.

"That's some distance away from here and I really don't trust driving this car that far. You must know one nearby?"

Simba paused, and thought about it for a while before finally answering.

"Me have a man further down Mountain View Avenue wha' look after my bike, but him is really a car mechanic. Him ah de best inna de east still."

He looked at her again, more warily this time. It was strange for a woman of her social standing to be so accommodating to someone from the ghetto. He placed his shades back over his eyes.

"I'll follow you," she said, "then, perhaps — to say thank you — you'll let me invite you to a meal after."

"Fair enough," the Ranking readily agreed.

"Okay," Monique said. "Lets go."

She had never done anything like this before. It was crazy, but in the few minutes they had talked her attraction had grown. *It must be purely physical,* she reasoned. How else could this youth make her feel like this? She'd only felt this once before, that was when she first met Hugh.

Monique caught herself watching Delroy's behind. Her heart raced at the thought of how sexy he was. He mounted the small bike and cranked it. His thoughts were on this beautiful uptown girl and why she was so grateful to him.

Driving behind his Honda 90, Monique was determined, whatever the consequences, to get to know this youth.

FOUR

"Ah my time dis, man," Simba Ranking thought aloud, as he leaned over the balcony of the villa in Negril.

He was thrilled, but kept that fact to himself. In public he would let his cool exterior hide the excitement inside like it was no big deal. Monique had introduced him to a side of life he prayed he would experience, but he had never thought it would ever become a reality.

Simba reflected again on how fortunate he was in meeting Monique, and how things had simply 'clicked' between them. He had expected to simply 'lick an' run', never seeing Monique again after one night of passion. She was a 'browning' from the hills who came down to the flats, to *look a piece ah dung town pedal an' wheel.* It wasn't a regular occurrence, but Simba had heard stories of certain 'cocks man' finding themselves in just such a situation. A novel experience to tell her friends about at whatever big office she worked at in Kingston. Such relationships could not be sustained, Simba believed. The inevitable would happen because they were two people with nothing in common except sex, which was fine for Simba.

But in this case he was wrong, Monique was not like that. He couldn't imagine her choosing a piece of yellow yam from a market woman down at Coronation, or helping to weigh a snapper fish at the sea front and bringing it home to scale herself, but in her own way she had a feel for street life.

Simba had nicknamed her 'counterfeit Risto' because she

seemed too willing to learn about the life of the sufferahs and she didn't need to. *Why?* he kept asking himself. Why did she want to be with a man like him, when there were bigger sharks with longer pockets out there. Was it that she was trying to escape from something? He couldn't tell. Throughout their 'friendship' he had not asked her about her background. The little she told him had satisfied Simba. But as time went on he became more curious.

He had been only too willing to tell her about his life and about the humorous and the serious day to day runnings of the ghetto. But when he tried to dig a little deeper about her past she would always keep tight-lipped, simply saying: "For your own good, darling, you don't need to know."

Simba had never asked her for anything; as much as he had wanted to, his pride had held him back. Fortunately Monique was free with her cash. She booked this weekend in Negril as a surprise.

It was hard for Simba to accept it all, because things never came this easy for him. Monique Saunders was rich, sophisticated, sexy and unlike any woman he knew. A month of seeing her had reinforced his belief that people are people whether they're from uptown or downtown.

Simba watched the pelicans circle on the horizon, his thoughts drifting with them. The amber-red orb of the sun hung like a ripe blood orange ready to fall. He could smell the salt water in the air, and as he listened to the sound of the sea lapping at the rocks he felt as though he were a million miles away from Kingston. It was hard to believe this was the same Jamaica he had lived in all his life. This part of the island was like an alien world to him. He rarely ventured further than Spanish Town or St Thomas, and that was with the sound system. In his world, little existed outside Kingston or the dancehall.

He knew now how wrong he was. He had missed out on the real natural beauty of Jamaica for so long. Out here in Negril, people were more relaxed, less concerned about politics and forcing their point of view down your throat at gunpoint.

Cool runnings.

Unlike the weather.

Even wearing a black string vest and knee-length designer shorts (a present from Monique) it was still humid, and even in the shade Simba could feel moisture trickle down his back. Still, he was quite relaxed, thanks not only to the sea breeze, which intermittently cooled things down but also to his bottle of chilled Dragon stout.

'Relax an' float' was an understatement down in Westmoreland. For the first time Simba tasted how the tourists and the rich people enjoyed the high life Jamaica had to offer — and he was envious.

Thinking about his continued hardships, the struggle with his mother to move out of the tenement yard to a real home of their own, his career in the dancehall and other things, he couldn't help but feel the Father had not forgotten him after all. How else could he explain Monique? She had turned up at exactly the right time. A businesswoman with money who was not satisfied with her life at the top, for reasons unknown to him, but who was attracted to the Ranking. And though he refused to admit it to himself, she held some power over him because he liked her. She was different, unlike the women he was used to but, most importantly, Monique was a challenge.

Behind him the villa door creaked open and he turned to see her stepping onto the balcony in a sexy black and white bikini.

"Are you enjoying the view, Delroy?"

She snuggled up to him.

"It's fantastic, isn't it?"

He nodded as he snaked his hands around her small waist, massaging the soft skin there.

"Have you ever thought of starting a family and settling down?"

Monique's question was sudden. It came out with a kind of practiced nonchalance. Simba grinned broadly, one of the few times she ever saw him so amused.

"Yout' like me cyan settle dung, baby. It nuh inna my

31

blood. Furthermore dem t'ings deh is fe man who can afford it. A man wid house, car, job. As a sufferah, yuh haffe be like my father fe start a family. Yuh mus' be either nuh right in yuh head or yuh love yuh woman like how my father love Mama Christy."

A frown of dejection formed on Monique's face which Simba did not see.

"Your family means a lot to you, doesn't it?"

"Daddy do de wuk and Mama carry me fe nine months, haffe respect dem."

They looked in the distance silently for a while.

"Yuh can forget 'bout de runnings ah town, yahso, man. Everyt'ing just easy."

He leaned back on her slightly.

"That was the idea, remember? We were supposed to forget about Kingston for a few days and just get to know each other some more. Flake out."

"Easy fe seh but hard fe do. While me deh yah wid you baby, Missa George an' Mama Christy still deh inna de day to day juggling business. Me nuh feel right 'bout dat."

Simba's expression darkened.

"I know how you feel, Delroy, but you have to learn to loosen up. You won't change things by worrying about them, but by acting. Now relax."

He didn't mind her using his Christian name, she seemed to prefer it to his dancehall tag. There wasn't much he minded about her at all. She moved behind him and started to massage his tense shoulder muscles. That relaxed him. He groaned with satisfaction, feeling the urge to lay her down on the patio so they could round off the evening with some hot loving. Simba imagined her going shy on him, as she protested that the neighbours might see them. Monique was 'safe' but there was something else he couldn't put his finger on. Somewhere, deep down in his subconscious, was a niggling sense of danger. For after one month, she was still a mystery. Something wasn't quite right about her past.

"So what de schedule, fe lickle more, baby?" Simba asked in a submissive 'Joe Grine' tone.

"Don't you worry about it," her small nose wrinkled into a smile. "You're going to enjoy every minute. Trust me"

"Ah you run t'ings, Mistress Saunders."

"I do, don't I?" she giggled and backed away from him "So I'd better get the ball rolling then."

She disappeared inside the thatched house and Simba lowered himself in a wicker chair on the verandah. He had already decided that he would make sure he found out more about her in time, right now he wanted to play her game, after all, he had nothing to lose. Nothing at all.

The evening sun was dazzling as they walked barefoot on the white sand of the splendid Negril beach, frothy waves lapping around their ankles. They held hands, joking and laughing and making slow but steady progress towards their destination. Many kilometres of the finest beach in the Caribbean and crystal clear waters the colour of emeralds, made the setting reminiscent of a Mills and Boon classic.

The private stretch of beach owned by Hedonism II, the hotel that overlooked it, was packed with people in various degrees of undress. The annual Negril Beach Bash was in full swing, jamming to the sounds of the Mighty Sparrow.

Monique had added a beach wrap to her bikini and looked ravishing as usual. Simba had dressed casual, and had a pair of black Hush Puppies slung around his neck.

Several upmarket rent-a-dreads mingled with the crowds, declaring themselves the unofficial hosts of the promotion. The liquor was free, but the red, sunburnt tourists were high on many other things besides alcohol.

Simba liked the vibes here but wasn't so sure about the people. These high-flyers, Jamaicans and visitors alike, seemed too carefree. He was used to seeing faces that reflected the struggle of day to day existence and the appreciation they felt at the release the dancehall gave them. In the concrete jungles of town a dance was a release from insanity. But to these people in high society a dance was simply a way of passing the time.

As for the white tourists, he was wary of all of them. He had heard enough about how they treated the black man living with them in their own countries. As far as he was concerned, their plastic smiles for the natives of Jamaica couldn't work on Simba Ranking. That's why he would never leave 'Yard'. Not for anything.

"Live a little," Monique whispered to him, noticing his pensive look. "What do you want to drink?"

They had drifted near to one of the speakers set under a shedding grape tree and the Ranking had to shout for her to hear.

"Me feel like a Dragon, still. A cold one."

She nodded.

"I'll make that two and a strawberry daiquiri for me. I'll be back in a minute."

Monique swayed off in the direction of the beach-side bar; a crowd of appreciative males followed her all the way there with their eyes.

Unuh can look bwoy, but unuh cyan touch, seen? Simba smiled to himself.

Monique returned with the drinks, stretching over to hand Simba his two brews. The deejay's rough fingers rubbed over hers as he took the bottles and he noticed the base of her wedding finger was moulded smooth, the kind of impression left by a ring.

Simba held on to her hand, placing his bottles on the sand beside him, and looked at her quizzically before asking the question that had formed in his head.

"You married?"

"I wouldn't go as far as to say that."

"Me nuh really care, all de same. If you waan keep it undercover dat safe. But me love fe know which man woman me ah fuck," Simba chuckled ironically.

There was no bitterness in the Ranking's statement. He had already guessed that something wasn't quite right, and he wanted to see how Monique would react.

He had no idea how difficult it was for Monique to decide to sleep with another man, even after all her husband had done to her. She was brought up to believe that there should be only one man in your life. And then along came Simba. She smiled as she turned to face him and said, "Whether I'm married or not shouldn't concern you. If you're comfortable with what you have, don't ask too many questions, okay?"

Another woman would have felt the back of Simba's hand for less, but Monique could get away with it. The Ranking glared at her knowing that the continuation of their relationship depended on how he reacted now. She was testing him, whether she knew it or not, and he wasn't going to let his hot temper mess everything up. His arm was flexing for release but that was the old style. Now, he felt like he was representing certain decent ghetto people who were classed as violent and criminal-minded but who were just simply poor.

His father never lifted his hand to Mama, he could follow suit. His voice calmer, Simba struggled to hide his annoyance.

"If a vexed husband ah come looking fe me because ah you, I hope you can pay de hospital bill."

Fe him.

"Don't worry, that won't ever happen. In time you'll know everything about me."

"Dat up to you," he said flatly. "Me know wha' me ah go do now."

"And what's that?" Monique expected some cutting comment.

"Me ah go hold two piece ah jerk chicken. Dat a'right wid yuh?" She looked at him surprised, and when he pecked her on her cheek without a sign of him being upset and walked off Monique didn't know what to make of it. Delroy smiled inwardly, knowing he had won a small battle, and dismissed it from his head.

As another calypso ended, the Ranking wondered if the 'drum pan sound' would ever get around to playing reggae. Calypso Rose belted out the next number. Simba decided that he would have to have a serious word with the selector.

The night eventually slowed down with smoochy soul music and the couples took the floor for the slow groove. Simba had just finished dancing with Monique and now sat back on a deck chair watching the security men patrolling the borders of the hotel's property.

Apart from the stretch by the Hedonism guest houses, the rest of the beach was public. Tourists, local residents and hustlers alike were supposed to be allowed to walk through the private section as long as they did not interfere with the guests. But Hedonism II wasn't like that. No one passed through except guests, and the hotel management prided themselves on the tight security surrounding their artificial world, where a holidaymaker's every need was catered for.

Simba eased himself back in the deck chair; he was counting the stars in the evening sky when Monique approached, accompanied by three Jamaican men. One, a man of middle age, was tall and very dark. The other two were younger and had lighter complexions. One was half-Chinese and the other half-white. They had been drinking heavily and Monique was clearly in no mood for their advances, but they were rich and arrogant and obviously didn't give a damn about anyone else but themselves.

The Ranking had seen their kind so many times before, but still they could 'sick him stomach'. As they approached, the taller man grabbed Monique's hand to stop her from walking too far ahead of them. She stopped and turned. Simba couldn't hear what she said but the way she turned her head away from him suggested that he had received a verbal slap to the face. The three men backed off.

"Damn idiots can't hold their drink."

Monique motioned to the three men as they huddled together singing along to the music. "They're pretty harmless, I suppose..."

She shrugged casually and knelt down beside him.

"Me know you can handle yuhself," said Simba, leaning forward, "but when a man nuh waan hear yuh fancy lyrics an' him waan get rough, what you ah go do then?"

Simba was watching the drunkards approaching them.

36

"The people I know don't resort to violence just because of disagreements, they try other ways to get you. I'm not sure what I'd do if I found myself in a situation like that."

Yuh bettah learn fast, Simba thought.

"So this is yuh yard, bwoy?"

The tall black man stood over them, his rum-scented breath wafting into the deejay's face. Simba winced at being called a 'yard bwoy'.

"A woman like you need a man to deal wid you," the man continued, "not a schoolboy."

He hiccoughed loud, and his cohorts behind him roared with laughter. Simba kept cool. He knew that if he opened his mouth now, he would get wicked.

"Will you jackasses leave us alone," said Monique, trying to control her temper. "You're wasting your time, I'm already here with someone and…"

"Not'n can go so, me dear," the man interrupted. "You can't have a lickle bwoy performing a man's job. No way."

"A true man," one of the others agreed.

"If you want a good time, only we can give it to you…" the third man said, reaching across to pull Monique to him.

That was Simba's cue.

"De lady seh, she alright, man. Yuh nuh understan' dat?"

The drunk continued unperturbed.

"You have mouth, yout'?" he slurred. "This discussion is for intelligent people, not fe a back-a-wall nigga…"

Simba didn't need to hear any more. He blanked his mind and kicked the deck chair from behind him. Monique pulled her hand away from the drunk man and fell backwards onto the soft sand. The half-Chinese man started coming forward. His dulled senses realised too late that Simba's foot was planted firmly between his legs. Fire seemed to explode out of his groin, shooting sharp pins of pain to every part of his body as he gasped and fell to his knees, then flat on his face. The 'white bwoy' was more brazen and was bearing down on Simba with a beer bottle in hand. The Ranking had already seen him and his open hand shot up suddenly, grabbing the bottle and then

37

twisting the man's wrist and pulling him down to his knees all in one fluid motion. A sharp crack cut through the music as Simba's knee connected with his mouth. The force of the blow whipped his head back and he fell awkwardly over his drinking mate, spitting out teeth and blood.

"Come nuh, pussy, yuh nuh waan test?" Simba goaded the tall black man who had already taken a step backwards. His mouth opened and closed but no words came out.

"Jus' bumboclaat gwan," Simba spat. "You ah waste time."

Security guards were quickly on the scene, and tried to make Simba out to be the troublemaker. But Monique would have none of it, and she forcefully explained what had happened. As the real troublemakers were being booked out of the hotel she and Simba decided it was an ideal time for them to leave too.

"So there's still a few more things I need to know about you," said Monique as they made their way through reception. A taxi was waiting outside, the driver holding the rear door open for them.

"I know you didn't learn to take care of yourself like that in the rough downtown streets."

The Lada pulled smoothly away from the hotel.

"Too many karate movies ah Majestic bound fe rub off," Simba replied simply. "An' anyway, if yuh comfortable wid wah yuh have nuh ask nuh question."

"Touché!" Monique said, feeling an apology was due. "I was wrong back there. I'm sorry I snapped at you like that. But I'm still a bit uncomfortable about saying too much. Right now I'm vulnerable…"

"Nuh worry 'bout it," Simba interjected. "When de right time come yuh wi' tell me everyt'ing me waan know."

She snuggled under his arm, playfully.

"That sounded like a threat, Delroy," she teased.

"No baby, dat is no threat. Dat is a promise."

FIVE

The tread of Hugh St John's Italian-cut shoes echoed through the cool, air-conditioned halls of Gordon House.

Parliamentary 'Discussion Time' had gone on for far too long. The Saint couldn't have spent another minute listening to the 'hog and goat' MPs and senators from the opposition party, and even his own party, ramble on about law and order, no matter what Mr Speaker felt about his hasty departure.

The Saint had heard all he needed to. He'd left the rest of his colleagues debating the ramifications of the Prime Minister's announcement, but as far as he was concerned there was nothing further to consider.

He had served his West Kingston constituency as an MP for almost six years now, and soon he would have enough property leases in the area to start moving out tenants to make way for his big building plans. The Prime Minister's sudden election announcement would be the perfect cover to speed up his recruitment drive of staunch supporters to his cause. Political violence was the surest means he knew of securing undying allegiance.

He smiled to himself. All he needed now was a Cuban cigar and a glass of brandy to celebrate the good news.

Deep in thought, he walked down the corridor to the House's lounge and restaurant. The bartender smiled as he took St. John's order, and a minute later Hugh took his drink and cigar to one of the bar's secluded seats. Two large photographs, of Sir Alexander Bustamante and Norman Washington Manley, hung on the opposite wall. The two great Jamaican politicians' portraits were soon shrouded in cigar smoke. Hugh raised his glass and mockingly toasted them.

"Without you gentlemen, I wouldn't be here. Salute!"

The brandy warmed his throat and then his stomach, relaxing him somewhat. Then he sank back into his chair and let out a deep breath.

"The likes ah you shouldn't be able to step foot into the House ah Parliament."

He recognised the voice, looked up slowly, and smirked.

"The Right Honourable Errol Peterkin...I thought we said everything that needed to be said the last time we talked."

Peterkin, an opposition party member, was never pleased to see him. He was a thin man with bright eyes that softened his dark stern face.

"How long do you think this pretence can go on?" Peterkin asked, disgust distorting his features. "You don't give a fuck about your constituency. You just want to bleed the poor people dry, fe yuh own ends. How do you sleep at night?"

"Mi sleep quite well, t'ank you."

The Saint rolled the brandy around in his glass and tapped his cigar in the ashtray, "An' fe your information, I care deeply about my people. That's why I try and improve their lives...you, on the other hand, want to jus' talk."

"Listen to me, man —"

Peterkin had lowered his voice, leaning forward to make sure that what he was about to say had the desired effect.

"—The only thing that can improve the lives of the residents of West Kingston is you standing down. What do you say, St. John?"

"Stop trying to be a comedian, man, yuh haven't got the timing fe it. My constituency can't come outta the shit because you ah send your gunman inna my area fe destroy we."

"That's a goddamn lie an' you know it."

Peterkin's outburst drew a confused look from the bar man, who was carefully drying glasses.

"De only thing I know is, a weak raas like you will never control not'n. You don't know what it means to be a winner, but I do."

"This discussion is pointless, me realise that now," said Peterkin, shaking his head. "You wrong-footed us by convincing the Prime Minister to call an early election. But even if it means working round the clock, me ah go expose you. Remember dat."

The Saint responded with a deep bass chuckle.

"Many have tried an' fail. But one thing dem all have in common is dem realise too late dat me control my business fully. This town's only big enough for one don, ah me dat."

Peterkin turned and walked away, and as he did so Hugh called loudly after him:

"Remember dat!"

The Saint poked the remainder of his cigar into the corner of his mouth.

"Fucking bastard," he hissed.

Peterkin stopped and turned; with an unusual smile on his face he called across the empty bar:

"Riddle me dis, riddle me dat, guess me dis riddle an' perhaps not? Which ghetto man ah fling sweet whine under the Saint's wife when he's away?"

Peterkin rubbed his chin, feigning puzzlement, before answering the conundrum himself.

"I don't know, but I do know whoever he is, he's younger and has a bigger cock…"

He disappeared through the door laughing loud.

"Wha' de bloodclaat yuh seh." The cigar fell out of St. John's mouth as he jumped up, overturning his glass and his table.

Nobody suggested that he wasn't satisfying his wife, or that she was seeing another man, and lived to laugh about it.

He reached for his gun like a desperate man, then on

touching the coarse leather holster under his arm he remembered where he was and decided against using it. If they hadn't been in the House, the Saint would have shot Peterkin dead in cold blood.

But outside was different story, a wide world of violence in which the opposition man could so easily become another unfortunate statistic. Still fuming, St. John stepped over the table and headed towards the bar, to calm himself. As his breathing slowed down, certain incidents of the past few months sprang into mind.

Peterkin's riddle had fuelled his imagination, and the odd veiled insult thrown at him during a debate in the House recently had suddenly taken on new meaning. He began wondering…the low snickering from the opposition that sometimes welcomed his entrance to a committee meeting: was that more than just innocent? *Did everybody in the House know something he didn't?*

Leaning on the bar, he looked over to the bartender who had heard the heated exchange. St John refused to believe that Monique would do this to him. *No way.*

She wouldn't have the guts.

He licked his dry lips. Or would she? Maybe he'd underestimated her; if he had, it would not happen twice. He stretched over the bar for a stack of napkins and dabbed at the brandy stains on his jacket.

He'd have the matter looked into. If there was the slightest truth in Peterkin's riddle then whoever the man was he would soon be staring down the barrel of an AK-47.

The Saint shook his head, his blue eyes smouldering evilly.

If there was one thing he could not abide, it was people keeping secrets from him.

Especially his nearest and dearest.

SIX

"Hugh St John is yuh husband?" Simba repeated. He laughed nervously trying not to show his shock.

It had to come. He hadn't known when or how, but he'd known something would upset the apple cart. Things had been going too smoothly, he and Monique enjoyed each other's company too much. She didn't make any demands on him and he still had plenty of time to go about his own business — with a little financial help from his uptown woman, of course. Perfect. Until now.

"So yuh real name is not Saunders but St. John. How come yuh feel fe tell me dat now?"

They sat together in the Carib cinema. The auditorium lights brightened slightly, giving the cinemagoers the opportunity to hurry to the foyer for popcorn and Coke before the main feature began.

Monique preferred the drive-in cinemas of New Kingston to the Carib, and never thought she would find herself sitting in the $20.00 seats watching a Chinese kung fu movie. But from Delroy's enthusiasm for the film she was convinced she'd enjoy herself. Simba propped both feet on the back of the empty seat in front of him. Monique's admission had changed his mood. He had been looking forward to the film; now he felt tense. And for good reason.

Unease over the upcoming elections was mounting slowly. There was sporadic fighting across the city between rival political gangs and stories of minor unrest were

43

increasingly being reported in newscasts. The Saint's name had been linked with the violence in the most volatile sections of Kingston; and now Monique was admitting being married to this political don. He tried in vain to stay cool. Dealing with a cuckolded boyfriend from downtown was difficult, but this was something entirely different.

He repeated his question.

"Yuh ah Hugh St. John woman?"

"I'm his wife, not his woman, that makes me sound like his mistress."

"To a man like dat it mek a difference?"

She didn't answer that.

"I should have told you from the beginning, but I didn't know I would *feel* this way for you. I just didn't think you would need to know who my husband was."

Simba was still finding the news hard to digest.

"Why yuh choose fe tell me now?"

Simba was digging deeper; he felt she had more to say.

"It just felt right, I think…"

Her guilty eyes dropped away from Simba's steady gaze.

"…And I owe you more than withholding something as important as this from you for too long."

Simba massaged his chin contemplatively before speaking.

"If yuh waan call it a day, baby, yuh can. You nuh haffe go through all ah dis. You of all people shoulda know Simba is a upfront yout'."

"Don't be stupid, of course I still want you." She paused. "If you still want me?"

Another one of her loaded questions hit Simba squarely between the eyes. Things had changed, it would no longer take a silver tongue to prove that he cared for her, now she was looking for commitment. That word had sent many an otherwise fearless 'rude bwoy' scurrying for cover. He swallowed hard.

"If me nevah want yuh, me wouldn't deh yah."

Monique relaxed noticeably.The Ranking just could not figure out why she needed to be reassured like this now.

"I wont blame you if you want to get as far away from

me as you can."

"Why me woulda waan do dat?" Simba said, sounding surprised. "De Ranking nuh 'fraid ah no bwoy, man. An' anyway him nuh know what ah gwan, so it nuh mek a difference."

But Simba knew it did make a difference.

"Usually everyone disappears after finding out who my husband is. You're the only person I know who is either crazy enough or who cares enough to date me."

She sounded grateful and relieved at the same time, but Monique had made up her mind to manage whether or not Simba had decided to stay.

"To how me see t'ings, if him dida do him wuk right, I wouldn't deh yah so. Fe him loss ah my gain. Somewhere dung de line him fuck up big, big or else there is no way a woman like yuh woulda even deh wid de Ranking."

Simba collected his thoughts, staring at the screen.

"Hugh coulda bad like 'yaas' baby, ah only you can stop dis from gwan."

Monique felt like holding him close to her and just remaining in his embrace until the fear that was gripping her disappeared. She simply sat there lost in thought.

A man in a large cap and dark glasses, squeezed along the seats in the row in front of theirs, then the lights dimmed and Simba placed an arm around Monique's shoulders and whispered in her ear:

"Yuh have a lot fe tell me."

She shuddered slightly, fighting back the dread of that prospect and the trepidation she felt at telling him the real reason she was so worried. It wasn't about Hugh; that would be a problem later. It was about her. Something special had happened between them, special and unexpected. And even though she feared what Hugh would do, for Simba's sake she had to either keep it from him or just stop seeing him altogether.

But could she do that?

Monique needed time to think before she made a decision that she didn't even know she was capable of making.

Stay with Hugh and live in a comfortable hell devoid of any feeling?

Or be with Simba — happy, but uncertain of the future.

The credits rolled on the screen while, for the first time in years, Monique prayed for an answer.

The Volvo's wipers fought off the heavy rain splashing against the windscreen. Hugh St. John twisted in the driver's seat as he manoeuvred his bulletproof car around the winding roads of Beverly Hills. His bodyguards had gone on ahead after escorting the Volvo from Duke Street in downtown Kingston, and would be at his gate waiting eagle-eyed for his arrival, ready for any attempt on their boss' life.

It had been one of the most difficult days he'd had in a long while. He was tired and frustrated after heated discussions in the cabinet over the passing of a bill on the financial disclosure rules. That goddamn bastard Peterkin was trying to force the members of the house to lay their business interests open to public scrutiny. *Bullshit!* A bill like that would make his life very, very difficult. He had protested forcefully, maybe a little too forcefully.

Percy Sledge's silky tones filled the interior with *Cover Me* and helped to relax him, but Percy was no substitute for a stiff drink and a back-rub.

The familiar slope levelled into a plateau and he slowed as a dirty green Lada came into view, snuggled into a bush. The Saint shook his head in disgust. He wondered how his imbecile bodyguards had passed by without noticing the car. If the car had belonged to some less than friendly hit men, he could be dead. What was he paying those idiots for?

The Saint pulled up across the road from the Lada and calmly lit up a Craven 'A'. Within seconds the Lada driver had slid out of the car and was running swiftly across the road. Dressed in a long army raincoat, old-fashioned leather weatherman cap and combat boots, he seemed unaffected by the mild tropical storm. He stopped and stood beside the Volvo. The Saint paid him no attention and finished his cigarette before he lowered his electric window.

"Have you found out anything?" he asked quietly. The man nodded. "Well, Maskman, gimme the details, nuh. Do you think I enjoy sitting out here in this godforsaken weather wid you?"

The Saint rapped his fingers on the dashboard as the man dropped a small piece of lined paper into his lap.

"Simba Ranking?"

The Saint read the name out loud.

"Who the raas is that?"

The man's head was bowed as he answered. His voice had a gravel like edge to it.

"Him is a deejay, very popular wid de ghetto people dem. A known cocks man roun' town."

"A ghetto man ah fuck *my* wife behind my back?"

The words exploded from the Saint's mouth in a spray of saliva and incredulousness. The horn sounded as he slammed his fists on the steering wheel angrily.

"Are you sure?"

"Not a hundred percent, boss. We sight dem together twice, outta town, dat's all. Yuh wife is being very careful."

"Have you got a photograph of dis scruff?"

Maskman shook his head.

"I want you to be a hundred percent certain, you hear me? I want to know everyt'ing 'bout him. You got that? Then if it's him, we'll see how he can perform while I slice his cock off bit by bit and ram it down his fucking throat."

Maskman didn't need further instructions. He turned and crossed the road as silently as he had approached. St. John watched him drive away.

"Simba Ranking," he rolled the name around in his mouth and then eased the Volvo forward. "You are a dead man, yout', and you don't even know it yet."

SEVEN

It was twelve noon, and Monique had just saved the files she was working on. She had woken up early, which was unusual for her on a Saturday, and decided to write a report she had been putting off for weeks.

The news broadcasts on the radio talked of more deaths and unrest in the city. Monique re-tuned to uninterrupted music on FM and turned it down low. She sat in bed with her laptop and mobile and worked away. Business gave her some relief from her worries, but that didn't last forever. As soon as she shifted her attention away from the office, the problems came rushing back into her mind to upset her.

It seemed in business, as opposed to her personal life, decisions had never been this difficult to make before. Maybe it was just that whatever she did at work there was always a network of people behind her. A decision was never made alone. Monique massaged her temples feeling a stress headache coming on.

Time had gone by quickly. She only realised she had not eaten breakfast when she felt a niggling ache in her stomach, and the onset of a migraine. She pulled herself out of bed and headed for the kitchen.

Peace and quiet.

Monique had demanded her own space away from the bedroom she had shared with the Saint for three years. Hugh didn't like it, but she didn't care what he thought. The second-largest room in the mansion became hers, as far from the master bedroom as she could get.

The house was big enough that they didn't have to really meet at all if she stayed in her portion of the house. The huge living room was where she relaxed, watching wide-screen television or listening to CDs. Some days a few words would be exchanged, some days they said nothing.

Monique padded down the corridor in her fluffy slippers with less trepidation than usual because the Saint was away on a political rally in St. Thomas. She stood in the customised kitchen feeling lost, wishing Maude had not gone to the market today. Monique decided on something unusual for her, cornmeal porridge. It was funny how she had not eaten the staple Jamaican breakfast in…well, years, but now she had a craving for it.

Half an hour later it was ready, and she was about to pour the piping hot liquid in her dish when a buzz on the intercom connecting the guard hut to the house surprised her. She pressed the talk button. It was Marshall the guard.

"Sorry fe disturb yuh, Ma'am, but me have a man ah de gate wid a parcel. Him seh it must be delivered to yuh in person. It very important. Ah so him seh anyway." His voice lowered. "Him look like a teef to me."

"You're a judge of character all of a sudden," she said, getting frustrated. "Just find out what courier company he is with and why he can't leave it with you. You must be able to make the signature on my behalf."

There was silence for a while and then low muttering in the background. Someone cursed. Marshall came back on line, flustered.

"Dis feisty bwoy seh him nah tell me. An' him seh if yuh nuh come yuhself an' sign fe it, him ah go bring it back to de company. Yuh waan me throw him backside out?"

"He did say it was very important, didn't he?"

"Yes, ma'am," Marshall replied, not knowing where it was leading.

"The office could have sent me those acquisition

documents they were compiling." She thought aloud. "Why didn't they just call and say they were sending them over?"

Monique focused again.

"Okay, Marshall. Tell him to wait. I'm on my way."

Monique dashed down the corridor to her room and slipped on a track suit, tied back her hair and headed outside towards the gate.

She entered the guard hut and saw Marshall, looking like he was waiting for the slightest reason to pull his revolver on the courier, who had his back to her. She knew he was simply being careful.

"You had a package for me to sign for," she said to the courier.

Simba turned with the parcel in his hand an amused smirk on his face.

"Mistress St. John?"

Monique stuttered awkwardly, her eyes wide with surprise.

"Yuh parcel arrive."

He took a sip from his half-finished Dragon.

Monique was mad as hell. She quickly ushered Simba into the house, ordering Marshall to take lunch. The guard felt it was strange to be given a break so soon, but he didn't question it.

Simba smiled all the way into the house. Monique was using some expletives he didn't think she knew existed, but he wasn't worried. He knew she couldn't stay mad with him for long. Anyway, the Ranking was too busy taking in the splendour of this magnificent house to worry about Monique's protests.

It was better than he had imagined.

He finished the stout en route, then put down the empty on the plush carpet of the vast sitting room. It took what seemed like ages for Monique to drag him to her room. She slammed the door. In here she could scream at him with less restraint.

"Simba Ranking, you must be crazy or drunk. Suppose Hugh was here today, what then?"

"De Saint haffe cool man. Ah de Ranking dis y'know. Yuh forget."

"Damn it, you're impossible."

Simba held her hand, but she pulled it away.

"Nice place, baby."

There was an amused look on his face.

"De bwoy have taste."

The Ranking continued the pretence. He knew full well from the papers that the Saint was in St. Thomas for a major political rally. But poor Monique didn't know he knew that. His game of being 'a bad bwoy without fear' made him feel in control.

He loved that.

After some wild slapping on her part, she calmed down somewhat and Simba managed to get closer to her.

"Delroy, you shouldn't be here. It's dangerous."

She looked at him intensely.

"Suppose Marshall reports this to my husband when he gets back. What then?"

"Yuh worry too much," was his casual reply. "Marshall just t'ink me is a messenger bwoy. End ah story."

"I'm trying to protect you, can't you see that?"

"Me know, but me nuh need no protection. You just look after yuhself."

He pulled her closer to him and this time she did not resist.

"You're insane, do you know that?"

"It tek one fe know one, now just cool an' open yuh parcel."

Simba handed the plain wrapped parcel to her. Monique looked at him with accusing eyes and ripped off the brown paper to reveal a brown and white cuddly rabbit. Forgetting herself and her anger she cried out excitely.

"Me know yuh love dem t'ing deh."

"It's sweet. I'm going to call it Simba."

For a while all was forgiven and she hugged and kissed him. The bunny would be given pride of place amongst the rest of cuddly toys on her bed.

"Thank you...darling."

She kissed him again, and then he knew her anger had completely gone. Somehow he knew she would not have understood the risks he had taken to get the toy. But to him, leaving the 'wild' west for even an hour of tranquillity and seeing Monique was worth the risk.

His day had started with gunfire.

He had to first run a gauntlet of bullets 'busting' from Jones Town and Tivoli, then find Push 'Mout' Lorna, the higgler from the market, to finish paying for the soft toy. The security forces were out in force, patrolling the streets in their notorious cut-off-top jeeps.

The trip was much easier because he was riding his pride and joy, the new Kawasaki Ninja that Monique had presented to him saying it would enhance his image. How could he turn it down? This was his little way of saying thank you, and turning up unexpected at her 'palace' was an added bonus.

In his small way Simba was stamping his authority over her and it felt good.

After all, me run t'ings, t'ings nuh run me.

Simba was getting too comfortable at Hugh St. John's mansion. He lay in bed with Monique, his hands roving all over her sexy body, wanting desperately to make love to her, but she wouldn't let him. *Not in her matrimonial home,* she had said:

"I just can't bring myself to do that."

It was a principle Simba didn't like, but he accepted it.

She left his side soon after and went into the bathroom, thinking. Once again Simba had succeeded in cheering her up and arousing her at the same time, but she was uncomfortable with him here. He just could not stay for any longer. She was going crazy expecting Hugh to step through the door any minute.

Every sound affected her; every slamming door, every rattling window made her jump. It was good seeing him and *God*, she did want him to stay, but that was tempting fate. He would have to understand.

It had just started to rain in Kingston and the high Beverly Hills altitude frosted the breeze ever so slightly, causing Simba to shiver. He went over and closed the louvered windows gently. Dusk was approaching and the sun began to dip behind the lush green hills. He heard Monique come out from the bathroom and looked round to see her carrying his shirt.

"You left this on the floor, Delroy."

She stood before him, arms akimbo, in a flowing cotton night robe. Delroy looked at her with a glint in his eye as the robe opened slightly along its length. Her caramel skin was smooth and unmarked, the crescent of her firm breasts just showed behind the cut of the gown. She walked towards him, swaying her hips like a catwalk model.

"Listen, darling," she cooed,"as much as I hate the idea of you leaving me, you know as well as I do that you being here makes me extremely nervous. Hugh is an unpredictable man."

She held him tight around the waist, her skin touching his, and gently placed her head on his chest.

"Please…"

"Why yuh stay wid de bwoy, if yuh nuh happy, Mon?" Simba was not a hundred percent sure why he asked her that.

She sighed.

"All that I've ever worked for is tied up with that man. I did something stupid in the beginning of my marriage to him. When I think back on it I must have been lovestruck or stupid. But the long and short of it is that I made sure Hugh got building contracts for government buildings which were supposed to be tendered out fairly. It was fraud on a massive scale. He can destroy me just like *that*." She snapped her fingers.

"Only you can destroy you, man. Yuh too smart fe him trap yuh. Him cyan stop a determined woman. Just pick him off like ticks."

Monique clung to him tightly, rubbing her finger gently along his spine, then said:

"You know, you're right," she twisted her head to look up at him, "but I need to convince myself of that first."

Simba didn't like Monique's moody reply. She was more positive than that in the worst of situations...he was beginning to realise something was wrong.

He took the shirt from her and slipped it on. She kissed him tenderly and led him down the corridor through the washroom to the kitchen. Monique pointed out the route back to his motorcycle.

"Promise me something," she said, after silently staring into the depth of the pouring rain for a few seconds. "Never come here again."

"Why?"

"Promise me, Delroy," she insisted

"A'right, me promise, nevah again. Cool."

"Cool." She squeezed his hand and opened the door.

Simba looked around the grounds of the St. John home, at the landscaped gardens, the swimming pool, the security cameras...the Ranking craved this lifestyle as much as he did the woman, but right now he felt he had no real control. He kissed his teeth and bounded off down the slick concrete steps towards the security turnstile. The electrified fence was switched off as Simba discreetly disappeared through the groundsman's entrance. Beyond that was his bike and and an unwelcome journey back to Coronation Market in the rain.

From an upstairs window Monique watched him go. She knew he was vexed, but he had given her the courage she needed to do something very important, something she had been putting off for far too long. Right now she needed to be alone.

It had to be done.

The very thought of what she could discover frightened and excited her She shuddered as she walked slowly towards the bathroom, her hands clasped, sweating and trembling.

EIGHT

Walking down King street go straight ah Parade,
De people seh Pupa Josey yuh nuh 'fraid,
No my bredrin you must be mad,
As long as me pray to almighty God
Kingston hot. Lawd a God
Ah me seh Kingston hot,
Mek me tell you seh Kingston hot,
Ri-i-i-i-ight!

Downtown Kingston.
Fifteen days from the June General Elections

Night time fell reluctantly over the war-torn Jamaican capital. Josey Wales' words were like a prophecy of things to come, summing up the deep-felt fear and anguish that the forthcoming general elections seemed to instill in Jamaica, but in Kingston in particular.

The body count was 720 dead and mounting daily.

The desperate citizens of the ghettos were busy burying their loved ones, gun-toting bad bwoys and innocents alike.

Yet the Gold Street massacre still managed to shock a country growing numb to daily atrocities. Nobody had ever witnessed anything quite so appalling as this recent killing of a dozen youths at a waterfront dance site.

Tonight the residents of Pink Lane, a cramped back road in the Coronation Market area, were enjoying a welcome respite from the conflict. It wasn't the lack of sound that made the night so calm; the howls of agitated dogs and the wailing sirens of security force vehicles could still be heard.

What was missing was the constant volleys of gunfire.

Bullet-riddled walls and burnt-out premises lined the narrow lane, mute testament to nights of heated gun battles. The empty husks of homes and once-viable businesses bordered the lane on either side, with zinc sheets dividing the gutted buildings and cramped tenement yards. Most of the residents were taking full advantage of the unexpected lull in violence, and enjoying some undisturbed sleep.

Simba lay quietly, unmoving, snuggled tightly between his linen sheets and listening to Mama Christy's snoring. He watched his father getting dressed in the flicker of the lamplight. Simba's waking eyes took in the familiar room which served as his family's dining room, bedroom and sitting room all in one; that was the reality of living in the 'hungry belly' ghetto.

As Simba watched his father prepare to leave, not wanting to sleep, he thought about his mis-spent youth. At sixteen Simba thought he knew it all. He listened to no one but himself, and was proud to be labelled as 'bad bwoy'. As his crew 'bigged him up', he began to feel petty crime was the only way of survival, and questioned his father's motives for going to work every day.

Him a fool man, Simba had said, caressing his shiny black .45 special, *dis ah de only t'ing dat can tek me outta de ghetto.*

But that was before his bredrin died before his eyes from the carbine of a trigger-happy rookie in a roving police unit. His crime was to snatch a gold chain from two country folks. His sentence was death.

Simba was much luckier.

Looking down the barrel of a Kalashnikov, he stared death in the face for the first time. The panic that had ensued at North Parade had saved his life. But the mental scars of that day would stay with him forever. It was then, in that crazy instant when the bullet exploded his friend's chest all over the sidewalk, that Simba came to understand his own mortality.

He now understood exactly how his father could get up at some 'bad' hours of the morning, against the backdrop of daily politically-motivated murders in the area, and do the back-breaking work of a fisherman; all for his family — for him and Mama Christy.

Now Simba's ambition was to leave the ghetto and to give his parents an easier life. The thought of vacating the decrepit, cockroach-infested tenement yards of Pink Lane and moving to the new housing developments in Portmore made Simba almost swoon in anticipation. His duty now was to support his family as much as he could.

Simba and his father had had many conflicts in the past, but the funeral of his spar two years ago had spawned a new sense of reality in his young head. And though he missed sparring with 'de ghetto yout' dem', 'badness and mix up' would have landed him in Gun Court or, worse, on a cold slab at Sam Issac's morgue. Becoming an 'artical don' deejay was his best chance of realising his dreams now, and he had dived into his new image with relish.

He had even offered to help his father on his small boat, something he would never have thought of doing when he was running it hot with his idrens. His father, who had been surprised by Simba's offer, had told him:

"One fisherman inna de family is enough, bwoy."

There was a slight chill to the early morning air. At about 2am Mr George flung on his old camouflage cap, setting it neatly on his spotted grey hair, and wiped his face with his weathered palms as though he was trying to smooth out his wrinkles. He bent over to check the bag with his fishing gear for the packed lunch Mama had prepared. He sighed, and something made him turn and look towards Simba.

"You awake, bwoy?" he asked, his voice a hoarse croak.

"Yeah Missa George, couldn't sleep."

"You too. Me t'ink ah only me have de sleepless nights." He walked quietly over to Simba and sat beside him. "Yuh see dis, yout'?" He pulled his jacket forward and grimaced. "Dis is not de life fe you an' Mama. But circumstances mek it so fe now." He focused his moist eyes on his son and placed a caring hand on his shoulder. "When some ah dem pastor tell you money is de root ah all evil, dem ah raas liar. Dis is de root ah all evil."

His eyes swept the interior of the room, a look of distaste on his face.

"No matter what you haffe do, widout hurting a man, mek sure dis nuh happen to you. Yuh understand me?"

Delroy nodded, a wave of compassion for his father

flooded over him. He straightened and answered with as much gusto as he could muster.

"Dat nah happen to me, Missa G, me promise yuh dat. As long as breath nuh leave de body, me ah go mek t'ings better fe you both."

The old man smiled.

"I had me doubts about you, bwoy, I must admit dat. But you grow up fe de better, an' me proud ah you."

He paused as he stood up.

"You start mek a name inna yuh music business, able to even buy a bike fe yuhself. You done good. Now get some sleep, you ah go need it. Remember, you ah help Mama down ah market tomorrow. I will see you later."

"Lickle more, Missa G," Delroy answered, yawning.

Mr George left as quietly as he could, closing the door behind him gently, but their dogs, Rambo and Tyson, howled farewell to their master from out in the yard. Simba listened to the sound of his father going down the lane, then put his head down and sank quickly back to sleep.

Mr George ambled down the lane, his bag slung over his shoulder and his dirty hat drawn down over his eyes. The stark, uninspiring terrain ahead of him was poorly lit by street lights too far apart. But he had walked this way many times before, and it held no surprises for him. He was known and respected by all the roving 'gundileros' of the area and even though he did not want to admit it, he had taken root in this place that he wanted to curse every day.

Half way down the lane he stepped over a discarded tyre and thought he saw a movement at the corner of his vision. The old man rubbed his eyes, looked again and saw nothing, dismissing it in his mind as Miss Murtle's 'black puss'. He quickened his pace. Choppy, his fishing mate, would be sitting in the old Lada at the corner, no doubt with a 'bighead spliff' which he had fired up while he was waiting for him. He could just about see the rear of Choppy's old 'salad' in the distance, when a sharp metallic sound shattered the silence of the lane behind him. He turned to see several men in uniform coming towards him carrying M-16s and Kalashnikovs.

Mr George recognised the men as being from the notorious Hammond Barracks police section. Their white combat helmets and dark blue fatigues distinguished them from the rest of the constabulary. This was the government's Operation Eradication squad, a rapid response unit deployed to combat the rising tidal wave of violence on the island.

"Ole man," one of the men called out, "we come fe yuh, bwoy! Whe' you live?"

The fisherman shook his head in disbelief, squinting and shuffling backwards, his eyebrows knotted in confusion. *Why dem want Delroy?* He had no idea, but he knew that these men weren't about to start giving explanations.

"What de raas unuh want him for? Him nuh live yah."

He angrily tried to dismiss their questions.

"You ah lie, ole man , we nuh have time fe no liar. I want you to give yuh bwoy dah message yah, an' nuh leave not'n out, understan me…"

They cocked their weapons.

BLAM! BLAM! BADDAP! BADDAP!

The gunshots startled Simba awake. He rose bolt upright. They sounded as if they had come from just down the lane. Had he dreamt it? He rubbed his eyes. How long had he been asleep? Was it a minute or an hour?

His heart was pounding in his chest.

Mama Christy stirred in her sleep but didn't wake. The night was silent again, but Simba was still anxious and lay tense listening for any sound.

All he could hear at first was his own breathing, then he heard the sound of running feet, stumbling and frantic. Someone crashed through the gate and skidded to a stop right outside their door. Fists slammed on the shaky door frame.

"Mama Christy! Mama Christy! Fe God almighty sake, open de door!"

The Ranking shot out of bed in his shorts and string vest and pulled the door wide open. Choppy stood in the doorway trembling uncontrollably, his eyes filled with tears and his thick lips trembling with anguish.

"Him dead, man!" he bawled. "Dem kill him, Delroy, Jesus Christ him dead..."

He pointed out at the street.

Mama Christy came up to the front door still groggy and disoriented with sleep. But by then Delroy had tumbled out of the door in his shorts and was running in the direction his father took to work every night.

A group of dreary-eyed Pink Lane residents were standing in a circle — women 'bawling' wringing their hands and men running around helpless, like headless chickens. They parted as Delroy ran through, almost stumbling over the figure sprawled across the sewer, his dripping blood colouring the slow-flowing water red.

Hot tears streamed down Simba's face. He stared down in horror and sheer confusion at his father's crumpled, bloody body.

Mr George was hardly recognisable, his body shattered with bullet holes. His hat lay near him.

Simba fell to his knees and sobbed as he had never done before, hugging the blood-stained body of his father.

"Dem kill him! De man dem kill Missa George!" Simba howled like a wild animal. "Unuh ah hear me? Whoever do this to me ole man ah go pay wid dem raas life. Unuh ah hear me, star?

"WHEREVER UNUH DEH, UNUH AH GO PAY!"

NINE

It had been days since she received the outcome of the tests and Monique had still not recovered.

The first shock had come about a week ago, in the form of her late period. Monique's cycle had never been this late before. Though she was worried, she simply put the tests off day after day. But with every twenty-four hours of anguish that passed, it became more evident what was wrong. The home test kit confirmed it, but she still wanted a second opinion. The results from the pharmacist blew away any remaining doubts.

She was pregnant.

Monique was devastated. All the meticulous care she took to protect herself had ended in an accident. Simba knew there was something wrong too, but there was no way she would discuss this with him until she knew what her options where.

If she had any at all.

She tried to reason out her dilemma logically.

Monique knew the Saint well enough to realise that if he found out about this, he would force her to abort the child.

Then there was Simba. He wanted his freedom to roam unrestricted. Monique couldn't see him accepting the responsibilities of fatherhood. She loved him, but music came first to Simba. That left her alone and confused. It took her some time to stop feeling sorry for herself and realise that this could be a blessing in disguise.

Monique had always wanted children — and she couldn't deny she was feeling a steadily-building sense of elation — but if it was going to happen she didn't want it to happen like this. She didn't want her child born to a backdrop of lies and infidelity. It would seem that the decision to leave Hugh had been made for her.

But she would have to do this alone.

There had been little else on her mind all day, and when she finally arrived home from work in the early evening she poured herself a large rum, which she drank neat to help calm her nerves.

She was on her third glass when she heard the front door click shut and Hugh's footsteps nearing the living room. Monique sat up straight and tried unsuccessfully to control her racing heart. She would not scurry away intimidated but she hated it when he came in and saw her relaxed, off guard. Hugh had been his usual irascible self when he'd come in the night before and Monique had simply tried to ignore him as usual. But this morning, following a brief phone call, she noticed that his mood became lighter.

The room was dark apart from the flickering light from the colour television as her husband entered and flopped himself into a leather easy chair. He grunted something, stretching out and closed his eyes. Monique followed his movements in the gloom, saying nothing. Her heart said to tell him straight, there and then, but she knew she had to bide her time.

"Can't you pour your weary husband a drink, woman? Or do I have to call the maid to do it?"

He kicked his shoes off and glanced in Monique's direction.

A man in his late forties, Hugh St. John was moderately built, with the 'rich man belly' often associated with Jamaican men of his social class. His hair was dark brown, blending evenly with his tanned skin and his deep blue eyes. They were a legacy from his English parents, aristocrats who had fled the embarrassment of a bankrupt business and the very real prospect of poverty. Borrowing money from family they left Britain for the altogether more attractive ambience of Jamaica, where their blue blood was held in high regard.

Monique didn't want an argument, she got up silently and walked to the elaborate bar close to where he was sitting. She reached for a crystal glass, dropped two ice cubes in and poured three shots from a bottle of Ballantine Gold Label whisky.

The Saint took the glass eagerly and sipped it with both hands. He looked up at Monique standing before him.

"You are not in a very talkative mood, me dear," he rasped. "What have you been up to these last couple of days? Any new projects on the way?"

The question itself was harmless enough. But his tone seemed to be edged with sarcasm...or was it her imagination? Monique stood there thrown off balance for a moment and chewed on her bottom lip trying to conceal her nervousness.

"Why the sudden interest in what I do?" she snapped, a little too quickly. The Saint picked up on his wife's nervousness and smiled inwardly. He knew her well enough to know when she was uptight.

It's okay, darling I know, he thought. *I know how you're fucking Simba Ranking, but let me have my fun first and then later...*

"But what is this?" The Saint's voice was low, threatening. "Don't get feisty with me, woman. It's a simple question, why is it making you jumpy? Are you hiding something?"

A sardonic smile ran across his lips.

"I've got nothing more to hide than you have when you're fucking the maids, dear husband," Monique reminded him icily.

"I *expect...*" the Saint stressed the word "...my wife to show me respect, not this 'independent woman' bullshit I've been getting over the past months."

He wagged his finger threateningly at her.

"You want us to have an understanding, then get with the program, gal, because I'm not standing for any more of it."

"Respect, did you say, Hugh? Is that what you want from me? You better learn to give some and you might get some. You married your equal, darling, when are you going to learn that I'm not some servant girl?"

The Saint turned on the balls of his feet, as if he was buoyed up by his wife's reproach.

"Don't raise your voice to me, gal!" he barked.

"And don't call me 'gal'!" she responded quickly. "What's eating you this evening, frustrated are we? Well, I have a suggestion. Why don't you take the new maid up to our bedroom? I hear those ghetto girls have the 'wickedest slam'. Maybe that will help you to calm down."

The Saint's eyes bulged. He would have slapped her there and then, but he had already decided on the ultimate way to humiliate her. He wanted to catch them together, and then show lover boy the real meaning of pain. With effort he controlled his temper.

"You think you're smart, eh?" he asked. "But try not to use it with me. I control you."

She kissed her teeth. He calmly walked over to the stereo unit and touched play on the CD. The sounds of James Brown filled the room from the low resistance speakers. The Saint set his glass down on the crystal side table and walked towards Monique, who was standing by the cocktail bar.

"Don't you realise yet that I own all of you? Everyt'ing! You...are...mine. My property."She laughed humourlessly.

"Get real, Hugh. I'm not one of your woman outta road. Wake up. You don't own anything but your sorry self."

The Saint snickered.

"You of all people know how I do business. Nobody stands in my way. I win or nobody wins. Anybody standing in my fucking way has to pay for it."

He paused, stooping down beside the bookcase. He picked up an empty Dragon stout bottle and looked at it with interest.

Jesus Christ! Monique thought wildly. How could the maid have missed that? Then she remembered it was the maid's morning off. She cursed herself for being so careless

Hugh walked slowly towards her.

"If, for instance, I ever discovered that you were keeping another man with me..."

His voice became a whisper.

The suddenness of his words rooted her to the spot, taking her unawares.

He knows! The bastard knows. The Saint stood in front of her with a sinister grin on his face. He studied her features closely, then took her chin in his hand and massaged it gently with his thumb. Monique closed her eyes, unable to move, as he ran his fingers over her nose, her lips, her cheeks. She could feel his cigar and whisky breath, hot on her forehead.

"I don't like competition in business." He rasped "But if a man try compete wid me for you — heh! People die Monique, families die, when them try dat. Do you understand?"

Monique said nothing.

The Saint started rubbing his palm over her nose and mouth with more aggression each time, then held her jaw in a tight grip.

"Do you understand?"

Monique shook her head loose and knocked his hand away defiantly, stepping back beyond his reach. She knew these where not idle threats. The Saint continued:

"What a bangarang if dat scenario was a true one." He laughed.

Trying to make light of his previous tactics of intimidation.

Then suddenly he switched the emphasis back to the stout bottle in his hand, pointing it at her accusingly.

"By the way, who did leave dis bottle of Dragon here? I don't drink de stuff... or have you started to hit the bottle? In which case you could have chosen somet'ing more in your bracket."

He's playing games again, she thought. *Why doesn't the bastard just come straight out with it? He's trying to trap me.*

Monique looked up at her husband's searching eyes. Fortunately she didn't have to think long or hard to come up with an answer, Simba had provided one.

"Well pardon me, the next time a courier delivers anything to me, I'll make sure they leave their drinks outside," she countered sarcastically.

"You do dat."

St. John toyed with the bottle some more, as if deliberating over her answer. Then he replaced it on the floor.

"You've been a good girl, then Monique." He walked over to her slowly. Monique backed away, matching his steps and eyed him keenly. "And for being a good girl," he breathed deeply, stripping off his jacket and loosening his tie, "you can have the pleasure of this."

He unzipped his trousers and jerked out his hardened penis, holding it firmly with his left hand.

"With my compliments, me dear." He smiled.

"Not even if you were the last man on earth, Hugh."

"Then you will go without a man." He screamed. "That is a much better alternative!" She fired back and stormed off.

It was moments later, as she bolted her room door, that her stomach knotted, and the realisation that he knew more than he was saying dawned on her.

TEN

Oh, what a ruff old life
What a tuff old life
For a ghetto man an' his child
Oh, what a ruff old life
What a tuff old life
You haffe give it a fight
Rough Life, Shabba Ranks

The rain fell in dark waves across the white tombstones of May Pen Cemetery. Unusually, today there was a reason other than work to brave the elements. The huge crowd at the cemetery had one purpose and one purpose alone — to pay their last respects. The many umbrellas around the graveside formed a weather-proof covering, protecting elaborate hairstyles and expensive clothes.

Father Justin Ho stood on the moist red mud, surrounded by people, his head uncovered, his purple vestments dripping with rain. Simba's parish priest and good friend had buried so many victims of violent death in his district over the past five months that he had become hardened to it; victims who had so much to live for but who got caught up in the political madness that was engulfing the city.

He slowly recited the burial prayers over another innocent. Mr George may not have been a regular churchgoer, but the fisherman always donated part of his catch to feed poor people through the Catholic church's aid scheme. To Father Ho, Mr George was like one of those selfless characters in the Bible, for even though his family were struggling to survive themselves, 'Maas' George gave as much as he could. Those who were close to him remembered that one of his favourite sayings was 'de more you give ah de more you get'.

Delroy stood on top of the hillock and stared down at the gathering around his father's graveside. The wind whipped

67

at his jacket while his mind raced through past and present.

Mama Christy concerned him more than anything else. She was taking it all so very hard — not sleeping, not eating and her small market stall business was suffering. She had been unable to get over the shock of losing her life-long partner. It was not supposed to be this way. Her husband was a hard-working man who never did anybody a wrong, so how could they have killed him?

Simba sighed as he thought about how much his mother had wept over the last few days. Nothing he said seemed to ease her anguish. He decided that he needed to move fast on his plans of lifting his mother out of poverty's shackles. His father's untimely death had hit home hard, and Simba feared that he might lose the opportunity to ease his mother's burden, even for a part of her life.

For Mr George the move they had dreamed of as a family, to a better life outside the rat race, was never to be. Nothing could change that. But Simba was not about to give up. His father's memory was worth much more than that.

The day after his father's death, Simba got on his bike and searched for new accommodation. He and Mama Christy could never feel safe in their home, while Mr George's killer still roamed the streets. They had to get out. He eventually found a place in Harbour View that was cheap enough to rent and far enough away from the bad memories. The area was quite neutral, politically speaking, and the residents were a few rungs above the rock bottom sufferah class. It was a sanctuary in the Ranking's eyes.

Monique had come through for him again with moral and financial support, even crying openly when he told her about his father's death. She helped to soothe him when he was able to be with her, and was only too willing to help with the deposit on the apartment. Monique had long transcended the novelty status he had unfairly given her in the beginning of their relationship. She was 'de real McCoy', but Simba was not the settling down type and even if he was, what about the Saint…?

With the new home by the sea, Simba had felt a tangible

weight lifted off his shoulders, until today. Today the horror of his father's death came rushing back.

He turned away from the mourners in sorrow. His gaze was drawn to the unkempt graves behind. He read the inscription on one:

Here lies Digital,
A ghetto youth
Who lived life to the full
And payed the ultimate price

Delroy bowed his head. He had been lucky in the lottery of life. He could have been buried there beside his friend. Why had he escaped with his life when his friends weren't so lucky? And now his father murdered. Why did ghetto living have to be like this?

Survival on every level.

If you couldn't get a job (and be certain you couldn't with a ghetto address), how where you supposed to survive? The only option was to juggle. But life was cheap in the ghetto, and the risks were too high.

After Digital and Speng had been shot dead in front of his eyes, Simba had buried his gun and tried to forget his bad bwoy days, but now, with the death of his father, it was like he was being drawn back into the life he had shunned, to take revenge. It was as if life were playing a game with him; his restraint had dissolved into nothingness.

Going legal had been an uphill struggle, but he had stayed humble and waited for his time patiently. The small dances he had kept around town, amidst everything that was going on, had been successful beyond even his expectations.

Now, with Monique's help, he was finally on his way to promoting his first major dance, and it all seemed worth it. Or was it? One thing he did know was that if he found out who killed his father, revenge would be taken. He would never rest. What else could he do to ease his grief?

With a clenched fist, he 'bigged up' his dead brethren for

the last time. His face was a mask of determination as he turned to rejoin the mourners.

He walked over to his mother and hugged her. His eyes roamed across the unsmiling faces of the mourners, tightly crammed together. The churchgoers' respectful gazes and their lack of familiarity with the changing face of fashion stood out among the throng. They sang mournfully, their voices lifting up above the patter of a light rainfall.

Ashes to ashes, dust to dust…the priest's handful of dirt hit the coffin below and triggered a distressed wail from Mama Christy as the realisation hit her that this was it, the final goodbye. Her legs buckled but her son was there in support absorbing her sobs as they vibrated through his body. The loss and anger welded up in him like a volcano about to erupt, but Simba could not bring himself to cry.

Choppy stood beside him, immersed in his own turmoil. He could have been lying beside his friend in a burial plot, if he hadn't kept a low profile in the car as the gunshots exploded. But then, as the killers passed him, Choppy had recognised one. He had been asking questions around Wellington Street, saying he was a promoter looking for talented deejays. Now that 'raas' face was burned into his memory.

He was torn between telling Delroy what he knew and saying nothing. Looking across at the anguish in his eyes he accepted the youngster had a right to know. But at the same time he knew Delroy to be a wild youth from his school days, and feared that the boy would get himself mixed up in something he couldn't handle. He was sure that Delroy would want to go after his father's killers regardless of the consequences, but that kind of attitude would only serve to increase the bloodshed. Maybe it was better to let sleeping dogs lie. Mr George was dead and gone and no amount of revenge would bring him back.

But withholding the information was not as easy as Choppy imagined. He felt uncomfortable when Delroy came over to him and thanked him for everything he had done. Choppy felt like a villain himself for not telling what he knew.

Choppy stretched across to touch Delroy's elbow.

"Yout'man," he said. "We must talk. Is somet'ing important I t'ink you need to know."

"It cyan wait, Choppy?" Delroy asked. "Me waan bring Mama home, still. You know how it go, she nah tek this so good."

"Mek Skilly tek her home," Choppy suggested. "This is important." He paused to think. "You know de bar at de corner ah Matches Lane?"

Delroy nodded.

"After this meet me deh."

Choppy had made up his mind, he would tell Delroy everything.

Simba watched him walk away, his head lowered, pellets of rain soaking him through, and him not even caring.

A man wid nuff t'ings 'pon him mind.

Simba would soon realise how true that was.

Five days later, a happy officer strutted down the Denham Town police station stairs on a sunny Sunday evening, already imagining his girl's 'sweet' rice and peas dinner waiting for him at her home.

He could practically taste the cool carrot juice washing down the delicious food, and savoured the anticipation of some serious 'bed wuk' afterwards. He grinned broadly and patted the .38 special under his arm. He could do with two days off from the beat. This election was tiring him out.

In times like these being a 'red seam' was a hazardous occupation, the only perk he enjoyed were the profitable little odd jobs he performed for his boss. And they were coming very frequently. Most times these tasks were dangerous, but the money was good. Very good.

But he had to be extra careful about flaunting his earnings, or driving his 'criss' Honda Accord to work. That would be asking for unwelcome attention from his constabulary colleagues, the last thing he needed in his

71

already stressful life.

He slung his bag over his shoulder and trotted across the road to the bus stop in front of May Pen Cemetery. The sooner he was away from this battle zone the better, he thought.

There were no pedestrians walking the streets, and he didn't really expect to see any. It would be dark in three hours and these parts were to be avoided at all cost, even by those with a reputation like his. Just three days before the country's general elections, spirits were high.

The polls all predicted a closely-contested election. For himself, he simply wanted a change, a new guard and some serious opportunities to make money from young politicians like his 'boss'. They would be doing their part, at least for this area of Kingston, to make sure that the seat would be won by the only man who could turn things around for the neighbourhood.

The off-duty policeman flicked out a Craven 'A' from his pack and resigned himself to a long wait. The mild smoke soothed him as he exhaled through both nostrils.

Then he heard the urgent screech of a car braking behind him. Startled, he turned around to see three men wheel out of an old Escort, assault rifles trained on him as one screamed out:

"Tu'n round, beast bwoy an' keep yuh hand up high where me can see dem!"

The policeman spun around immediately and his hands shot up. One of the men frisked him, pulling out his .38 special from his shoulder holster and laughed, a coarse chuckle.

"Ah this yuh government give you fe protect poor people wid, bwoy?" He fired a shot into the air from his captive's .38 and the other men caught on to the joke and started laughing as well.

"A one pop dat babylon," he scoffed. "Hear dis…" He released a booming volley from his weapon, which made the revolver sound like a cap gun. The policeman was in shock expecting a swift end. His ordeal had only just begun.

A brown paper bag was rammed over his head and he was jostled into the car and driven away.

Estimating the drive at about twenty minutes, he sat passively, trying to figure out the twists and turns of their route. He had been forced head down into the foot space in front of the back seat, while two of the men rested their dirty boots on his back and buttocks.

Finally the car stopped. The policeman was unceremoniously pulled out and dragged over what seemed like an open stretch of land. The parched dirt underfoot crunched with every step he took. They walked him for about a hundred metres before he was stopped. His clothes were cut off him with ratchets, he stood naked and was kicked to the ground. Before he could even catch his breath, he was grabbed and tied to a post. He tensed as he felt the bite of electrical wire gnawing into his wrists and ankles. He let out a wail of despair, his fate, he knew was hanging in the balance.

"Why unuh ah do dis to me, man? Wha' me do unuh?" he pleaded from beneath the paper bag.

"Jus' keep yuh raas mout' shut, beast bwoy. Me ah ask all the questions round yah so."

The officer wished he could see the bastards' faces properly, so he could deal with them at a later stage. But then he thought again — dead men tell no tales, nor do they take revenge...

He tensed again as he felt the pole being lifted behind him, then he was dragged a few yards and thrown into a ditch without warning. He hit his head as he crashed down, but fortunately for him the earth beneath him was soft. Within seconds he heard the sound of a spade shovelling and then felt earth fall on top of him. The realisation of what was happening hit him like a bullet.

De fucker dem ah go bury me alive.

He panicked, but with his hands and feet tied to the heavy pole on top of him his frantic wrenching and twisting were to no avail. He coughed and spluttered and gasped for air as more and more earth fell on top of him. He made use of his last moments on earth to say a prayer.

"Me have some question fe yuh, pussyhole."

The voice was emotionless. The shovelling stopped.

"An' yuh better answer dem up front, seen?"

If I'm going to die anyway, why should I answer any questions?

Silence wasn't what they wanted to hear, and the man with the spade used it, quickly and effectively, on the policeman's knee. The pain seared through his entire body and seemed to penetrate to his mind. That scream would echo in the ears of his captors for days. He was a lot more cooperative after that. Questions came thick and fast from all around the blindfolded man, confusing him.

"Who send you fe kill a man 'pon Pink Lane de other day, bwoy?"

"Who pull de trigger?"

"Wha' for?"

"If you want fe come outta this alive, Babylon, yuh bettah answer de question. De longer you wait, de more we ah go lick yuh raas."

Then another whack from the spade on the same knee, but this time the policeman's cry died in his throat as a lump of earth slipped into his mouth. When he recovered, the answers came flooding out.

"It was a mistake, boss," he bawled. "Ah de wrong man we shot. It was a big mistake, boss man, believe me..."

"Who bust de shot dem?"

The officer stuttered and squirmed.

"Me was the lookout, boss, me nevah see who fire de shot dem. Believe me, man, me nevah see," he pleaded, tearfully.

"Ah who sen' you then?"

The same unfeeling voice fired the question with impatience.

The policeman hesitated.

He felt the cold touch of the spade pressing down on his

neck. He tensed and screamed:

"Me nuh know, boss!"

It wasn't good enough.

"You t'ink we ah ramp wid yuh, bumboclaat bwoy?"

One of the interrogators stamped the policeman in the groin; he stiffened, his body jerked outwards and a muffled dumb note came from his lips. But still there was no answer to the question. They looked at each other silently, wondering whether the 'beast' was speaking the truth.

"Me ah go ask you again, bwoy, who ordered de hit?"

His voice was just a weak moan:

"Me tell you a'ready, man…me nuh know who run t'ings…rasta know me ah tell de truth."

A voice that seemed to float from a distance pierced the tension.

"So you 'fraid ah dis man yah more than yuh 'fraid fe dead, bwoy? Then hear me nuh. Whoever yuh boss is, him jus' lose a good man."

The shovelling resumed, as the officer began to scream for mercy. His captors didn't stop shovelling until only his face was left uncovered.

This time they would let him live, for he might eventually lead them to the truth. And they knew with certainty they would find out who had ordered the hit.

Long run, short ketch.

Mr George's memory deserved no less.

His death would not go unpunished.

ELEVEN

Monique lay beside him on the bed fast asleep.

Simba was feeling a mixture of excitement and concern, and could not sleep even after making love so passionately. He sat silently on the edge of the firm four poster bed at a motel up town, admiring the smooth curves on his new Bally shoes. His mind wandered for an instant as he looked through the louvered bedroom windows at the orange haze of Kingston sprawled down below. Town was beginning to stir for its Saturday night grand performance. The nightclubs would soon be full, the cinemas bulging and the dance halls rampacked despite the politics and violence.

Simba looked around him and his earlier feeling of depression and despondency rose up to tease him again. He kissed his teeth.

Today had been a frustrating one. He had learned nothing new about why his father had been shot dead by the police. The story of mistaken identity he had been told by some outraged Rema man did not settle well with him. There was more to the shooting than that, but he couldn't find the missing piece of the jigsaw. In the meantime he needed someone to be around, someone to take his mind off his worries. That someone could only be Monique.

Earlier he had called on her mobile and she had seemed eager for them to meet. Simba interpreted her urgency as a sign that she was missing him badly, but discovered later that was just a part of the problem.

They met at the Motel La Barge at the foot of Beverly Hills, a plush establishment with only fifty rooms, which was full of pretentious rich people with social problems, well known for its discretion and a staff who kept their mouths shut. Simba wasn't about to complain. With the pain of losing his father, he had forgotten how much he detested these bogus uptown people. As for the surroundings, this was as good a place as any to meet up.

What he needed was some good, good loving and right now it didn't matter to Simba if he got it uptown or 'dung inna de ghetto'.

Monique had arrived at the motel gates with a split lip, swelling on her arms and dark glasses covering her tears. She had said it was an accident, but couldn't lie successfully to an accomplished liar like the Ranking.

He knew the Saint had done it.

And Simba was livid. He wanted to give the fucker a taste of his own medicine, and see if he could take the kind of punishment he dished out so readily.

But that was wishful thinking.

The Saint was much too powerful for Simba to even consider hurting, yet the Ranking kept playing with the idea in his head. It made him feel better.

As soon as they settled in the motel room Monique had sat him down and calmly explained to him that she would be going away. She needed time to think and be away from everything, she said. She felt that she was losing control. At one time the Ranking would not care one way or the other about one of his gals' problems but, contrary to the cocks man code of conduct, Simba was involved with Monique up to his neck.

There was no point in him protesting either, he wanted her in Kingston with him but for once he refused to think just about himself. He encouraged her to go, because he knew the Saint was capable of anything. Her home life was hell and becoming more dangerous daily — and something more was up. Throughout the evening she had been on the verge of telling him something, but each time he asked what was on her mind she would say:

"Oh, it's nothing."

Simba sensed that whatever she had been keeping from him was tied up in some way to the drastic move she was planning.

He lay awake staring at the ceiling, thinking about tonight's big dance. This was his test, the move from more modest promotions to 'big t'ings'. He hoped it would lay the foundation for him to claw his way out of poverty for good with his own efforts.

Monique murmured faintly as she slept. Simba turned to catch a soft word or two. She was sobbing and calling her husband's name.

He kissed his teeth, cursing the Saint's very name and rose up from the bed slowly, squinting to see in the darkness of the room. He walked to the windows and drew back the curtains to allow in a streak of light from the security lights outside. It was bright enough for him to see his reflection in the full-length mirror. He stared at himself keenly, studying his new haircut.

The top was cut at an angle, with a peak. The sides were cut low, with two short parallel parts near his left temple. *A wicked trim, Buckey,* he said to himself — congratulating his barber from Nine Miles — and gave a rare gold-toothed grin, then flicked some dust off the lapel of his black and brown Cerati silk trouser and shirt suit which was a a gift from Monique. It had come all the way from Milan, Italy, and had been specially tailored for him.

Tonight he would have to boost up his bredrins for sure, or else he would be coming home without a shirt on his back. 'Cyan no yout' can touch 'dis style yah'.

He reverently swung his heavyweight 'cargo' chain around his neck to add the finishing touch. *Don ah don an' idiot ah idiot,* he thought snickering. It was time to go. Simba went over to Monique, who was still asleep on the bed, and kissed her lightly on the cheek. They would meet up before she left for the country.

"Little more," he whispered to her, and he left.

The night was warm with a slight breeze. The frequent rainfalls of the last few weeks had all but finished, and it was the perfect weather for Delroy to be modelling his new superbike. The Ninja stood like a sleek red and black beast on its kick-stand. Simba caressed the gas tank lovingly.

Is a good t'ing me have my PhD in riding dem road yah, he said to himself. *This baby yah will do de job nicely.* He stroked the handlebars, placed the matching helmet on his head, and glanced at his watch. *Mus' leave yahso now,* he thought, hoisting himself onto the bike and turning the ignition key.

He had just one stop to make, at Constant Spring Mews, to collect some blank cassettes from a 'big batty t'ing', who wasn't able to make the dance tonight. He didn't want her to be vexed with him or his monthly 'one touch' would be in jeopardy.

With a 'bumpa like dat' it was the least he could do.

Uptown was buzzing as Simba rode through. The plazas along Half-Way Tree and Constant Spring roads were seething with youthful activity. Soon the flashing panorama of high-rise buildings deteriorated into a haze of greyness, and appearing from this came the more austere — and painfully familiar — surroundings of western Kingston. Simba decided to take his own tried and tested short cut to the Rockfort area. He slowed the bike down to a near crawl and broke left into a zinc-fenced side street. As he wound his way through familiar alleys and backstreets, dodging the frequent potholes, memories of times he'd spent at these old haunts flooded back, filling his mind with a mixture of good and bad emotions. Those experiences had played a major role in his survival and progress.

The dance would start soon, and he would relish the look on the faces of Pablo and the crew if he got there on time for once — and rolling up on the 'criss' Ninja at that. They would have to change his nickname from 'Always-Late-Fe-Dance' and start calling him 'De Eva-Ready Kid'. He would have to earn that title, though, and so there was no time to waste. Simba pulled his bike up into a roaring wheelie, and noticed the walls of Vineyard Town were strewn with his own flyers:

NUBIAN HI-POWER CHARITY DANCE
proceeds for Lane Community Centre Fund Action
takes place at
OUR FATHER'S PLACE, ROCKFORT
on
26TH MAY
GIRLS SKIN OUT AND DO THE BOGLE AND
BUTTERFLY
with
BUJU BANTON
CAPLETON
DADDY SCREW
BERESFORD HAMMOND

The message was plastered over nearly every flat surface Simba passed, and he smiled at how effectively the Pink Lane 'juveniles' had his dance advertised all over 'town'.

It was an astonishing line-up, so many stars on one bill and all happy to perform free of charge, agreeing that the majority of the money should go to the restoration of the local community centre. The skillful negotiating behind this had all been down to Simba and because this was a Ranking Promotion there wouldn't be any problem with unreliable entertainers who didn't turn up. It was widely known that the Ranking was able to deliver the artists as promised.

A short ride later, Simba was at the dance. Even before he got to the gate, it was pure roadblock. A mass of people had assembled outside and 'de crowd ah people' were becoming excited. Orderly queues were an alien concept to the dancehall fraternity. Men and women who had taken meticulous care and patience to look their best for the evening were now being squeezed and mauled at the head of the crowd by other revellers screaming and pushing to get inside.

The women always won hands down when it came to looking 'trash'. Triple-pierced ears, diamond-studded noses and the elaborate 'dung town' fashions were designed to race the pulses and raise the nature. Nothing was left to the imagination in some cases, with everyone from the loud-mouthed 'pancoot' from west to the pretentious 'browning' from east dressed in their finery.

Around the edges of the crowd, the sounds and smells and hustle and bustle of the vendors created almost as much excitement as there was at the head of the crowd.

When a dance was 'ram' it brought business to many sectors of the community, and everybody wanted to cash in on the success. The peanut cart vendors whistled for business as the steam from charcoal-heated nuts forced mist through their little metal chimneys. The lisped cry of 'Nuttsy! Nuttsy! Salt nuts and Ital nuts!' sounded from an old dread whose cart was surrounded by peckish revellers. Another dread sold sugar cane, chopping through the tall stalks with his machete.

Revellers were spoilt for choice; the line of vendors went on and on. You could buy everything from Wrigleys to jerk chicken and if you were 'fat wid cash' or fancied your chances of making more 'corn' before you entered the dance, you could play a little 'crown and anchor'.

Beyond all this activity a sleek black Mercedes Benz rumbled forward, full-beaming its headlamps into the unsuspecting bystanders, blinding everyone in its path. The driver, hidden from view behind the darkened windows of the 190E, parked as far from neighbouring vehicles as possible.

A short distance away, a youth leaning proudly on his spruced-up bicycle kissed his teeth loudly, but when he noticed the license plate 'DREAD 4 U' he buttoned his mouth swiftly and focused his attention elsewhere.

The front doors of the Mercedes swung open and two men stepped out.

"Wha' de bloodclaat ah 'appen yahso, man?" the taller of the two men called out, his short locks bouncing on his head as he spoke. Through beady red eyes he looked around him at the crowds gathered outside the dance.

"It look like me underestimate my bwoy. Him seh to me before me leave fe Washington that it would be a small t'ing. No need to get involved, Mikey, it's fe charity, him seh. But look 'pon dis…"

He motioned with a wide sweep of his scrawny hands.

"Him ah try mek I man look like a fool. Using my sound fe raise money fe charity. You believe dat?"

The second man, who was fat and stocky, laughed hoarsely.

"So you mean seh, you nah line you pockets from dis dance yah, star?" he asked with an edge of sarcasm. He already knew the answer but he wanted the question to pain his employer.

"De only man making any raas money tonight from dis dance is de one Simba Ranking. Him tek me fe idiot. I will deal wid him inna my own way an' inna my own time. Him t'ink him can bandulu de dread an' go tell him frien'? Yuh mad!"

Mikey Dread's nostrils flared and his red eyes seemed to burn. He turned towards his fat minder.

"Come mek we go inside an' surprise de prento promoter, nuh?"

The fat man smirked.

"Your kinda surprise mek man end up inna board box, Mikey."

"Ah t'ink fe once, Fat Man, yuh right."

The two men moved quickly into the inner core of densely packed bodies. Fat Man cut a path before him by barking, in his booming baritone:

"Mikey D. ah come thru! *Watch it! Watch it!* De boss waan pass, seen? Small up yuhself, nuh!" His voice carried over the noise of the crowd, and everyone knew enough of Fat Man's reputation to obey his command and make way.

Mikey Dread was walking casually behind as the fat man made like a latter-day Moses parting the Red Sea. He understood the importance of a reputation in town. Especially in the dancehall business. If you didn't have respect, you couldn't make it as a promoter, for you would definitely get dissed by the prentos eager to take over.

At Mikey's level — top level promotions — he needed respect from everybody. The only person he wasn't getting it from was the one Simba Ranking. Even the tough-looking bouncers at the gate were in awe of the man who was cutting a swathe through the massive. The gatemen's eyes locked on the 'maaga' dread as he approached them grim-faced. Their collective surprise showed on their faces as the boss strode past them without a word of acknowledgment.

"Boss, we didn't expect to see…"

One gateman tried to explain, but Fat Man and Mikey Dread were already past the doors and heading into the lawn.

"PAM-PAM!"

The deejay's voice exploded through the speakers placed around the lawn as Mikey Dread approached. *Criss!* the Dread reflected in admiration, *no sound in Jamaica can play like dis.*

Ghetto people were skilled at exaggerating a situation to what they would like it to be, just through a name. And so the 'lawn' was actually an open air concrete enclosure, where no grass could grow, purpose-built for dances and named in honour of the garden parties held by the rich on their lawns.

The twinkling stars shone in the night sky above the revellers, adding a romantic air to the session. The control tower was set into the far end of the semi-circular floor plan. The lighting was dim and hung on a few poles scattered around the compound, and a bar shed to one side provided liquor, soft drinks and light snacks.

The air felt heavy with bass. Reggae bass.

"I man cyan believe dis," said Mikey D. to no one in particular.

"My promotion dem nevah cork like dis."

Fat Man said nothing as he advanced towards the control desk.

The operator was oblivious to the approaching men. He stood poised over three turntables and an array of equalisers and amplifiers, poking and prodding at dials and knobs and lining up needles to records. He bobbed his head to the music like he had no control of it.

A pensive Mikey Dread stood a few feet away, watching Pablo, the operator and his excited prancing. Pablo spun the next 'criss biscuit' on the turntable without noticing the Dread's presence. When Mikey had seen enough, he reached forward and pulled the earphones off Pablo's head.

"Wha' de raa…!"

Pablo's angry eyes shot up ready for a fight. As recognition struck his face froze, and then melted into a grin for his boss.

"Missa D, me nevah expect you back from de States today, boss. I was looking fe you end ah week."

"Change ah plan," Mikey said abruptly over the din of the music.

"Whe' de bwoy Simba deh?"

Pablo cleared his throat nervously, aware that Mikey was in a bad mood and immediately guessed why.

"Him shoulda deh yah by now," he looked around wistfully.

"Ah him ah introduce de dancehall star dem."

He looked at the digital time display on his console and shrugged.

"You mean dem artist really ah perform yah tonight?" the Dread asked. "Dis ah nuh some con de yout' Simba ah try work up?"

Pablo shook his head, but said nothing.

"Straight up?" Mikey probed persistently.

"Fe real, Missa D," Pablo confirmed.

The Dread experienced a sinking sensation in the pit of his stomach. It seemed that whatever his protege, Simba, turned his hand to in the music business succeeded. The impressive turnout at this dance *could* have been a fluke, but he couldn't help thinking that his efforts to keep the Ranking's talents in check were coming to nothing. The possibility of losing the title of Jamaica's premier sound man and promoter to this young upstart crossed his mind. If he could hold a one-off dance like this, what would stop him deciding to go independent on a permanent basis? Simba Ranking was obviously more than capable.

Mikey knew better than anyone how exceptional Simba Ranking's talents were, especially since he had produced and distributed three of Simba's tracks in the States and England. The response had been phenomenal and the royalties brought him a handsome profit. He had even received a couple of letters from some woman at Pony Records, expressing an interest in his artist, but he had destroyed them after reading them.

Simba was hot and so Dread had decided to keep hold of him until he was in a position to control his actions. Then Simba could sign a million dollar deal of which he, Mikey Dread, as 'producer', would be the main beneficiary. Until that happened he would keep the news about Pony Records' interest hidden from Simba.

Now, though, with the success of this dance, Simba would be more difficult to control.

Ah push up him chest like ah him run t'ings.

What grieved Mikey Dread the most was that Simba's success tonight was made possible with the use of his own Nubian Hi-Power sound. Why oh why had he agreed to let Simba use his equipment for even something as innocent as a charity dance?

It would not happen again.

Pablo was just placing the needle on another vinyl, as the sound of Pinchers came through the speakers. The Dread studied him intently. "Whe' him get de corn from fe pay all dem artist deh?"

Pablo looked blank, then stuttered a reply.

"H-h-him nuh use no money, boss, most ah dem man yah grow up inna de ghetto like Simba. Them all understan' de need fe a community centre yahso. Is jus' a sign ah respect, Missa D."

The dread winced.

"Respect!" he bawled out. "Ah respect you call it? Inna fe me book me call it disrespect! Imagine, a hurry-come-up bloodclaat bwoy from Pink Lane ah come test de Dread? De yout' couldn't read or write until de other day, an' him ah try fe move in 'pon my livelihood an' getting de respect from big time entertainer over I."

The Dread slapped his chest in defiance.

"I jus' ah tell you how I understand it, boss."

Pablo held his arms up in submission.

"Me jus' ah tell you how me get it."

Fat Man remained silent throughout his boss' outburst. His job didn't include cooling Mikey's hot temper. He wasn't paid to comment, just to protect.

His anger vented, Mikey Dread lit a cigarette and leaned back on the wooden post behind him, waiting for Simba to arrive.

Outside, the crowd seemed to have dwindled somewhat as some of the revellers had become resigned to the fact that it would be near impossible to get inside, and had gone home. Others decided to do their jamming outside for free, listening to the sounds from within floating out into the street. But the entrance to Our Father's Place was still blocked by the 'tegereg gal dem' and the 'name bran' man' standing firm at the gate, trying desperately to convince the stone-faced gatemen to release the door.

So when three unmarked military jeeps pulled onto the shallow verge across the road no one took the slightest bit of notice. A number of men in casual clothing climbed out and walked purposefully across the road. Then a hush fell over the crowd; the revellers could sense the new arrivals meant trouble.

Eradication!

One of the men strode forward, confident and self-assured and placed himself unchallenged before the biggest gateman. The gatecrasher was a tall man of medium build with caramel-hued skin and a vicious gash over his left eye.

"You know who me be, baby face?" He snarled at the gatemen blocking his entry.

"Wha' me suppose fe do, 'fraid ah you?" He asked slightly amused in a country drawl. "You cyan jus' come on yah so an' expect fe get in." He sized him up. "Me nuh know yuh bwoy and me nuh waan know yuh."

It was an open invitation to hostility, and the inexperienced gateman was about to learn — the hard way — that some men should be accorded the utmost respect.

The man looked down at the gateman's feet, his eyebrows concealing burning red eyes as he asked:

"Yuh nuh know me, *pussyhole?*"

The gateman moved forward, his mouth falling open with shock and anger at the insult. He was about to lunge at the red skin man when he noticed the butt of a gun stuck in the man's waistband. He stopped in mid-stride, wide-eyed, his stare fixed on the black-handled Desert Eagle.

"Officer Dillon, we nevah recognise you, boss," the eldest of the group of security men interjected nervously, trying to diffuse the situation.

"You haffe forgive de yout', boss, him is a country man an' him just learning how town run, y'know how it go. Him still green, man…"

He prayed his quick thinking would save his colleague's life.

Detective Talman Dillon said nothing; his searing gaze spoke volumes as he zipped up his windbreaker. He moved into the dance signalling to his entourage to follow closely.

As they entered, Buju Banton's husky voice delivered a blinding version of his 'ghetto anthem':

What more!
What unuh want de massive fe do
When every dance run, keep
Unuh mek dem get curfew

What more!
What unuh want de ghetto people do
When every dance run
'Bout unuh mek dem get curfew

Curfew of de century
Search of de year…

The 'crowd ah people' were responding to Buju's every word excitedly. But Dillon was unaffected by the atmosphere as he made his way grimly through to the control tower. Pablo looked up from his decks, saw Dillon and slowly took the headphone from his head. They exchanged a few words and Pablo nodded in the direction of Mikey Dread who was a short distance away, engrossed in conversation with his minder.

Dillon turned around, surveyed his henchmen and smiled. He felt satisfied with the operation so far. He walked casually over to the Dread.

"Me nuh t'ink me ah go try again fe get inside this session yah tonight, it too risky yah, man," said a youth wearing a Kangol hat, his arm around his girlfriend.

"You sure you witness Talman ah enter de dance an' ah threaten de gateman with gun, Dougie? How everyt'ing look safe to me," his friend queried.

"I was there, papa. Check out de gatemen dem nuh, you nuh notice how dem just jam to one side fe de pass half hour an' de gate still nuh open yet? Dat nuh strike you as funny, star?"

"You ah get paro boss," his friend Peter argued. "Maybe it just cork an' dem cyan get nobody else in. Just relax an' cool, man, de gate soon release."

Peter was used to Dougie's exaggerations and was determined not to let a case of mistaken identity stop him from enjoying himself tonight.

"Come yah Dougie, mek we go home," urged his girlfriend who had started feeling edgy. "Me glimpse Talman 'matic meself. Him up to somet'ing serious tonight and me nuh want to be in de crossfire if him decide to mek arrest."

Peter shrugged his shoulders, still unbelieving.

"So you see him as well Rita? An' you really t'ink him woulda cause disturbance inna charity dance, while gunman deh 'bout ah Jungle? Naa, man!"

"Him do worse than dat in the name ah de law, don't you read the *Gleaner*, Peter? Dis man yah capable of anyt'ing," Rita said seriously.

"Anyt'ing," Dougie agreed. "You t'ink Bigga Ford an' Trinity can touch dis man yah? Him get three gold star fe sharpshooting in de force, you nevah know? You can tek all de risks you want, star. *Me — ah — go — ah — my — yard!*"

"Cho!" Peter exclaimed, disappointed in them but still not about to give up. He folded his arms as he smiled at them. Then, from nowhere, a hand rested on his shoulders. He jumped and turned.

"Simba Ranking! Bwoy yuh dance ah bomb, super. Boss, if I..."

Delroy stopped his enthusiastic rambling in mid-sentence. He hailed up his friend briefly, then turned to Rita with a serious look on his face.

"Yuh seh you see de Babylon bwoy Talman enter the dance. You sure ah him?" Delroy's tone was coloured with urgency. Rita answered slowly, her eyes not leaving his for a second.

"Him come in wid about seven or eight man. Me cyan mistake him, no way."

Alarm bells sounded in Delroy's mind, a legal killer like Talman at his dance spelt danger. Detective Dillon was here for a reason, and Simba wanted to find out what it was. His men with him complicated things even more. *What did they want? More importantly, who?*

For some reason Choppy's words leapt back into his head.

"Dem did ah wait fe him, Delroy. Dem know exactly wha' dem did ah do. Dem did want yuh father dead."

Talman was known island-wide, and had expressed his dislike for west Kingston openly. He hated the ghettoes and blamed their lawlessness for most of the city's ills. His presence at the dance was not a good omen, he was definitely not making a social call.

Simba would have to think quickly.

He thanked Rita for the vital information.

Forewarned is forearmed, he thought as he turned to go.

Delroy landed lightly on the mall surface, his knees bent to absorb the impact. He crouched low and allowed his eyes time to adjust to the darkness, then looked around the enclosure.

It was the general refuse area for 'Our Father's Place', and contained the usual garbage bins, disused electrical and electronic equipment and cardboard boxes. He listened carefully, but there was nothing out of the ordinary to be heard. As Delroy started to relax, a sharp movement on the edge of his vision tensed his muscles again. Something shot out from a pile of crates on his left.

He straightened his frame immediately, spinning in the direction of the commotion, his fist clenched in a fighting stance. A frightened cat, clambered up the wall and Delroy grinned nervously. He continued on into the darkness with both hands outstretched feeling for concrete or metal. His palms rubbed against a solid wall. *De kitchen,* he thought, and he edged slowly to his right, finding his way by touch and hearing alone. His fingers crossed cold flaking metal, and he knew he was at the kitchen's back door. He dropped to his knees to move the boxes and bags out of the way.

The back door was heavy-duty, steel reinforced and there was no way he could get through it. But there was a smelly, rusty utility hatch hidden behind all the debris. Cooks used it to get rid of refuse without opening the security door, and the odour from it was stomach-churning. But he had no other choice.

He felt for the handle and pulled the cold vertical trapdoor outwards, cringed at the nerve-grating squeal from hinges that had forgotten the taste of oil, and squeezed through the narrow gap into the kitchen.

He closed door behind him; what a fool he would look if this was a false alarm…but he didn't think it was.

He had a bad, bad feeling about this.

He inched forward slowly to see what was going on inside.

Mikey Dread was calmly smoking a spliff. Talman stood before him with a Red Stripe in hand and an empty crate beside him. The Dread watched the ash from his spliff spiral down to the ground.

"I don't want to be running up and dung Kingston if yuh fail fe kill Simba Ranking," he said.

"Yuh already decide dat you will close down my sound fe good if I don't co-operate with yuh inna dis trap." He drew hard on 'the big head' and it flared to life as smoke filled his lungs. "Me nuh worried 'bout dat. If ah money you want name you price, but as far as me concerned my sound mus' keep playing no matter what."

"What de bloodclaat you tek me for, sound bwoy?"

Talman's voice was low but carried enough force to be understood over the deafening beat.

"Yuh prento is a corpse. A walking talking corpse."

Mikey Dread shifted uncomfortably on the spot. The spliff threatened to fall out of his mouth at the detective's response. He held it between two fingers.

"Me nuh want no dead bodies in yah, dat would destroy me business reputation. This is not a bad bwoy sound, I have to keep me image as a neutral sound, me haffe cater fe both politics party. Me need —"

Talman interrupted suddenly, "Me *want!* Me *need!* You nuh have nuh needs boss, unless me decide you have dem. Fe de next few hours me run t'ings yah so. When you talk 'bout dead bodies pray to God — or 'Jah' — you don't end up as one."

"Jus' cool man it ah go…"

"You chat too much bongo Dread, and you not telling me what I want to hear — like why you agree so quickly to kill a man I know from surveillance you dida bring inna de business?"

The Dread considered the question, exhaling a stream of cannabis smoke as his mind churned through the many petty reasons behind his dislike for Simba Ranking.

"Me nuh like competition."

As far as the Dread was concerned, "De bwoy" was too "nuff", too ambitious. Simba had been 'teefing' him smartly' and this dance was the final straw. Detective Dillon had simply made the proposal at the right time, how could he say no?

Talman viewed the man before him with cold eyes and felt the tug of empathy between kindred spirits; he smiled.

"You know people t'ink him own de sound," the Dread continued. "No way me can have dem chat deh." Mikey Dread forced himself to look away from the policeman's penetrating, accusing eyes.

"You do right fe nuh look inna me face bwoy, becah you worse than me to raasclaat," said Talman. He spat on the ground.

"My sound system means more to me than any one man. You played de hand and me draw bad card. His life fe freedom from man like you."

"Simple!" Talman snorted, placing his half-empty beer bottle to his lips. He gulped thirstily, closing his eyes as the cool liquid flowed down his throat...unaware of any movement behind him.

The ink blot figure stepped out of the pitch darkness behind Talman silent and unseen. He moved with uncanny speed, aiming for a box of records and using the gloom, the concrete wall and the speaker box as cover, stepping nimbly closer. He reached down and grabbed a vinyl 45 from the box, then quickly moved back behind the standing men, retracing his steps in the shadows until...

Mikey Dread looked up suddenly into the darkness, seeing something move but uncertain of what it was. A smashing sound came from the speaker box closest to him. The Dread turned, recognising the duppy-like form emerging from the darkness behind the boxes, but too late.

It happened quickly. He could give no warning to the policeman as the jagged edges of the broken vinyl record pressed against Dillon's jugular. Talman stiffened and dropped his bottle, which hit the top of his foot and rolled away. The policeman's hand fell submissively to his side.

Simba looked towards the cowering dreadlocks one step away. He coolly dipped his hand under Talman's jacket and wrenched out the stainless steel-framed Desert Eagle Magnum.

The Ranking was impressed; just about the only thing more powerful than this handgun was a rocket launcher. He pushed the big pistol into the waist of his trousers and shuffled back into the shadows, adding more pressure to Talman's throat.

"Step forward dutty dreadlocks, me want you 'tan up whe' me can reach you." The Dread walked briskly forward and stopped at arm's length away from the Ranking, his mouth open and eyes wild.

"Talk to me, rude bwoy," Delroy growled in Talman's ear. "Tell me slowly who send you fe lick me and why."

The 'Babylon' squirmed, but Delroy held him firm. "Me nuh know you...and me nuh have nothing...fe tell you bwoy...you a bumboclaat idiot."

His angry words came out in interrupted spurts. Delroy jerked his makeshift knife up against the soft folds of the man's chin. The serrated edges broke the skin, causing a rivulet of blood to trickle along the grooved surface of the record. Talman thrashed as Simba brought his head further and further back, then suddenly Simba eased up on the pressure. Talman gasped for air like a thirsty man, knowing for the first time whoever held him was not 'skinning up'.

Mikey Dread considered running for his life, but the threat of a quick draw and a shot in the back kept him motionless.

"Yuh know ah who this, batty bwoy? Ah Simba Ranking. De man unuh ah plan fe wipeout." Talman strained to move forward as he heard the name, but the 45 was pressed even more firmly against his jugular.

"Unuh two pussyhole gimme most ah wha' me waan hear, still. But you, rude bwoy Dillon, me need some answer."

"Me nuh know not'n..." Talman rasped arrogantly, his throat a gravel pit.

"Don't *fuck* with me, beast bwoy. You t'ink I man woulda hesitate to cut yuh throat? T'ink again. Right now me have not'n fe lose. Now who sen' you, bwoy?"

Delroy's tone was impatient. He shot a glare at Mikey Dread.

"So you decide to come back from de States early, eh? Whe' Fat Man deh?"

The dread was wondering the same thing himself.

"You lucky him nuh deh yah." He croaked but his ill considered threat had no effect at all.

The Ranking eyed him. He could so easily pump a bullet into Mikey right there and then, but instead he turned his attention back to Talman. "You ready fe talk, Babylon bwoy?"

Dillon wasn't about to reveal anything too easily, but he just didn't know how far this yout' would go. But he knew for sure this wasn't his day to die, and this wasn't the place. He would call Delroy's bluff and give out just enough information to buy more time.

Dillon played his hand smoothly.

"You ah talk to de wrong man, prento. Me only follow orders...but just t'ink back to which man woman you ah fuck an' maybe you will have yuh answer."

Simba stiffened.

So that was it, that was what this was all about! The Saint had finally found out about him and Monique. And if the man was crazy enough to send an army down to get him, he must want revenge badly.

In the silence Talman sensed the deejay's uncertainty and seized his chance. Simba felt the detective brace forward and try to break his hold, but he reacted quickly. Hauling him backward with all his body weight, he rammed his knee hard into the base of Dillon's spine. The detective slumped forward.

"Wha' you ah try do beast bwoy, escape?" Simba grinned. "Get up, man. Haul yuh raas up!" He struggled to a standing position; Simba tried to overcome the urge to kill him there and then. For now he needed Talman Dillon alive.

"So...you an' de dread decided fe tek de Ranking out an' fail."

Simba pulled the huge gun from his waist and pointed it at

Mikey Dread.

"Wha' me shoulda do wid you dreadlocks?" he asked.

"Me couldn't do not'n, don..." Mikey tried to smooth his way out. "De man was threatening to kill I."

He was lying and Simba knew it.

"You haffe let me go, man. It cyan end jus' so. A long time me know you, yout'. Gimme a bly, nuh man," the Dread said solemnly.

"Ah beg you ah beg me dreadlocks. Jus' give me one reason why me shouldn't just shot yuh inna yuh head?" The question was rhetorical. "Nuh worry still dread, Me nah kill you today, star, jus' cripple you. An' nuh worry yuhself me lion, me ah come back. Trust me 'pon dat." Simba threw the makeshift knife into the gloom and poked the Magnum into Talman's ribs.

"Come to me, bwoy,"

The uncertain dreadlocks complied, no questions asked. He stepped warily into the gloom where Simba and his captive stood, not knowing what to expect. Simba swung the gun at his head, knocking him unconscious. He crumpled to the ground and Simba rolled him over roughly into the shadows.

"Now it's just me and you bwoy." He nudged Talman. "We will tek a easy walk outta yah, just mek sure none ah yuh prento dem step outta line cah me nah go skin fe blow yuh brain, seen? Now walk!"

He pressed the gun to Talman's back and they stepped out of the shadows towards the exit.

The move had to look normal, just two 'bredrin' walking casually to the main door. Delroy used his gun hand to prop Talman up, hiding the gun and giving the impression that his friend had had too much to drink. As they skirted the wall on the far left of the lawn, Delroy kept a look-out for Talman's men. Delroy was so close to the wall that his left sleeve was grimy and soaked with mildew and condensation. He kept his eyes peeled, regularly checking behind and beside himself.

Then he saw a movement, people shifting out of the way of some disturbance. Delroy knew that meant major trouble.

Two of Talman's 'soldiers' came into view, sticking out like a bad sore. They had the characteristic look of police officers or soldiers — standard untucked striped Arrow shirts, casual windbreakers and well-barbered hair.

They came directly into Delroy's path, with grins forming on both their faces as they reached inside their jackets. He slammed the handle of the Magnum hard into Talman's ribs and the detective grimaced, let out a gush of air and stumbled to his knees, gasping.

"Tell you bwoy dem fe back off, seen!" Delroy hissed, tilting the pearl-handled Magnum in their direction to show his intent. Talman strained to breathe, flashing his hands wildly. They immediately got the message, and moved back into the crowd of dancers, keeping their beady eyes on their boss.

"You alright, star…"

The squeaky, high-pitched voice came from a young woman trying to help Talman. Delroy turned to face her. She was ample-bodied, but had all the right curves in all the right places, and cute eyes. Her green organza jacket allowed you to see her firm bust as it flowed into a black lycra catsuit with matching green trimmings. She smiled broadly as she recognised the Ranking and swayed her broad, sexy hips as she approached him.

"Him okay?" she asked Simba, who quickly responded.

"My bredrin cyaan ease up 'pon the liquor baby, so him haffe tek some air before him drop dung. We alright though."

He could see she wanted to say more to him, do more to him, but this was neither the place nor the time.

"I'll come check you out later, seen?" Delroy said as she gave him that broad smile. She nodded.

"Alright then," she agreed, "me will look out fe you."

Delroy squeezed her arm reassuringly and moved off towards the entrance. The money collection dug-out was empty as Delroy glanced over there. No need to fret though, Lizard would take good care of the money. He could trust Lizard, no problem.

The dancehall artists would just have to perform without

their promoter; he hoped Pablo would invent a very good reason for him not being here. His feeling of loss at missing this 'boom' dance was great, but self-preservation came first.

He looked all around the place for the final time, zoning most of Talman's men with their helpless stares. And when he felt confident he could not 'pick up a corn' from behind, Delroy leaned on the door and forced it open. Talman looked like he couldn't believe that they had actually come out of the dance in one piece.

There was no time to waste. As the gatemen tried to greet him Delroy barked orders, cutting through their questions.

"Block de door fe twenty minutes, Bigga. Let no bwoy in or out."

They looked at each other amazed, but moved quickly to clip the massive padlock over the securing chain. By the time they'd done, Delroy and his prisoner had already disappeared into the gloom.

They headed for Delroy's bike, Detective Dillon walking slowly four paces in front of the deejay, who was training the Magnum on the back of his head.

"You cyan run, you know," said Talman. "There is nowhere to run to. You cyan hide, either. We will find you and then you is a dead man. But until then, all yuh people dem at risk, yuh mumma, yuh yout', yuh gal…"

"Me father!"

Delroy finished the list, delivering a searing side kick to Talman's back that shot him forward and sent him sprawling face . He spat out dirt and blood and tried to raise his head but Delroy's foot came down hard on the back of his neck.

"Ah *you* kill me father, nuh true, beast. *Nuh true!*"

Talman didn't answer. He needed to be certain.

"De Saint sen' you fe kill me old man."

Talman was resigned to death.

"Dig yuh grave, rude bwoy," Simba ordered. Talman hesitated. Simba spat out the word again:

"Dig!"

The policeman clawed at the dry earth with his fingers until they bled. He grunted weirdly, wondering how death would feel, as he listened to his executioner carefully.

"Yuh t'ink yuh can frighten me, dutty babylon bwoy eh?"

Delroy breathed deeply, snarling his resentment.

"Yuh t'ink you ah go kill I like unuh kill me father, like unuh kill some ah me bredrin dem?"

Simba lifted his head and listened keenly like his namesake on the prairies of Africa.

"Mark me face good, cah if anybody fe me get hurt by yuh boss, him life nah go worth living, seen? Me nuh give a fuck who him t'ink him is. Me ah go hunt him dung like a dog."

He spat out the words like venom, then lowered the gun and pressed the muzzle to the back of Talman's head.

"Why waste a bonafide bullet 'pon a Johncrow like you?" he asked. There was a silence, and then Simba blurted out:

"It wort' it!"

Talman squirmed in panic, letting out a low moan as Simba gripped the Magnum's retraction lever and forced it back. The policeman stiffened, waiting for a flash and then oblivion.

Instead a blinding pain exploded in his head as Simba hammered him with the gun butt, hard. He slumped down into the shallow grave he had dug for himself, unconscious.

Simba looked down at him in disgust. Should he let this scum live to haunt him again or kill him without knowing for sure that Dillon had murdered his father? Luckily for Talman, his principles were as old fashioned as Cariba Suits.

Jah will deal wid him, but if me find out fe sure dat ah him kill Missa George, then him raas is mine.

Simba ran over to where he had parked the Ninja, trying to weigh up what his next move should be. It would be safer to get away first and think later.

If the Saint knew where he was, and what he had been up to with his woman, then time was running out for them both.

Me must talk to Monique now, she needs to know what ah gwan.

He adjusted the Eagle in his waist and switched his machine to rumbling life.

TWELVE

What is dis looting an' a shooting an' a killing an' a rampage?
When will it cease?
Killing mother and father an' innocent children,
Mercy please,
All this looting an' shooting, an' killing, an' a rampage...
Rampage, Buju Banton

The motorcycle skidded to a stop on the Bull Bay Road, the acrid smell of burnt rubber mixing with the salty sea air of Harbour View.

Simba's mind was working overtime trying to figure out his options — if there were any! Whichever way he looked at the situation he was in deep water, that was for sure. He was a wanted man, a hunted man.

He lifted the Ninja onto its centrestand and considered his dire situation. Talman's threats had only spurred him on.

He had to contact Monique.

He had stopped off at the Harbour View Shopping Centre en route and called the motel at Beverly Hills, praying she hadn't checked out.

Monique was asleep when the phone at her bedside rang.

"Hello…"

Her voice was low. Simba got straight to the point.

"De pussyclaat bwoy try kill me, t'night baby," he said coldly. "Him know 'bout we."

There was silence on the line as Monique tried to shake herself out of her sleep and make sense of what he was saying. *Someone tried to kill him?*

"You hear wha' me seh!" Simba thundered angrily down the phone line. "Yuh red 'kin husband try kill I!"

It was what she had feared the most.

"Delroy, are you alright?"

"Relax, man, me safe."

"Thank God!" She let out a breath of relief. "I should

have followed my intuition. Hugh suspected, I knew it!"

"Yuh *know?*" Simba asked puzzled. "So how come is a bullet haffe sen' de message to me?"

"I didn't know for sure, it was just how he stared at me. As if he wanted to accuse me but was waiting for something to happen. He plays games. He loves the chase."

"Him know exactly wha' him ah do," Simba added.

"I can't believe this is happening..." she shuddered. Delroy had to get out of town fast.

"I don't think we should talk any longer, Delroy," she said quickly. "Someone could be listening in. But before you hang up, listen to me carefully. You've got to get away from Kingston as quickly as you can. He's going to keep on trying to kill you until he succeeds. I need you, darling, and I couldn't bear to see you...you die..."

She choked on the words.

"But wha' 'bout you? Me cyan jus' lef yuh to de bwoy. Him can hurt yuh, kill yuh. You nuh see dat? Come wid me ah de only way —"

"I *can't* Delroy," Monique interrupted.

She understood Simba's concern and she loved him for it. But no matter what he thought and how she felt, Monique couldn't leave her pampered lifestyle behind — not yet. She had to sit down and make a considered decision so she would have no regrets later. This situation was forcing her hand, and she did not want that.

But it was obvious to her that if she stayed there was more of a chance that Hugh would give up on Delroy. If she went with him, they'd be hunted down like animals.

She held back her tears and took a deep breath.

"He won't hurt me, Delroy, but he won't think twice about killing you. Get out of here while you can!"

She pleaded with him, but Simba stood his ground.

"Gal pickney come to yuh senses. Yuh ah play wid fire."

He tried desperately to convince her:

"De man is a *killa.*"

"Don't worry about me, I said, just keep running. From now on never call me or try to see me. He will be waiting for you."

Monique was sobbing.

"I don't know if there is a future for us after this, but if it was meant to be, it will be. Please darling...take care."

A tear rolled down her cheek as she cut him off.

"Monique! *Monique!*"

Simba shouted down the line but it was dead, just like he felt inside.

The Saint had rallied his forces to wipe out one man 'grinding' his wife. *Could he have sent the police to kill my father as well*? If he had, Monique could be his next victim. The thought of that made Simba weak and frightened. He locked that idea away in his head, afraid of what it would do to him. Now was not the time for thought, it was time for action; Mama Christy had to leave.

The Ranking leaped from his bike in one fluid movement, vaulting over the familiar twisted metal gate and into his sand-strewn yard. Nothing appeared to be out of the ordinary, but he scanned the surroundings anyway, checking that this ramshackle concrete house had not been broken into.

The front verandah, shuttered with metal burglar bars, seemed in much the same state that he'd left it in. At the rear of the building, light from her low-burning kerosene lamp glowed weakly through the frosted glass of his mother's window. Delroy edged along the dirty concrete wall to the entrance at the back. He was about to step onto the stairs when a shuffling sound stopped him in his tracks. He twisted his head in the direction of the sound and smiled when he saw his dogs, Rambo and Tyson, come padding towards him.

"Unuh alright?" he asked, rubbing their heads.

Delroy knew that nobody would have been able to set foot anywhere near the house — the Alsatians would have torn them apart. Rambo and Tyson bolted away from him, no doubt heading back to their warm spots beside the fowl coop. There wasn't much time.

He stood there unmoving for a few seconds, a twinge of loss and hopelessness knotting his insides. There was nothing striking about this drab-looking compound. Sand and pebbles made up the surface, and a solitary water faucet lodged beside the fence that connected them to the neighbours' yard. The chicken coop and doghouse jutted up from the back yard like two isolated teeth in a toothless grin. It was all they'd been able to afford. At least they had been away from the 'mix-up' of ghetto life — but not for long.

He went inside.

"Mama, Mama Christy!" Delroy whispered, gently trying to shake her awake. The room was barely lit; 'Home Sweet Home' etched on the lamp shade created dim shadows across the unrendered walls. The sharpness of the oil fumes and the pleasant smell of camphor relaxed him immediately. He couldn't help looking down and wondering about the woman stirring under the sheets. His usual feeling of sorrow came back to him when he remembered the many sacrifices she had made for his sake. She deserved better than this. At fifty-nine she should be enjoying life but instead he was bringing her more anguish.

"Son!"

Mama Christy hauled herself up into a sitting position and blinked.

"What 'appen, son? Don't you know it's early morning, now?"

"Yes Mama, me know…"

He bowed his head slightly, trying to find an easy way to break the news to her. But there was no easy way.

"We haffe leave yahso now, Mama. It's a life and death business."

"What you talking 'bout bwoy? *Why* do we haffe leave here? What is wrong Delroy, talk to me."

"It's a long story Mama, an' one me nuh have nuh time fe talk 'bout now," he insisted.

"Yuh have to go to Ms Pearline ah Rema until t'ings cool dung. Cousin One-Son will keep an eye out 'pon de yard.

An' him will bring you up fe feed de dogs an' fowl. Me ah go country an' will keep in contact wid you regular."

The garrison constituencies of Rema were no-go areas even for brazen policemen like Talman. None of his hitmen would dare 'fe cross de border', and Mama would be as safe there as she could be anywhere.

"But what about me market stall?" she protested. "You jus' expect me to pack up an' leave it all, widout a reason son? I cyan give up me livelihood. Dat lickle business has kept we from going hungry many a time."

Simba understood, but what could he do?

If she didn't have something to keep her occupied the outcome could be much worse than hunger — an early grave, even. And Simba couldn't stand by and be the cause of something like that. He decided she could stay and he would arrange for her to get protection as she sold her wares in Coronation Market.

He knew the right men for the job.

"Alright," he said. "Go ahead, Mama, run yuh business. Dat is no problem, but don't move until you hear from me or a messenger tomorrow. Yuh understand?"

Mama Christy listened in silence, and then started to cry.

"Me worry fe you, son, you is all me have lef. Me couldn't bear if anyt'ing happen to you."

Delroy sat on the bed beside her and pulled her close to him. The smell of bay rum floated up from around her as he kissed her on the forehead. A distant look came into his eyes as he recalled the lyrics by Garnett Silk:

Oh mama! You can depend on me now,
Cause I can see you tried your best,
Now it's up to me to do the rest

"Hush! Mama," his voice was a whisper. "Me safe man. You know I man grow up wid de best teacher any man could ask for…"

He smiled thoughtfully.

"After dem kill Papa is jus' me an' you alone. From now on, me mek a promise to you to change t'ings, an' me mean it. You can't climb de ladder, Mama, widout step 'pon corn-toe. Dem ah threaten me and you."

He squeezed her hand.

"Me cyan mek dem use you fe no trump card, Mama. Becah me nuh waan end up inna Gun Court, Jah know! Dis is de only way out, trust me."

Delroy stared down into her tired eyes and could see the hurt there. She sniffed, eyeing him carefully with her usual motherly concern and worry.

"I still don't understand who want to hurt you, and where you going to go. Who will look after you? When will me see you again?"

"Dat ah de least fe worry 'bout, jus' cool. Everyt'ing ah go copaset."

He hugged her again tenderly.

"Now start pack up Mama we need fe lef yah so now!"

He left his mother's room quickly and went through to his own bedroom. He went to turn the light switch on then decided against making his presence too obvious. The kerosene lamp in the far corner would do just as well. His room was stacked full of compact discs, 45s, albums and cassettes. Among them was his prized possession, a DAT master copy of a demo tape he had made at Ken Wong's 32-track studios on Trafalgar Road. Everything had been paid for by Monique, and he had five 'riddims' laid down on it which he hoped would one day make his name.

Monique had given him so much, and he had repaid her by running away. He couldn't help being angry at himself and the situation, but he had things to do.

Simba made a mental note to take his tape with him no matter what. He rushed over to a wood-veneered chest of drawers and began to pack his clothes, flinging them in flurries onto his bed. He filled two bags easily, then remembered he didn't have his passport. He plunged back into the chest of drawers, probing around until he found it. Delroy held it up to the lamp's light, thinking how different he looked now from the mug shot.

He licked his finger, turned over the page and noticed his US non-immigrant visa. Rubbing his fingers over the embossed stamp, he whispered Monique's name.

He had become so engrossed in his packing that he'd forgotten about his mother in the back room. He listened for any sound of activity but heard...nothing!

He pulled the Desert Eagle from his waist and ducked into the shadows of the hallway. The dogs were silent, but he was taking no chances. He rubbed his back against the rough passage wall as he edged towards Mama Christy's room. Then he took a deep breath and whipped his head around the doorframe to see his mother talking to herself quietly and concentrating intently on packing.

His heart was hammering in his chest as she looked up.

"Me soon ready son, just a few more t'ings to pack."

He breathed out, pushing the automatic into the back of his trousers and flopping his shirt over it again. Nothing would happen to Mama Christy, he repeated over and over again in his mind.

If he was wrong, he would never forgive himself.

Watching Mama's taxi disappear around the bend at St Benedict's church, he felt like a great weight had been lifted off his shoulders. Simba had made sure she had everything she needed, because he knew that it would be a long, long time before they could even think of living here again.

Now he had some spars that he had to ask favours of — spars who were scattered around the ghettoes, on both sides of the political divide. People normally avoided leaving an area controlled by one political party and entering an opposing party's territory, especially around a general election. But the Ranking was respected enough that he was one of the few men who could do this. His army of contacts had to be rallied tonight because he was still not sure how far the Saint was willing to go to get him killed.

The only leads he had so far were from 'de dutty bwoy' Dillon, and he wasn't sure the officer's words could be trusted even under duress. But trying to shake Talman's threats from his mind was near impossible. He suddenly remembered the killing of the political activist Claude Maputt. Everyone in the ghetto suspected the Saint had ordered his death through the police, and his message had been clear: don't fuck with the Saint.

Now Jamaica had become too small for the Ranking. He could run, but there was nowhere to hide. But even with nowhere to go, he was going to make himself a hard target.

The Ninja lay on its side, its metalwork dull with the settling of dust. Early morning goods trucks droned past with their heavy loads, air horns playing loud tunes as they came from St Mary.

Gripping the handle bars and hauling the heavy machinery up, Delroy pushed the Kawasaki onto the road and jumped into the saddle. As he did, two sets of bright beam car headlights stabbed from behind him. Jamaican drivers are notorious for keeping their full beams on when going around corners, especially when they want to 'fass' in other people's business. Ignoring them for a moment Delroy throttled his bike and then spun round to face the opposite direction. By now the lights should have gone past. Instead the cars seemed to be crawling in his direction, lights blazing. Simba blinked rapidly and tried to distinguish the two vehicles.

"Wha' dem man yah ah deal wid?" he said out loud. And then, too slowly, he realised exactly what they were doing. The two police jeeps screeched to a stop as the men inside recognised their quarry. Simba counted six men shuffling out of the two jeeps.

"Nuh de bwoy dat!" a voice shouted in his direction.

"Jus' mek sure you blow weh him raas, seen."

"Him can't get 'weh, boss. Nuh worry 'bout dat."

Callous laughter.

Simba analysed the situation with such rapidity only fear could fuel, knowing if he didn't act now the slim chance he had to go on living would become no chance at all. He ducked down and started his motor, and as the jeeps' doors slammed shut Simba surged forward. He was making up the rules as he went along, but there was no other way. The bike's engine growled as he twisted it towards the loose dirt of the hill on the right hand side of the road. It would take him no more than ten seconds to reach it, but in that short time the policemen would riddle him with bullets unless he could keep them occupied — *give dem somet'ing fe hold.*

He reached for the gun at his waist, keeping one hand steady on the handlebars.

They had been stunned by the speed with which Simba reacted, but now the officers were taking aim.

Simba fired the Desert Eagle twice. The massive recoil nearly separated him from the bike. They scampered for cover as a tyre exploded from the impact of the first bullet. The second .357 slug pierced one of the jeep's windows and tore through a policeman's arm, almost severing it at the shoulder.

Simba heard the screaming.

In seconds the bike had crossed the road and bumped onto the sidewalk, mounting the steep slope and skidding across its face.

The policemen opened fire, rounds from their M-16s thudding into the soft dirt of the hill. They fired indiscriminately at Simba's Ninja as it threw up dense clouds of dust. They could no longer see him for dust, so they shot at the sound of the Kawasaki's engine as it roared away, but without success.

By the time they realised what had happened the Ranking had slid back down the slope some distance ahead and was already 'burning rubber' to town.

The official police report would read: 'Policeman injured and a disabled vehicle attacked by unknown assailant'.

Nobody dared to tell their boss they had failed yet again.

THIRTEEN

A black Granada sedan lumbered to a halt before the plush Bohemian restaurant in New Kingston — a car out of place in its current surroundings.

The normal activities of the car's occupants were harassment and intimidation, but tonight their business was a little less clear-cut, and that made them very nervous. Their journey here had been a silent one and now Talman ducked out of the parked car as though he were anxious to get out onto the pavement. He rubbed the band-aid strapped across the bridge of his nose and adjusted the rim of his dark glasses around his bruised eyes. The memory of Simba's beating three nights earlier still caused him to 'screw up' his face with humiliation.

But he knew he was lucky to be alive.

Two other men got out of the car, and the three walked up to the restaurant's glass facade. Talman pushed the door open and entered, his associates following closely behind. They threaded their way through the packed restaurant, ignoring the chatter of dinner talk around them.

It was a classy place, frequented by foreign and local celebrities, and its award-winning cuisine was featured in gastronomic journals around the Caribbean. Little did the regular patrons know this place was one of the Saint's 'fronts' for arms and money-laundering transactions.

Mr St. John would be raking in the money tonight. Dillon hoped his mood would be a mellow one, but he reminded himself that appearances could be deceptive; and deception was one of his boss' main tools.

He didn't want to visit too often; stories circulated about the men who had 'disappeared' after heated chats with the boss in his office.

But Talman had to admit the organisation of St. John's operation was brilliant. He admired the set-up every time he thought about it.

From what he had deduced over his years of working for the Saint, on the first and last Thursday of each month his restaurant opened only to an exclusive 'clientele' — bankers bringing in cash from a contact the boss had in the Caribbean. What Talman didn't know was that the large sums of money coming into the Saint's coffers from abroad were actually a favour being done, for a fee of course, for a political colleague in the Bahamas.

The cocaine cartels of Colombia used a multi-millionaire friend in the Bahamas to launder some of their money. But some members of the Bahamian government were being investigated by a Royal Commission for their involvement in drug trafficking and corruption, so he had to shift a large chunk of his business to Hugh St John.

Money was wired to him or brought to the restaurant in person by couriers represented from the large Canadian banks, and he washed the dirty dollars clean through his contacts in the Jamaican banking community, leaving no trace of their origin.

To the Saint it was simply icing on the cake, just another business venture added to his growing criminal empire.

The men passed through into the slick floors and steamy pots of the kitchen. Ignored by the waiters and chef alike they left through swinging doors at the other end of the kitchen, then went down two flights of stairs to an imposing reinforced door leading to what looked like a storage room, but was in fact the nerve centre of St John's underhand business dealings.

A closed-circuit video camera focused on him as Talman pressed a hidden button and spoke into the intercom.

"Me have an appointment wid de boss, ah me Dillon."

The voice of Bones came back:

"Missa Dillon, de time delay lock ah go open in a minute, just push when it buzz."

Talman had been through all this procedure a thousand times, but Bones loved operating the machinery and felt it necessary to show off his meagre expertise every time.

"How t'ings, detective?" he asked when the security door opened. "You look like a man fuck you over proper, boss."

He was glad that Dillon's reputation had been tarnished. The man needed to be reminded that there were 'badda' men than him in this city.

"You nuh worry yourself 'bout dat every man deserve a lucky break inna dem life. But one is enough, I will settle this when I ketch him face to face and dat will be very soon. Nuh fret."

He ignored the snide remarks and snickers of amusement from the Saint's bodyguards as they lounged around. Dillon knew he would be given a second chance to take Simba's life, and then all 'dem dibi dibi ghetto youts yah' would have to eat their words.

The idea warmed him.

The trio stepped through the security room and into more formal offices. Dillon knocked on the solid mahogany door which led into St. John's private office.

"Come in!" the Saint's voice boomed, "Time is money, gentlemen. I don't like wasting any ah dem."

They pushed their way into the dimly-lit office, squinting to focus in the gloom. The only source of light was a brass gooseneck lamp that rested on an expensive-looking desk. Its light shone directly onto the desktop, making everything else around it sink into darkness.

Dillon stood a pace in front of the other two men and braced himself for the oncoming onslaught. The Saint was hidden behind a leather high-back chair, wreathed in cigar smoke. When his eyes had adjusted to the dim office, Dillon couldn't stop gazing over at an erotic oil painting on the wall.

"Detective Talman Dillon?" the Saint asked from behind the seat, catching Dillon off guard.

"Yes, boss."

"What good tidings have you brought fe me tonight, mister policeman."

Talman felt apprehensive for the first time in the nine years that he had worked for the Saint. He had never in all those years failed to get his man. Until now.

"Me sorry sah, we have no good news for you...except dat..." Dillon left his statement floating.

"Except fe what, man?" The Saint spun his chair around to face his men. He looked at each of than in turn, his blue eyes cold and evil.

"We — " Dillon swallowed, " — t'ink him leave town an' suspect him ah go skip Jamaica soon."

"Him do *what!*" The Saint slammed his hands on the side of the chair and stood up, glaring at the policemen.

"Are you trying to tell me that after dat unfortunate incident at the dance, you and your men still haven't learned you lesson yet? How can he evade an entire squad of supposedly competent men and then just decide to fly out ah de country like he didn't have a care in de world? Can you raas explain that to me?"

Dillon cleared his throat.

"Him anticipate nearly every move we mek, Missa St. John," he explained.

He'd never seen the Saint this angry and never before had it been directed at him. He knew he would have to tread carefully, in this case honesty had to be compromised.

"Me man dem even went de same night to kidnap him mother, but him bust shot 'pon dem an' escape," Dillon lied nervously "Him mother situate at Rema or somewhere desso, either way we can't touch her or him, boss."

"So you fucked up again, me friend..."

The Saint's voice was calmer now, measured; he sat

down and tapped cigar ash into his ashtray.

"You seem to have no luck with this elusive deejay. Him mek a fool of you twice now, so I will haffe see to it myself…"

His voice was beginning to rise again.

"My business is based on commitment and credibility, Dillon. I have people who try to destroy me name everyday, an' everyday me make people pay fe dat mistake. Suppose they were allowed fe get away wid it? Where would I be then? Incompetence is like betrayal to me — both are unforgivable. This business has blown up way outta yuh clumsy hands, so me will handle it personally."

Dillon's eyes widened, as he spluttered a protest.

"If you give me a chance me can tek de bwoy."

"You've used all your bloodclaat chances." The Saint spun his swivel chair around, ending the discussion.

The three men left the room in silence.

Alone at last, Hugh St. John was delving deep into his thoughts, breathing deeply to attempt to keep his hurt and anger in check. He couldn't understand why Monique had done what she'd done. He had given her everything. *And yet she was fucking another man.*

He shook his head. The thought of someone else touching her, sucking her breasts, laughing at him with every stroke, made him shudder.

He lowered his head, his stomach was churning with rage. This was no good, he couldn't dwell on this. He had to think of the things that had gone right. Like the killing of Simba's father.

Now the upstart had felt what it was like to be touched by an angry Saint. A fleeting smile crossed his lips.

That was some compensation for the damage the deejay had done. But not enough and it was far, far from the end.

Monique had been keeping a low profile, guessing that it would be best to stay out of his way. And she was right. He hadn't seen her for a week, but he knew she would be back.

No words had been spoken between them since Simba had escaped from the dance, but words weren't needed.

He knew, Monique knew, and the fear in her eyes was satisfying for him.

And her fear was justified. Her suffering was just beginning, and if she had any plans to sleep around or leave him she would soon forget them. This would be the first and the only time.

Monique would know in no uncertain terms that he needed her with him. And if not with him, then with nobody.

Something spectacular was called for to ram his message home — not just for Monique's benefit. The news of this was already on everyone's lips, and his reputation was on the line.

So catching the deejay was crucial, and everything else was secondary — even though the election was only five days away.

For his own peace of mind the Saint would make this deejay pay with his life for his sins.

FOURTEEN

Pa-Pam! Pa-*Pam!* Pa-*Pam!*

The night sky was heavy with smoke as firecrackers and sparklers injected a carnival atmosphere into the celebrations. Whistles blew with shrill squeals and the conk shells sounded in the streets as people celebrated the Saint's election win and his party's landslide victory, their third consecutive win. In homes throughout Jamaica, the common people were watching the Prime Minister's live broadcast from Gordon House.

But in Western Kingston another king ruled.

And his hundreds of followers were more interested in shouting party slogans in triumph, their rowdy voices echoing off walls and mingling with feedback from an ill-adjusted microphone on stage. Their bodies swayed to popular songs, some of which they had adopted as their anthems. There was no fear in their faces for once, they were among friends, the bloodshed that had marred the election forgotten.

The Saint's name was chanted even above the noise of the music by a few supporters, until the mass caught on to the chorus:

"Saint! Saint! Saint...!"

They cheered ecstatically as the man himself strode onto the stage outside his offices on Duke Street. He tapped the microphone to test it, then cleared his throat.

"You've worked hard fe this, people. I know because we did it together," he began thoughtfully. "Some have given even their *lives* for what we call home. All ah this — " his hands swept all over them, " — because we a proud people we never have any doubt who was going to win this. Ah we run t'ings yahso."

The crowd answered with rapturous shouts.

"Ah we run t'ings! Ah we run t'ings!"

"Yeah man, that's the truth."

He laughed over the microphone.

"And we ah go continue to do just dat, no matter how many times dem try to intimidate we. I'm proud ah you people, an' I want to thank every single man, woman and child fe dem continuous support to de party and me. The Prime Minister sen him respect an' I just want to finally say keep de faith, cah from now on ghetto people, de future ah fe we."

He backed away and raised the hands of his advisers in triumph.

The people of Western Kingston erupted.

In the constituency offices celebrations were more subdued than the noisy merry-making outside.

Businessmen and women chatted and sipped champagne to the backdrop of Soca and calypso. The party's yellow rosettes and posters of St. John's smiling face were everywhere.

Monique nibbled at an hors-d'oeuvre and glanced nervously over her glass as her husband watched her. They had been photographed earlier kissing and hugging. Just being near him sickened her to the core, but it was a simple exercise in good PR.

Her PR.

The longer she could keep him sweet, the better Simba's chances would be. But Monique had done enough for one day, and was now trying her best to avoid Hugh by mingling with the party faithful. Every chance she got Monique moved further away.

As she pretended to enjoy herself people came over and congratulated her for having such a 'dynamic' husband — a husband who had tried to kill her 'man' and then carried on as if nothing had happened.

The Saint wanted her to admit what she had done, and was applying all the psychological pressure he could manage. The tension at home was unbearable, as she worried about Simba and he gloated in silence while the hunt for him went on.

Monique did not think she could take the pretence a moment longer. The time she had spent away had made her decide to grab for what little happiness she could get, come what may. She would fight him all the way, no matter what it cost her, she had to get away from him.

In the distance, next to the rum punch bowl, the Saint raised his glass to her in a mocking toast. A well-dressed young lady joined him and he hugged her, his hands roaming all over the woman's breasts. She didn't seem shocked, as Monique had expected she would be. Instead she moved closer to him.

The Saint kissed her on the cheek and took her hand, leading her over to where Monique stood.

"Monique, this is my secretary, Margaret. Pretty little thing, isn't she?" He didn't expect an answer from Monique, and just grinned.

"Get me another drink, sweetheart, while me an' my wife have a little talk."

Margaret walked off, smiling smugly.

"You haffe tek it where you can get it, darling," he explained, studying his secretary's statistics from behind. He reached inside his suit for a Macanudo vintage no.5 cigar.

"Enjoying yourself?" he taunted her. Monique glared at him. "Yuh mind doesn't seem to be here...Is yuh conscience bothering you, me dear? Is there somet'ing you want to tell me?"

Monique looked at Hugh coldly. The confession he was looking for was forming on the tip of her tongue. The bastard was goading her, trying to humiliate her. If he would only leave Simba alone...

She smiled.

She hadn't smiled in weeks.

The Saint looked agitated.

"You make me laugh sometimes, Hugh," she said, quietly.

"You've always said you needed me. Like a trusting fool I believed you, even after all those women. I've stuck it out with you, not out of love, even *you* should have realised that, but because I wanted what I had worked so hard to achieve. I just don't care any more. I'm leaving you no matter what you do or say. You're a sadistic shit, Hugh. You can blackmail me if you want. And you can try to destroy me. But don't expect me to lie down and be fucked by you like I did in the past. I'm going to fight you all the way."

The Saint applauded.

"Bravo! *Bravo!*" he mocked, blowing his cigar smoke at her. He savoured the taste of it and smiled.

"*His* blood will be on your hands. Can you sleep wid dat?"

He turned to leave, nimbly lifting another glass of bubbly from the tray of a circulating maid. He lifted this glass to her too, in mock salute of his coup de grace.

Hugh always had the last word.

This time, he wouldn't.

Accidentally Monique had found a chink in his armour, something she had kept, for just such an occasion.

Weeks ago while she rifled through his files to find anything she could use as leverage against him, she had come across a letter from his physician, explaining a condition, Hugh had kept from her. The problem was his incapacity to father children because of an inherited trait that could not be treated.

God, it explained the rage that he carried around for her.

She bared the brunt of his misplaced rage for too long.

It was about to end.

She grabbed Hugh by the shoulder and spun him round.

He turned to her with an expression of false sorrow.

The words dripped from her lips. "I'm pregnant."

The cigar fell from his mouth. Monique's smile widened.

"Such a pity it took a real *man* to do what you couldn't."

The wine glass shattered in his hand as she turned away.

Hugh St. John stood speechless.

Monique savoured the look of hopelessness for some seconds. Satisfied, she nodded her head and smiled a second time, finally she had the courage to walk away. And she did.

FIFTEEN

"This just nuh right a raasclaat!" Simba mumbled to himself.

But who the fuck ever said that life was fair? He knew better than anybody not to expect that. For a week he had lived the life of a man on the run from the law. The Saint's law.

He feared every dark corner, and every face looked like that of a hit man. The Ranking could take no more.

Trying to outwit a man whose influence affected his every movement as far afield as St. James had drained him physically and mentally.

T'ings ah get too hot fe me inna de country, an' him ah get closer an' closer. Me jus' nuh waan no harm come to my people dem because ah me, he thought.

Simba strapped himself into his economy seat.

New York was his destination.

He had family there who would put him up. Maybe he could even start a new life there. The thought left him with a emptiness inside as he whispered his goodbyes to Jamaica, Mama and…Monique.

He still couldn't understand why she hadn't come with him. *Why did she want to stay?* The thought that she could be trying to get back together with the Saint made Simba mad. After all he'd *done* to her, all he *put* her through, she couldn't go back to him — not now.

Or could she?

The Ranking chose to call it anger, but he was jealous, jealous as hell. And as he stoked the flames of hatred for the man, reality struck. There was no way he could get close to the Saint now, especially after his win at the polls. The man must be sipping champagne and eating caviar even now, laughing at 'de yout' who tried to come test' and failed. But he wouldn't be laughing for long if Simba had his way.

Hugh St. John's time would come.

At least leaving the country would give him a chance to re-evaluate his position. Money was the only language the Saint spoke, and Simba intended to speak it fluently. In a few months he'd be back on his feet and he'd return to Jamaica eventually.

Then they would meet on equal terms. His thoughts returned to Monique, and what her psychotic husband was capable of doing to her.

His heart sank. If dat fucker ever hurt her yuh see...

But his threats were pointless, Simba had no control over anything that happened here now.

As the plane roared down the runway at Donald Sangster airport, he could only hope.

Was it possible that hatred between two people could be so strong that they could sense one another's movements?

Hugh St. John was *sure* that Simba had got past the men he stationed at the airports and left the country. The bastard had slipped through his net.

Now he stood in the deserted Portmore boatshed fuming at the way in which an illiterate 'ghetto yout' had made him feel inadequate.

He had never spoken to Monique about his own yearning for a family, the dream of having a son to continue his line. But how could someone like him, with his pride and ruthless image, tell his wife, tell the world, that he was incapable of having children.

Sterile.

And *goddamn*, the boy had succeeded where he'd failed.

She would have to have an abortion of course — no two ways about it. Another man's child; he couldn't have that. No, he would kill it with his own hands if he had to.

But right now there were more pressing issues on his agenda and his gun shipments would take his mind off the hunt for a while. He stared intently at the invoice sheet in his hand as his men busied themselves.

"Let's see," said the Saint, his bushy eyebrows tight in concentration. "We should have fifty guns. I want dem all laid out, counted and checked, just in case our Cuban friend t'inks he can make a quick buck at my expense."

He tapped the paper with his fingertip and scowled.

"Now mek sure everyt'ing is in order, alright."

He thrust the paper at one of his men and strode away to a makeshift desk built from Red Stripe crates. Two of his bodyguards stood smoking, watching their boss approach.

"Where de hell is Tuffy?" St. John wanted to vent his anger on someone, but restrained himself.

"Doesn't that raas realise that my business come first before anyt'ing else? Him shoulda be here by now."

Richie nodded and shrugged a reply.

"Him seh he had t'ings to finish up, Missa St. John. It was short notice, but him seh him would be here 'pon time."

"But he's not, Richie and dat worry me considerable..." He paused. "Now...what about Simba?"

Richie pulled up the sleeve of his blue Puma tracksuit and shook his head.

"De contact at Air Jamaica seh his flight jus' lift off, boss, from Mo' Bay. De bwoy deh 'pon him way to York."

"Shit!" the Saint cursed. "Now me haffe change my plans. If Tuffy wasn't so good at what him do, you see..."

He bit into his bottom lip, cutting off the sentence before any threat could emerge.

"You want me send some man out fe get him?"asked the other guard.

"No, leave it. I've wasted enough time worrying about him. When him come, him come. De custom man dem at JFK will give him a reception that will last him a lifetime."

He grinned and turned to his men and their gun cache.

An older man in a greasy khaki shirt had checked the

guns. He called out to the Saint:

"All ah dem deh yah boss an' in working order. You want fe test one?" The gunsmith handed him a metallic grey Browning Hi-Power 9mm. The Saint examined it, pushed in the clip and jacked a round into the chamber. He aimed the gun at a stack of cement bags in a corner and fired twice. The shots boomed in the confined space; the bags exploded; cement dust showered the corner.

He turned the gun over in his hand.

"Good work, Mr P.; you can load dem up now and you and the bwoys can bring them to the warehouse...and remember, round de clock guards as usual. Okay."

"Not a problem, boss." Mr P. went back to organising the men and finishing his job.

Good men, the Saint thought, *but expendable, ten a penny.*

He was turning to face his bodyguards again, a question forming on his lips, when suddenly loud voices and the sound of a scuffle drifted in from outside.

"Move unuh bumboclaat, de boss waan see me. Seen?"

The voice coming from just outside the shed disrupted the Saint's thoughts, and announced the one man who would be brazen enough to storm in past the sentries.

"Tuffy!"

The Saint turned towards the guards at the door

"What's wrong wid you? Me ah wait fe dis man. Let him through."

Tuffy swaggered towards him, a permanent 'screw' on his vicious face and an air of invincibility about him. The Saint could not help thinking that his immediate problems were about to be over. He turned to face Richie, wording his instructions more carefully than usual.

"Now dat he's here, I want you to contact Rustler in New York, tell him his contact will be there today, and on what flight. Tell Rustler to meet him at the airport and to be prepared. Yuh understand?"

Richie nodded.

"Then move!"

SIXTEEN

Country life was driving Monique crazy.

She gazed out from the wooden verandah at the dirt track that meandered in front of her gate.

Maas Wilbur ambled slowly past on his donkey, right on cue, like Father Time — old, grey and patient.

Everything was slow and uninspiring in the hills of Hanover. The days came and went slowly, leaving her glued to the television for solace. Time dragged out here when you were doing nothing and though she felt she should be doing something, she realised that this place was doing her the world of good.

At least she was away from him. Safe. Such a pity her conscience was a more difficult thing to get away from.

She rested one hand on her still-flat stomach and with the other fanned away the buzzing mosquitoes. It was cool as night fell and the aroma of Maude's cooking drifted forward to the verandah.

The radio played low and moodily in the background and for a fleeting instant everything seemed to be trapped in time.

Her mind flitted from one memory to another; she was always thinking. In this environment you had to — there was little else to do.

She felt so different now from election night, the night she had left Kingston. She had been frightened and confused and even two days later she couldn't shake the memory of the twisted, deranged look on her husband's face, as he had spoken about her unborn child.

"Go kill de raas pickney, or else I will do de job myself."

She shuddered as she recalled his threat.

If that feeling of hopelessness had not overcome her maybe she would still be there, living with him and making excuses.

She tried to imagine how the Saint would have reacted when he realised she'd gone for good. She didn't care.

Now, as far as she was concerned, he was history.

It was obvious to her now that she had not really known the man she married.

When they first met, her guiding principle was simple. Her children would not grow up without a responsible father at home as she had. She had been preoccupied with men of means, and the one she married was supposed to make her perfect family dream come true. Then the dream had turned out to be a nightmare.

But what was done was done.

A new chapter in her life had begun.

She was going to be a mother, after all this time and she was learning to live with it.

It felt good.

She stretched out some more in her chair, counting herself lucky that her relationship with Maude the cook was a good one. The old woman had worked for them for as long as they'd been married, playfully adopting Monique as 'mi daughter'. When Monique had come to her, frightened and desperate, Maude had immediately welcomed her 'daughter' into her home in Hanover.

But they both knew the Saint wouldn't give up possession of his wife so easily. His people could be out there now, watching, waiting.

A shiver ran through her.

But in a moment the worries for herself gave way to a greater concern for Delroy.

Their last phone call looped through her mind...the last time they made love. She missed him so much.

123

A JBC news flash came on the air. She listened to the announcer's voice coming from a small radio in the front room.

'The body of a well known deejay and promoter was found in a Kingston gully today...'

Monique gasped, her thumping heart rattling in her ears.

'Earlier today reports came in to the Cross Roads police station that shots were heard by residents this morning in the Papine Gully area. A police investigation took place shortly afterwards and the body —'

She moaned, her stomach tightening and her head reeling.

"Delroy — no!" she whispered.

' — of Tonto Radical was found bound and gagged with two gunshot wounds to the head. Police intelligence suspect a gangland-type execution.'

Relief came over her in waves, weakening her as she flopped back into the chair.

"Simba!" She spoke only to his memory. "I don't know how much more of this I can take."

Delroy was not the type of man you could flush from your memory easily. In bed he fulfiled her like no other lover and as a friend his honesty and strength made her admire him. Simba was a unique character, the way he spoke, the way he walked, and his hunger for success drew her to him. He was wild, and though he would not express his love for her openly, she knew he loved her. Any woman would know. God, she missed him and had to be with him. Monique promised herself, whatever it took she would find him.

At that moment in time nothing else mattered.

SEVENTEEN

Simba sighed wearily, his head throbbing from the hour-long questioning and frisking an eager customs officer had subjected him to.

He hadn't expected any less. Simba had heard about the way Jamaican passport holders and other black travellers were treated in airports the world over. He even knew of many Jamaicans who had travelled on false documents and who were later involved with mostly drug-related crimes before 'dipping back to yard'. Some of these deportees had only the shirts on their backs to show for their troubles.

'De good haffe suffer fe de bad', they say, and his experience proved it; American customs officials were now targeting flights from Jamaica.

Simba followed the exit signs to the Main Hall, his sneakers squeaking on the shiny slick tiles. As he took in the unfamiliar surroundings and the many expectant faces, he spied a dreadlocked mane on the other side of the partition.

He guessed that would be his uncle, Moses, and relaxed. He'd reached New York alive, so maybe he could start to feel comfortable.

The Saint would have no idea where he was, and now he would have the time and space to further his career and plan his revenge.

His uncle had seen him too, and waved his nephew over. Simba smiled as they embraced like long-lost brothers. They had only met once before, when Moses was on a six-week vacation in Jamaica, but in that time they had forged a solid friendship. Simba respected Uncle Moses, there were few men he could say that about. That respect grew when Moses shared his experience of his good old sound days with Studio One and Sir Coxone.

De old man ah look good.

Moses was Mama Christy's half-brother and was in his mid-fifties. He was a dedicated family man, knowledgeable and softly-spoken, and would help any member of his family without question. But Simba knew he was pushing family loyalties to the limit — even if his uncle wasn't saying anything, he was worried about why his nephew was here. Moses knew it meant trouble.

"Me sorry from de bottom ah me heart, young bwoy, 'bout Mr George."

He patted Delroy's back affectionately.

"Up to this day ah can't get over it."

Simba looked distant for a split second.

"Respect, Uncle, but life haffe gwan said way."

Moses nodded in agreement.

Simba looked tired, so Moses decided that questions could wait until he was rested and refreshed.

They checked Moses' wheels out of the massive car park and drove home, laughing at past jokes, genuinely glad to see one another. When they arrived at his apartment block, Simba stood outside for a while admiring the neighbourhood. It was a far cry from the tenements of Pink Lane, and looked like a nice place to live. Would he ever be able to provide a place like this for his mother, and see her content for once?

A warm family welcome met him as he entered. It was a heartfelt reunion as Simba hugged and kissed Moses' wife, Aunt Gee, and touched fists with his cousin Courtney.

Courtney was the youngest of his uncle's children — the others, Leroy and Carol, lived in other parts of the States — and he had spent his earlier years in Jamaica. He was about Delroy's age and had the looks of a rugged *Ebony* model; smooth skin, firm jaw-line and piercing brown eyes.

Back in the days of Kingston College his looks and Delroy's

'lyrics' proved to be a lethal combination. Their names were called constantly in the halls of the famous girls schools of Queens, Immaculate Conception and Alpha.

Those were days to remember.

Delroy warmed to the memories and took his time to settle in after the boisterous 'howdy-dos'.

The sitting room of their well-kept home was spacious and the carpet was a rusty red. The leather couches matched the floor with a lighter colour of cherry and they shone with the regular polishing from Miss Gee, a woman who took pride in her home.

The walls were hung with family photographs old and new and mementoes of Jamaica. Opposite the TV and video was an elaborate stereo and massive speakers. CDs, cassettes, records and videos were set in a orderly fashion in a wooden cabinet beside fancy shelves adorned with a wide selection of books. Delroy's eyes couldn't miss the essential item in any old Jamaican home — 'de whatnot', which in its American form was a fashionable display and storage facility for cups, glasses, plates and silverware. The place had plain magnolia coloured walls which added to the light, comfortable airy feel.

He was calm, which was a welcome change, but far from being totally relaxed. He wondered if he ever could be, without Monique around.

He smelled the welcome, mouth-watering aroma of home-style cooking forcing its way into every corner of the apartment. Simba had not eaten on the flight; the airlines food didn't meet his fussy standards — no dumplings.

But if the culinary delights that were in store for him later tasted half as good as they smelled, the wait would have been worthwhile.

A couple of hours later, Simba had settled in.

Moses had gone out to the local shop for Dragon Stout, and Miss Gee was concocting a punch. Courtney was on the phone.

Sitting back in the easy chair, Delroy scanned through the myriad of television channels. He caught a news report from

JFK and his heart skipped a beat.

He turned the volume up:

At approximately five thirty-five this evening an unknown man stabbed one customs officer to death and critically wounded another.

'The scenes of carnage that you will see shortly were caused by accomplices of the killer who riddled the viewing gallery with bullets — among their victims, police officers, security guards and innocent bystanders.

'Highway Patrolmen later found a European sports car abandoned at a nearby service station, but no trace of the killers.

'An amateur video cameraman recording the arrival of his grandmother caught the entire incident on tape.

'The NBC news team has acquired a copy of the tape, and we now bring you these extraordinary scenes...'

They ran the tape; people were coming through the arrival gate waving and smiling...then the shrill scream of alarms...then security men rushed into the hall with guns drawn...then everyone panicked...the camcorder zoomed in on a black man using a woman nearest to him as a shield. He was cursing loudly in a Jamaican accent and was holding an implement, scarlet with blood, to the woman's throat...then three men, impeccably dressed in Armani suits and designer overcoats, stepped into the chaos.

Overcoats — in this heat? Simba thought to himself. Then the three men produced Uzis and MP-5 automatic weapons from under the coats...and opened fire...the knife man flung his hostage to one side and bounded towards the firing men, sliding between them like a cricketer lurching for his crease...then they shifted their attention to the doors, shattering them with bullets and backing through the broken glass to make their escape.

Simba slumped back onto the sofa with a heavy sense of foreboding. *This couldn't have anything to do with me, could it?* he asked himself. No, he was just over-reacting, still highly-strung after his past exploits in Jamaica. His nerves were on edge. The disturbance of the airport was just *too* much of a coincidence — too close to his own arrival.

"Wha' you ah watch?"

The voice startled him and Simba looked up to see his uncle holding a large brown paper bag in his hand.

"Ah nuh not'n, boss," he lied. "Jus' a news report ah some shoot-out ah de airport."

"Welcome to New York, yout'man," Moses smiled. "Gunplay ah de name ah de game yahso, man. Is Kingston dis inna de States. De only difference is everyt'ing is for sale yahso but 'pon a bigga scale."

When Moses had finished his chores he settled down beside his nephew, bringing all the materials he needed to 'build a spliff' on a Snakes and Ladders board. He hadn't talked to Delroy face to face in a long time and he was keen to catch up on events back home. His first trip back to Jamaica after twenty-one years had been just five years ago, and since then they had only spoken occasionally over the phone. Moses had taken to his nephew immediately in Jamaica and 'dem lick head together'. They had travelled everywhere together, more like good friends than uncle and nephew. But now the boy looked withdrawn and worried.

"From you ole man dead, Delroy, an' we talk over de phone, me nevah too like how you sound." He placed his hand on the younger man's shoulder.

"But me get frighten even more when a few weeks after dat you call an' tell me seh t'ings ah get hot ah yard, an' you need to leave quick. I man start worry, young bwoy."

Delroy nodded.

"Me did ah worry too, Moses. But is jus' like certain t'ings inna me life start go wrong from dem kill Missa George. Is like a move me mek inna de past decide fe ketch up wid me."

Moses looked away momentarily as he licked the segments of Rizla paper in his lap, sticking them firmly together.

"Moves...what moves coulda cause you to run from Jamaica like dis? Yuh widstand de worst ah de elections?"

This seemed all too familiar to Moses. He'd run into some bad trouble in Jamaica back in the sixties and now the same had happened to Simba. What other reason could there be? He thought back to his last weeks in Jamaica before fleeing.

There was a fight in one of his Blues dances, a knife was

brandished and the man 'chucking the badness' was fatally stabbed. He was blamed for a murder he didn't commit, and had to make choices very quickly on where his future lay.

Moses prayed nothing like that had happened to Delroy. He felt around the floor by his chair for the plastic bag he'd rested there.

"Yuh haffe understan', Uncle, dat over de years people attitude ah change ah yard, drastic. Politics and gun. You haffe be Jesus Christ fe nuh mek no enemies. An' me mek de mistake, I mek a big time one."

"Who dat?" Moses asked, dipping his hand into the bag of sensi and sprinkling it on his Rizla.

"A politician name Hugh St. John."

"*What!* You serious, bwoy?" Moses was so shocked the half-completed spliff nearly fell to the floor. *How in Jah-Jah name had Delroy managed to cross that man, of all people?* "You know who dat raas man is, Delroy?"

"Me know him too good, boss," said Simba, lowering his voice.

"Then if you know him, young bwoy, you should know from what me hear 'bout a man like dat, you lucky to be alive."

Moses felt his own heart beating desperately at the thought.

"How you manage fe get mix up wid politicians after all de t'ings you see inna de ghetto? You of all people should know better than dat, especially inna election time. You could be dead, dis time…"

"Dis time," Delroy interrupted his uncle's words of concern, "me ah relax yahso wid you, boss, until t'ings blow over, him nuh know whe' me deh, an' it ah go stay dah way deh."

Moses lit his spliff and sucked gratefully, allowing the smoke to trickle through his nose.

"Give t'anks…" he sighed heavily, "…you come 'weh wid you life, son. You can't underestimate people like dem yard politics man deh."

"It cool now, uncle," Simba reassured him. "Just mek sure you keep it between me an' you, seen?"

"Alright." Moses changed the subject. "You smoke?"

"Nuh cigarette but if ah sensi, me will burn it wid you man."

"It good fe you yout'," he laughed. "Calm you dung."

And it seemed to do just that. Soon Delroy had leant back feeling completely calm. They talked about Jamaica, Mama Christy and the elections as they puffed. Delroy filled in the gaps in Moses' knowledge, and soon the conversation came back to Hugh St. John.

"Why dis man Saint want you so desperate?" Moses asked

"A woman," Delroy answered, giving only part of the reason. "De Saint will forget the whole t'ing after some time. And I man will be back ah yard no problem."

Simba wasn't sure who he was trying to convince — himself or Moses. He knew this 'bangarang' wouldn't be resolved so easily.

"Well, you deh yahso, now yout'," Moses smiled, trying to make light of the situation,"dat's de important t'ing. It will all work out, man. You will have money in yuh pocket because yuh ah go help me wid de painting an' decorating business, an' in no time you will deh back ah yard wid Mama Christy."

Simba nodded uncertainly. The two sliding shutters on the wall slammed open. Miss Gee's head popped through the opening, her sing-song voice rising with excitement.

"Aren't you two bwoys hungry? De food is all ready and waiting. You don't want it to get cold, do yuh?"

Simba smiled. Miss Gee hadn't changed at all. She was a kind, down-to-earth and supportive woman.

"Wha' deh 'pon de menu, Miss Gee?" he asked.

"Nothing much me son, just some stew peas and rice, fried plantain, soft yam, mixed salad and some Dragon punch."

"But what is this, woman?" Moses laughed out loud, throwing back his mane of locks from his shoulders. "How come we, de immediate family, never get dem treatment yah?"

"Yuh face fava!" she grinned.

"Nuh follow him auntie, don't ease up, seen."

She laughed. Simba followed Moses into the kitchen, wondering what his mother was doing now.

EIGHTEEN

Mama Christy stood in the corrugated zinc kitchen, poking and prodding the assortment of dumplings, yams and bananas floating inside the bubbling pot. Droplets of sweat dampened the edges of the 'tie-head' wrapped around her white plaited hair as she hummed a hymn of redemption. The lines under her eyes told a story of hard times and worries.

It was evening over Rema, the sun having lowered its position in the cloudless sky, staining the shanties and tenements in a blood red hue. Little children were wheeling their tyres up and down Little King Street and 'de corner man dem' were holding court sipping a 'Stripe' or Dragon and burning spliffs.

The old woman leaned against the crumbling window frame and thought of her son. She couldn't bear to lose him as well.

Since Mr George had been killed, it had felt like her heart was being ripped from her chest every single day that had passed. The vacuum he left in her life after twenty-five years of marriage had threatened to consume her.

She had come through her grief, but now her son was in danger and she felt helpless. His letter tried to reassure her, but her 'flesh and blood' could not convince her not to worry. Mama Christy yearned to do something to help and prayed for an answer. And hallelujah, God had heard her prayers.

An answer came in the most unexpected of ways.

That morning she had been awakened by her younger sister. Pearline had burst into the room shaking her awake excitedly.

"Sis! Sis!" she half-whispered, half-shouted. "Wake up nuh, me have something important fe tell you."

She was out of breath, her chest heaving and dots of perspiration lodged on her brow.

"Sister Christy, wake up nuh woman, you sleep too sound."

The old woman opened her eyes, turned over from her stomach to her side, and yawned.

"What is de matter now, girl child, why you love frighten people outta dem sleep so?" She glared at her younger sister. "You want fe gi' me a heart attack, or is it somet'ing dat important why you haffe frighten me so early?"

Pearline stared at her. "I t'ink it's someone to do wid Delroy! An' she seh she will wait as long as it tek."

Mama sat up instantly, her eyes now focused, watching her sister carefully.

"So who is it Pearline, me know dem?"

"Me nuh t'ink so, Sis, but she seh her name Monique and she have to see you. It important to Delroy."

Mama Christy swung her legs out of the bed and reached for her nightgown.

"Hurry up an' go keep de lady company, Pearline. Me will come meet her in a minute."

Pearline left her sister and led the stranger through into the front room in silence. Mama Christy walked in soon after.

"Good morning," Mama said bluntly. "Me hear you have somet'ing important fe tell me 'bout me son…"

Monique looked up, suddenly lost for words. Everything she wanted to say and more was gone from her mind, blanked out by the light of this woman's penetrating stare. She had pictured this scene over and over in her head, imagining an ugly, big-breasted Mama Christy arguing and threatening her.

133

Monique found Delroy's mother to be a hard-working woman with a kind, wise face and easily confided in her.

"I'm the reason why Delroy's on the run."

Monique braced herself for what could come, but the statement hung in mid-air ominously.

If it had affected Mama Christy at all she was not showing it. Then a blink from her grey eyelashes announced she was about to break her silence.

"So yuh is de cause of me son suffering," she snapped. "You nuh do enough fe wreck we life? What else you want from me an' me family?"

Monique lowered her head, the old woman's anger striking a chord of shame in her. She tried to ignore it.

"You don't understand…I haven't come here to lie to you or make excuses, but to tell you the truth. I've had to live with all this too. I want you to know the reason why Delroy is running and why I need to be with him."

"Why now? Why you t'ink you can help him now? Him could be dead by this."

Monique recoiled. And for those fleeting seconds the sheer terror in her face told the truth beyond anything this high class woman could have said.

The girl was in pain too.

Mama was at least willing to listen now. And she did, as Monique answered her questions.

Why hadn't Delroy got involved with a decent single girl from the area? Mama Christy wondered. *Why had he chosen somebody else's wife — especially the wife of a politician?*

But for all these questions, there was still something about Monique which her 'spirit' took to immediately. This was a woman not used to even being around people like her.

Rema had an ugly reputation for violence and danger, Monique had taken a risk coming here to find her son. Mama was impressed by the girl's determination.

Mama Christy adjusted the flames on the kerosene cooker, then hobbled to her window, taking in the last of the evening sunlight. "Who God bless, no man curse," she said philosophically. "Who God bless, no man curse."

NINETEEN

In New York, Tuffy was like a man come home.

He loved the city's greed. It scurried in the sewers, shone in the faces of the inhabitants and was in the very air you breathed. The Almighty Dollar was God in the Big Apple.

If he had had his way he would have been back here much sooner. He hadn't wanted to leave the drugs 'runnings' in the first place, but the boss had his own agenda. At election time the party came first, and Tuffy and others like him had to go and protect 'de border line'. So he had patiently anticipated his return to the Big Apple, when he would again be 'running t'ings' with Jungle Ites Posse. Then the good times would be rolling again.

He was looking forward to fucking a few 'young t'ings' and also paying back some old debts from the Shower and Spanglers Posse, who were 'edging up' into his territory slowly but surely. But that was on the back burner now. He'd been given the job to 'blow weh' a deejay 'bwoy'.

Simple enough.

But things had gone wrong as soon as he arrived on American soil, when the 'twist face' customs officer had realised Tuffy's American passport was fake and tried to apprehend him. He had been lucky 'de Jungle man dem' were there to provide covering fire.

Tuffy kissed his teeth and shuffled back into the shadows, keeping his hands firmly planted in his long coat. He watched a black Porsche arrive at the house he was staking out.

Cho!

He could think of a million things he could be doing between Pinky's smooth long legs in Flatbush that would be more pleasurable than standing here in Harlem.

But he was being pressured by the boss, who seemed to want him to spend every waking hour searching for this raas deejay. The Saint wanted results, and until now Tuffy hadn't provided any.

Jah know! Tonight would be different, his first decent lead in three weeks into where that pussyhole Simba was hiding, he wasn't about to let it pass.

A long-standing associate from the projects had greeted him warmly after not seeing him for nearly a year with the words.

"Just fuck off bwoy!"

Touching.

It only took a few seconds of male bonding and gentle persuasion to produce the information he needed without further hesitation. The Crack junkie Ratty realised his intentions were honourable when he felt the less than friendly end of a Sig Sauer automatic pointing between his legs. They had an immediate rapport from then on.

Acting on that information he had been waiting impatiently in an alleyway for the last forty-five minutes, watching an apartment building across the street. He checked his watch.

It was 11.30 pm, and there was no sign of him.

Tuffy hoped for Ratty's sake that he had given out the right information. Even though the building he watched was a personal address, every Friday night, according to his informant, it housed a high-stakes game frequented by Vibesman, an unscrupulous Jamaican promoter. And if anybody would know where an entertainer from yard would be holed up, he would.

The only problem was that the man he needed to talk to was was very security-conscious. He never spoke to anyone he did not know or did not want to know, and he always travelled with two heavily armed 'gorillas' for protection.

Tuffy knew the odds were stacked against him; but that was

just how he liked it.

He could have had 'x amount of bad bwoys' with him even now if he contacted his spar the don, Rustler, who led the Jungle Ites posse, but he didn't want to involve anybody else.

He was the one who had been given the job.

And he was the one who would finish the job.

Tuffy turned his back to the street and pissed on the wall.

A dog barked.

When he heard the screech of tyres, his head whipped round in time to see the car he was waiting for pull up — a metallic blue Lexus and customised 'criss'.

Before the big car could park, Tuffy had already straightened himself up and was crossing the road towards it, unbuttoning his coat casually. The car had come to a stop under a streetlight, which made it very difficult for Tuffy to see inside the car clearly, but he counted three silhouettes .

He was still moving towards the car, coolly considering his options, when suddenly the passenger door facing him flew open.

One of Vibes man's bodyguards must have had seen him approaching and was probably about to ask unnecessary questions.

Tuffy didn't wait for the man inside the car to plant his feet on solid ground, before He side-kicked the door with all the force he could muster.

Metal slammed against bone and the man's head shattered the door's window. As he crumpled to the street the interior erupted in panic. Tuffy had to calm the situation right away. He quickly slid onto the back seat, the gun in his right hand pointed at the back of the driver's head. He smiled wickedly.

Tuffy growled at Vibesman who was moving toward the other door. "Ah wouldn't do dat if I was you, blood. Before you mek a step, bwoy, me can blow you driver marrow an' you after. You nuh want dat?"

The driver shook his head vigorously in agreement. Vibesman groaned.

The semi-conscious bodyguard out on the road murmured something. It seemed to amuse the 'gundelero', who placed his foot on his chest.

"Now, star!" Tuffy continued in a more relaxed tone. "Me a look fe a man you can help me fin'. An' guess wha', rude bwoy. Yuh life depend 'pon it."

Simba's thoughts wandered back to Jamaica; his hammer came down hard on his thumb, shattering the illusion that he was a seasoned professional.

Moses' laughter nearly toppled him off his ladder with roller, paint and all. Tippa and Tristan — two 'country bwoys' who had been given the opportunity to work in the States — followed suit, telling their new workmate to stop using the sensi so early in the morning.

Simba himself was too absorbed with the pain in his throbbing thumb to see the humour of it all.

To the Ranking this was the last straw. He wanted to tell Moses and the rest of the crew to fuck off and keep this whole trade business to themselves, but he wasn't going to be ungrateful. His uncle meant well, and Simba appreciated what the man was doing for him. But at least in Jamaica he could hustle for himself. Here he had to work; conventional work.

This was the third apartment they had worked on in three weeks and, apart from the money, the only thing he had to show for it was paint under his nails, splinters in his hands and now, maybe, a broken thumb.

This nah wuk out a bumboclaat.

He was working around the clock and not spending enough time on what he really wanted to do — dancehall business.

Moses kneeled down next to Simba and gruffly grabbed his hand, inspecting the thumb for broken bones.

Tristan and Tippa watched in silence. The two of them were inseparable — like a demented version of Bella and Blacka.

"How dat feel?"

Moses twisted it left and right. Simba resisted the urge to grunt, biting into his lower lip.

"You will live, sweet bwoy," Tristan concluded

138

immediately, and then laughed.

"Me see man tek off dem whole fingernail wid dat, you know."

Simba bit his tongue and ignored him.

"Ah hope you know, wuk done fe de day," Simba grunted to no one in particular.

"Jus' becah ah dat little tap?" Moses asked.

Simba kissed his teeth, irritated by his uncle's comment, and walked casually over to a chair to get his coat.

"No disrespect, uncle, but me nuh inna de bum…inna de mood fe this, seen."

He threw the coat over his shoulders and turned to leave.

"A'right! A'right, young bwoy," Moses conceded, feeling a bit guilty at the undue pressure. "Just relax. Mek we jus' pack up yuh t'ings an' you can tek de res' ah de day off. No problem. Tristan an' Tippa will hol' de fort 'til me come back, yes."

'Bella' and 'Blacka' nodded.

"Cool!" They said in unison.

The boulevard was just about fully awake as Delroy and Moses walked along it in silence. The early morning sun was already steaming off the moisture left from the slight drop in temperature the night before; it was going to be another blistering day.

The area was a mix of cultures distinguishable not only by the ubiquitous black faces but also by the types of music blaring through open windows. People from all cultures 'hailed up' Moses when he went by. In this part of the city he was a highly respected man.

It wasn't an opulent upper class area, but a place like-minded black people were happy to call home, bringing up their children in some degree of safety.

"You nuh really want to do dis painting t'ing, nuh true?"

Moses' question came as Simba's mind started to drift. Simba sighed out loud:

"Ah nuh me dis Uncle," he said finally, touching the paint stains on his trousers. "Me jus' cyan fake it. De money good an' widout it, me woulda a walk street bruk. An' nuh seh me ah diss you, Moses, me coulda nevah do dat. But me waan spend more time ah do my t'ing. An' ah dat me know me ah de champion for."

"Music business," the elder dread said flatly. "Will dat feed you, Delroy? Keep a roof over yuh head an' keep you warm inna winter? You feget yuh responsibility to Miss Christy."

His voice took on a slight edge.

"You is all she have, an' de poor woman need fe live a more relaxed life in her ole age. She need money, not promises, Delroy."

Simba curled his lips and sucked air through his teeth. He understood what his uncle was saying, but he still felt shocked that a man who had actually been in the business didn't empathise with the magnetic lure that the dancehall had for him.

He knew he had to stop thinking only of himself, his dreams of success and revenge.

But it was hard.

The image of his father was always there reminding him, 'Nuh get caught inna de ghetto son, use de talents God give yuh fe get weh an' nevah look back'.

Simba stopped and leaned on a mesh fence, Mr George's words dissolving away. He squinted shielding his eyes from the sun and opened his arms submissively to his uncle.

"You mek yuh point clear, boss. An' you right, Mama need me. But yuh see me, my plans haffe go through said way. Dat is one t'ing me nah ease up 'pon. Believe me."

"Ah nuh fail me waan you fail young bwoy," Moses sounded apologetic, "but ah jus' reality."

"No, boss," Delroy countered. "Dat ah fe yuh reality, an' me nah cater fe dat. Me wi' work inna yuh business, nuh get me wrong, but as soon as me start fe bruk out, you deh 'pon yuh own."

Moses stared back at his nephew, saw his arms folded defiantly, his face twisted into a 'screw' and knew he would not budge.

The dread cleared his throat.

"Me know how hard it is fe mek any headway inna de reggae business, 'memba me try it. You haffe have de right contacts, money, an' even gun sometime. It nuh worth it. Concentrate 'pon a trade yout' man, you wi' have dat fe fall back 'pon. Me jus' ah mek sure you nuh mek de same mistakes me make."

Delroy grinned.

"It gone bad a'ready, boss. You, ah one man who inspire me fe go inna de dancehall. Me nuh know wha' happen to you, why you waan elbow de business, but you see me," he slapped his chest with the palm of his hand, "me is a deejay dead or alive."

If Moses realised that his nephew's mind was made up. And whether he was living in Jamaica or in the States he intended to follow his dream. Moses had to admit that he felt a little envious. His own sound business hadn't been as successful as he'd hoped. Maybe Simba's attitude was what it took.

The atmosphere between them calmed as they neared home; Simba's mind was already on what he should be doing now that he wasn't going to be working.

Since he arrived a month ago, he had scouted the place by train, car and bus and felt familiar with the surroundings. Today he would check out the few recording studios in town he hadn't visited yet. He was still trying to decide whether he should produce a special in New York or approach one of the many record labels. But then, if he was successful, his whereabouts would be known to too many people. So if the Saint still wanted him dead — and he probably did — he could find him with no difficulty. That thought made his heartbeat quicken.

He had faced his fear and decided to go ahead with his plan regardless. That meant his first stop would be Vibrations Recording Studios in Brooklyn, one of the last studios on his checklist. The engineer at HCF studios in Long Island had recommended it as bonafide. This afternoon he would see for himself.

Moses had stopped walking, and was now some way behind him, talking to a young girl with bright red ribbons in her hair. Simba turned back to join him. It could take hours to get anywhere when you were walking with his uncle.

Simba was about to explain that he was on a runnings when two beautiful black women turned the corner ahead and walked straight towards them. Both women beamed their recognition of Moses with smiles and, in return, Moses' face lit up.

"Where have you been, girl child? I haven't seen you fe months."

"I could ask you the same, Moses," the taller woman said, her eyes intelligent and warm. "Since Momma left for Jamaica, I've sold the house and rented an apartment in New York state. I'll be joining her in Kingston in about two months, and you wouldn't know how I'm looking forward to living and working there." She squealed childishly as she held Moses' hand. "I'm so busy it's hard for me to link up with you guys…"

"You mus' mek time, Donna. Me nuh want you fe leave to Jamaica an' me nuh get to see you. Miss Gee asks fe you all de time, and even if it's fe her sake, come an' see we."

"I will, I promise, Moses."

"Now you do dat. "Oh," said Moses as if he had only just noticed, "this is my nephew, Delroy, jus' recently in from Jamaica." He motioned to the women in turn. "Delroy, this is Donna, de daughter of a frien' ah mine and her friend."

"Sharon," Donna added.

"Yeah man, Sharon."

Delroy greeted both women. Sharon smiled amorously back, but the Ranking's focus was on the dark-skinned Donna. She was a long-legged ebony beauty, slightly taller than Monique. It was strange how every woman he came across, he subconsciously compared to her. He had tried to tell himself that they would never meet again, just get on with your life but a niggling doubt remained about the truth in that statement.

Donna threw him a quick glance and smiled. When both women turned to go, Simba caught Donna's eye again.

She played cool and he liked that, but he wasn't about to push his luck. They would meet up again, he knew it.

TWENTY

The cab pulled up outside the gates of Vibration Studios. Simba's first impressions made him relax immediately.

It looked like a large chunk of Jamaica had been airlifted and dropped onto an empty lot. Someone with artistic flair, and probably too many ganja spliffs, to his name had made sure his creation would command attention and its stark architecture had been given extra vibrancy and life when they had painted the building in the Jamaican national colours; green, yellow and black.

There were about ten people out front in the yard. Some were standing around talking, some drinking, some playing cards and others arguing over a game of keep-up as the ball being juggled on feet between five people fell on the ground and rolled away. It was so like a scene from the streets of Jamaica — Simba smiled to himself. He liked what he saw.

He strolled over to the main doors and pushed them open, a surge of artificial coolness welcoming him into the reception area. Adorning the walls were pictures of reggae artists young and old and Simba wondered if all these greats had actually passed through here. This had to be the place for him. He idled over to the deserted front desk and rested his arms on the counter.

The receptionist sat up suddenly, filing her nails.

"Can I help yuh?" she asked with a clipped tone. Simba's presence seemed to be an imposition. She stood up grudgingly, placing her nail file down beside the telephone.

"Me woulda love talk to yuh boss. Him deh 'bout?"

"You have an appointment wid Missa Morris?"

"Me nuh need dat!" Simba replied. "If him deh yah jus' tell him ah Simba Ranking from yard, deh 'bout man."

The receptionist's eyebrows arched with surprise, and she punched a three digit number into the phone on her desk.

The extension rang but no one answered.

"Yuh want to take a seat until me can contact him?" she asked. "Me sure him nuh leave de studio yet."

Simba picked up a studio price list and wandered away from the desk. He looked at more of the photographs on the wall and noticed a large light-skinned man in expensive clothes was featured prominently. He wondered if this was Vibesman. If so, that evil lopsided grin said he was not a man to be taken lightly.

That face did not fill him with confidence, it reminded him too much of the Mikey Dreads of the world. He reminded himself that sometimes you have to compromise if you want to progress. Simba looked back over to the receptionist and made his way back to her desk to ask about the man in the photograph.

There was an agonising shout — the sounds of someone in extreme pain, coming from the stairs behind the reception desk.

He froze, as a body tumbled down the steps and slammed to the floorboards. The receptionist squealed and jumped up from her chair. The Ranking looked on in disbelief.

A man lay crumpled and moaning at the bottom of the stairs, his arms and legs tangled around the banister and a trickle of blood running from a gash across his forehead.

The receptionist rushed to his aid, then stopped herself as a muscular T-shirted dreadlocks came leaping down the stairs two at a time. At the bottom he hammered both feet into the shoulders of the stretched-out man. His victim rolled away in agony.

The dread checked his Karl Kani boots for scuff marks,

grinned and slowly looked up to see Simba watching him.

The receptionist turned away.

For long seconds Simba became the natty's centre of attention while he pulled his victim into a standing position. A gurgling laugh came booming down the stairs from above, soon after.

"Hector...*Hector!*" the voice teased. "You nuh know seh nobody cyan come ah my place ah business an' then call me a teef 'pon top ah it. You will dead, boss."

The man behind the voice came slowly downstairs, followed closely by another henchman.

Simba studied his evil lopsided grin.

Vibesman kissed his teeth and delivered a fierce punch to Hector's stomach. Hector gasped and fell to his knees, coughing.

"Once a man sign to my label, bwoy, him sign fe good until me finish wid him, right? Dat is how my business run. Yuh cyan hol' onto a demo-tape fe my artist. Dat is my property."

Simba kissed his teeth loudly and leaned on the reception desk.

"Ah so yuh do business boss, three man ah beat one man?"

For the first time the Vibesman noticed Simba. He looked him up and down. The face seemed familiar, he wasn't sure why. But he *was* sure this unknown 'mout' ah massy' was in 'de wrong place at de wrong time'.

The producer signalled to the receptionist to leave and she scurried away quickly.

Simba remained where he was, watching the men keenly. Trouble was not what he came for, but he was involved now and he couldn't back down.

"Who de bumboclaat you be?" Vibesman asked, then decided he didn't want to wait for an answer. "You know what? Jus' feget 'bout wha' you see, an' we can call it a day, right? Yuh nuh know me an' me nuh know yuh. De door deh over desso, batty bwoy. Use it."

The Ranking's left eyebrow twitched as if he had just

been slapped. He looked briefly at the door, then back at Vibesman.

"Bad bwoy!" Vibesman shouted. "Pop up him raas, Maxi."

"Come nuh! You t'ink Simba Ranking easy, fe tek dung nuh, pussy?"

The name jolted Vibesman's conscious mind into slow recognition.

"Simba Ranking…" he murmured.

Tuffy's man.

Too late.

Maxi was already charging over to Simba throwing a searing right hook and connecting air. Simba saw another one coming his way and ducked behind the reception desk. He came back up quickly clutching a solid crystal ashtray which he used without regret. Ashes and cigarette butts flew into the air as he slammed it into the side of Maxi's head, sending him sprawling to the floor.

Simba was taking no chances. He leaned over the moaning man with the ashtray held high, and rummaged through his jacket without taking his eyes off Vibesman. Surprise, surprise — he pulled out a gun. He clicked the safety off and pointed the Smith and Wesson at Vibesman and his minder.

"Who waan tes' de Ranking first?" he teased.

Both men looked at each other.

The dread attempted to reach in his coat…

"Don't do it!" Simba hissed. "You t'ink me nuh know how fe use this, bwoy!"

The Ranking didn't want any bloodshed now, but he didn't want to die either. The dread's hand fell away from his coat, to his side.

Simba breathed out.

"Keep yuh hand up high, rude bwoy," he told the dreadlocks. "You alright, star?" Hector nodded. "Then search de dreadlocks fe him gun."

Hector pulled out an old Taurus revolver, passed it to the Ranking and turned to face Vibesman.

"You t'ink ah you one can inflict damage?" he asked hoarsely. "Watch me."

Without further warning he lifted his thin leg and delivered a thunderous kick to the producer's backside, then followed up with a jaw twisting 'box'. Vibesman grunted and staggered back, off balance.

The dreadlocked bodyguard stood his ground, a grimace on his face. The urge to protect his boss was strong but respect for the 'matic in Simba's hand won the day. Hector's job finished, he limped away from his tormentors to lean on the reception desk weakly.

"You is a dead man, yuh know dat bwoy?" Vibesman wiped the blood from the corner of his mouth. "De two ah you."

"Yuh haffe join de line, boss. Many a man promise me death, an' see me yah."

He touched his sleeve with the automatic.

"It will come, deejay bwoy, nuh worry. Yuh t'ink you a bad bwoy, but badda man deh out deh ah wait fe you."

"Then sen' him come nuh, an' tell him fe choose him spot ah Dovecot careful. Cah me nuh miss."

Vibesman looked into his eyes and knew that these were not idle threats. He said no more.

"Lie dung."

Simba barked his command through clenched teeth.

"An' you, ugly bwoy, cover yuh bumboclaat mout', me ah smell it."

The producer kissed his teeth. He had missed a golden opportunity to hand the 'rough neck' deejay over to the gangster Tuffy. The yardie had been breathing down his neck for too long already. He'd have to find another way to dislodge the monkey from his back.

As he lay spreadeagled face down, he promised himself he would get Tuffy out of his life, then put Simba in the burial plot he had talked about.

It would be a pleasure.

Simba rubbed cigarette ash from his hands and ejected the magazine out of the automatic, then flung the gun behind the waiting room chairs.

"If me even see this door yah open before me drive 'way, me go start buss shot 'pon anyt'ing dat move, seen?"

Simba and Hector backed out of the building, leaving Vibesman and his bodyguard sprawled in silence. Hector gestured to his car outside the gate and they hurried over.

"Drive!" Hector said breathlessly throwing the keys into Simba's hands. "Me will thank you later, boss."

And Simba drove, not knowing where he was heading, but sure that it would be as far away from Vibration Studio as possible.

Delroy drove across Brooklyn Bridge unsure of whether he had done the right thing. It wasn't exactly how he had planned to get back into the music business.

Records not bullets.

Every time he tried to make some progress, he met some resistance. He couldn't have done anything else, the situation he found gave him no choice but to act. Sure, he had walked out without a deal, but the sight of Vibesman nose down in the carpet, his big quivering backside shooting to the ceiling was ample reward for doing the right thing.

Simba glanced at Hector, a man about his own age with a thin, but muscular frame, bright, intelligent eyes and the word 'SEX' cut into the back of his hair.

"Him ah go pay fe this!" he kept repeating to himself.

Simba put the pieces of the story together: Hector had gone to the studio to confront Vibesman about a stolen master tape. The producer had responded to the accusations with violence. Delroy had caught the end of negotiations. And Hector had come away with a few bruises and gashes, a bashed ego…and no tape.

"Simba Ranking," he said with a Jamaican twang. "Ah long time me respect you as a entertainer you nuh boss. Long time, man. Yuh waan see when you come out wid dah tune deh 'It Cyan Dun', three years ago, ah just fe yuh name ah New York dem did ah call. It did big, star."

Simba stared at the road ahead, unable to believe what he was hearing. *His second single had reached abroad and had done well, and 'de dutty dread' Mikey had pocketed every penny.*

Delroy remembered the dejection he felt when Mikey told him he had not made the grade for a 'farrin' release. He shook his head in disgust.

"Nuh tell me you nevah know?"

Hector knew the reaction of surprise and anger well, he had seen it many times before with entertainers who had dealt with the 'cowboys' in the business.

"Another fuckrie promoter or producer, tu'n yuh over, nuh true?"

Simba said nothing, which confirmed Hector's theory.

"You nuh haffe tell me man, cah me know, dat's why a big time artist like you Ranking can do much better than Vibesman. Me a show you man. If certain producer know seh you up yah, dem a come fe you bodily. But me can gi' you a better deal." He plucked at his nose in thought. "Hear wha', me owe you more than jus' me livelihood but me life star, an' if me can help you set back up inna de business, you have me support, no problem."

"You can help me?" Simba asked, a little too rashly.

"Listen, Ranking," he laughed drily, gripping his bruised ribs as the pain speared him. "Me is no big time producer or promoter, star, but me have some wicked contacts, an' hear wha'—" he grinned, "—me nah rip you off."

Simba had to admit he liked Hector. It was difficult not to. His enthusiasm and confidence were addictive.

But mout' mek fe chat.

News of today's altercation would spread around the other studios like wildfire. If he wanted to go ahead with his original plans he needed some inspired thinking. If he was 'bonafide', Hector could be the man to help. That was a big 'if', but what choice did he have?

So had he sunk himself even deeper into an already difficult situation or was he on his way back to the top?

Time would tell.

TWENTY-ONE

Simba left the apartments he was decorating in Queens with a clear idea of what he wanted to be doing that afternoon.

Usually he would have spent his lunch break in the local record store, checking out the new releases and chatting with the owner.

But today he had bigger fish 'feh fry'.

He wouldn't return from lunch, and Moses and his crew wouldn't see Simba for the rest of the day. He didn't give a damn what they said about that. He had a prior engagement.

When he got back the apartment was silent, the smells of breakfast still in the air. Miss Gee was working, and Courtney was away until the next day.

Nuff t'ings can gwan.

Simba had not been with a woman since he left Jamaica. If he could blame anybody for that, it would be Moses. The early mornings and late nights had thrown his life into chaos.

He had only the memories of Monique to warm him but the effect on him was so strong that he found it more and more difficult to remember the times he had had with other women. What struck him as strange was how, every time he even thought of sex, Monique popped up in his head like a niggling conscience. He knew now she was one in a million, but his life had to go on.

He could do nothing to locate her, and she would never

find him. Simba missed her much more than he would have admitted even to himself, and would do anything within his power to be with her now — but his hands were tied.

Time wi' tell.

Until then, 'nuh pretty gal was safe.

Donna had called yesterday and they'd talked for over an hour on the phone, leaving him with a fire in his boxer shorts that would not go away.

She was leaving New York for good the following week, and Delroy had quickly insisted that she come round at lunch time today to say her goodbyes. Donna had agreed — and her parting words had made it clear that she had every intention of seeing him again before she left the country. He knew that she wanted him, and that she was a skilled warrior in the battle of the sexes. But she didn't count on the resilience of a hard-up 'yard' man.

Delroy smiled as he shaved, remembering her last words: "save your best moves for me". Slipping on his tracksuit pants, he checked his pockets for his 'water boots'. He'd need the condoms soon enough. He slipped on a large mesh Ganzi, then headed downstairs to wait.

The doorbell rang soon afterwards.

Delroy was a portrait of control as he opened the front door.

"Hiya!" Donna chirped as he ushered her inside. She was wearing a body-hugging brown cotton skirt and a loose fitting white shirt which lay delicately over her bosom. Bra-less, her nipples cast fleeting shadows on the material as she shifted around. He could feel himself getting hard just from looking at her.

"Where is everybody?"

He sat her down on the chunky black leather sofa before answering her.

"You waan see Donna, certain t'ings come up fe Moses an' Miss Gee ah de wrong time." He paused, trying to look really apologetic. "Miss Gee get delayed but we deh 'bout later fe see you. Definite."

He watched Donna's reaction keenly.

"I guess I'll have to wait round a while, because I'm not sure when I'll get the opportunity to come here again…"

The corners of her red lips twitched into a smile.

"…But in the meantime I'll just make the most of your hospitality."

The Ranking grinned his approval, snaking his hands under a cushion to retrieve the sound system's remote control. Sensual lovers' rock teased its way out of the speakers.

"I'm impressed," Donna cooed.

"You love dem music yah?"

"Of course I do but I was talking about this…" She turned around, gesturing in a sweeping motion. "Music on hand, the coziness of everything…I'm getting suspicious."

Her concerned look softened as she smiled a sexy smile. Simba feigned guilt.

"Me cyan tek de praise fe dat, Donna. Miss Gee ah de woman fe dat."

"Okay, okay," she laughed, teasing him, "but you know I just love to see that guilty twitch of your mouth, when you're backed in a corner."

"Me!" he laughed a course cackle in response. "Me is a bad bwoy, man, me up front wid everyt'ing me do. You nevah know?"

"You Jamaican men never cease to amaze me."

"A dat mek we special, baby."

He stood up and gestured towards the kitchen.

"Drink?"

She nodded.

"De hard stuff?"

"Beer or wine will do, thanks."

"Relax, man," the Ranking said in parting. "Soon come!"

He poured her beer in a glass and cleaned the neck of his, drinking straight from the bottle. A revival tune wafted in from the living room.

"This tune brings back so many memories of my growing up in JA," Donna murmured.

He came back through and sat down beside her. She

daintily took the glass from him.

"Who sang it?"

There was a lapse in concentration for a moment as Simba was eyeing her with every sip of the cool 'juice'.

"Ah Delroy Wilson do this riddim yah. Yeah man," He pondered ruefully, "Is a pioneer dat."

They drank and talked — Delroy of his life in Jamaica and his involvement in the world of reggae music, Donna of her time in the States. A couple of hours later they were completely relaxed in each other's company.

The beers were soon gone and Donna slipped off her shoes and slumped back on the sofa. Simba replaced the revival sounds with modern lovers' rock, and lowered the music a few decibels. They were sitting very close now and, Simba was stroking Donna's shoulders.

"So wha' you ah go leave me…fe remember you wid Donna?"

"What about the memories of a good conversation?" she joked.

"Dat nuh good enough, baby."

His voice lowered to a whisper.

"Then what do you suggest…?"

"Suggest…" Simba smiled as he leaned forward and started to lightly kiss her neck. His hands moved to find her nipples, already taut and hard with arousal, and in response Donna's hands probed his back. She massaged his tight muscles through the mesh T-shirt, trailing down to his buttocks with the points of her nails and gripping the cheeks of his backside tight when Simba's flickering tongue excited her.

They hit the floor, their impact absorbed by the carpet. Simba's hands under her shirt massaged her firm breasts, inadvertently popping the buttons as his hands moved up and down her smooth chest. Her mouth opened and they tasted each other with relish, his tongue battling hers for supremacy.

Donna's shirt came off and landed beyond the sofa, leaving her topless and open to the Ranking's eager mouth, licking and sucking her dark brown nipples. He eased her out of her skirt and, without waiting for Delroy's eager hands, she slipped off her thong panties and went for him with the ferocity of a wild animal, pawing at his sleek body and ripping off his Ganzi and tracksuit bottom. She was not disappointed as she held Simba's throbbing penis as it eagerly sprang from his shorts.

Simba moaned.

"You're hard like a rock, Delroy," Donna gasped, smoothing her hand from the root of his manhood to its gleaming helmet.

"Come into me!"

The Ranking said nothing, but expertly donned his 'boots'. He found the hot dampness between her legs like a heat-seeking missile and drove into it.

She licked her lips and gasped with every stroke. But Donna needed to feel more of him inside her and she skillfully rolled over without warning, positioning herself on top. His pole throbbed as she rode him like a wild woman and Simba bucked with her, keeping time and raising up intermittently to massage her firm breasts. Her rhythm suddenly became more desperate, and Simba felt the vibration trembling through her like a small earthquake. Donna stiffened then, her red lips trembling and her eyes rolling back into her head and she cried out from the shock waves of her orgasm.

"Dah one de...a fe you, baby..." Simba moaned. "This one yah ah fe me, slow an' easy."

It was.

And so was the next...

TWENTY-TWO

Soon after Monique pulled out of Darliston, she noticed the red and white Ford Capri following her.

The car's occupants were either moronic amateurs or professionals who didn't care about being spotted.

They had made their presence known about three miles down the road. And from then on, as the bumpy highway forked or detoured away from the main route they stuck with her. When she thought about it, she realised the car could have been with her all the way from Hanover to Westmoreland.

Monique was worried. She'd had to come and see her mother, to explain what was happening. It had been risky but important.

Did her pursuers want her dead or alive? she wondered, and she fought to keep her panic at bay. The Saint would not give this madness up until he saw blood.

He had been searching for her without success for some time, and she found it hard to believe she would be safe forever. However, as much as she was frightened and trembling, she refused to succumb to her husband's terror tactics. That would have meant he was winning.

Not this time!

In everything she did, Monique took precautions and today was no different. She would go ahead with her trip to Montego Bay as planned, and if she kept her nerve they might still think she had not noticed them. Besides, if it came to a high speed chase, that old Ford wouldn't stand a chance against her BMW. Two could play his game of cat and mouse.

The speedo slowly inched towards sixty miles per hour as she flew through Whithorn, checking her rear-view mirror intermittently.

The Capri was still behind her, and as the hills and bush loomed they stayed close. She checked her watch, concentrating on the road and blinking as the sunlight broke through the shrubbery.

She thought about escape. Her pursuers would not try to capture her on these narrow meandering roads — it was far too risky. But when they reached the flats of Montpelier and Anchovy it would be a different story. She sensed that was where they would make their move and, if so, that was where she might have to rely on her BMW to out-run them.

The two cars sped up into the hills.

Monique was tiring from the tension and concentration but her pursuers were savouring the chase.

The man at the wheel of the Capri hoped she was a good driver. He didn't want to tell the boss that his wife had died before he had the chance to kill her himself. If she survived the twists and the turns of the rapid ascent, then capturing her on the flats would be a mere formality.

She hit the plains at high speed, overtaking every thing in her path. But the Capri had more power than she had given it credit for, and inch by inch it gained on her.

Then, as she flew over a rise in the road, her four wheels touching down all at once, she saw an unbelievable sight ahead.

A police road block.

A squad car and police jeep were parked on either side of the road, lights flashing as red-seamed and plain-clothes policemen stopped and interviewed drivers. She slowed to a crawl, watching the Capri in the mirror, holding her breath as she tried to figure out what its occupants were about to do.

Their engine was still turning over, idling noisily and the men inside sat motionless like cardboard cut-outs. A plain-clothes officer approached Monique's car and knocked on the window. He grinned. "T'ink you nevah did ah come, Miss Monique."

Monique wanted to jump out of the car and kiss her cousin Eva full on the lips.

"You alright?" he inquired, as he looked back at the two cars immediately behind her.

Monique answered him breathlessly.

"It's the Capri. They're Hugh's men."

Eva called out to some of his uniformed colleagues who immediately went over to the Capri and dragged the men out at gunpoint.

"You safe now, cuz. We will handle dem man deh, nuh worry you can gwan."

Monique squeezed his hand as he bent over she kissed him.

"Tek care," he said

"I will — and thank you."

He waved her through the roadblock. She slipped a Bob Marley cassette into the stereo, and as an afterthought decided to open her glove compartment again to check if all her documents were in order. The speed trap shrank into the distance as she floored the accelerator.

Passport and tickets all there. As if she had not known.

And then she was reminded again by Bob Marley himself.

Exodus, movement of Jah people,
Exodus, movement of Jah people,
Open your eyes and look deep within,
Are you satisfied with the life you're living,
We know where we're going,
An' we know where we're from…

The Saint sat alone at the vast dining room table. Classical music played in the background as an aid to his troubled thinking but the soothing sound of Vivaldi's *Four Seasons* had been completely locked out of his head for the last twenty minutes as he glared at the newspaper headline.

Ghetto man d'weet sweet

No names were mentioned or particular places specified but Hugh St. John knew the article referred indirectly to his private life.

He made a mental note of the journalist responsible.

"Freedom of press me raas!"

Only Simba's blood would compensate for this.

Thanks to the way *The Gleaner's* society column had poked fun of his private business it had become 'a big t'ing a town'. Try as he might to stop people from talking, it was on everyone's lips. As if that wasn't bad enough, some semi-literate deejay had made a record based on the exploits of his hero, Simba Ranking.

The Saint's name was being called downtown by the common riff-raff and this whole regrettable incident was a source of gossip to everyone from the shrimp woman on Kings Street to the taxi drivers at Parade.

It was a deteriorating situation, but he would have the last laugh.

No one around him dared to make even a fleeting mention of it. But who could stop the people on the street from 'spreading rumours' about a ghetto deejay who had fucked a politicians wife 'an breed her'? That was the stuff of which legends were made.

That riled the Saint: but what riled him even more was the fact that he couldn't be in New York to witness Simba's death. His presence there, no matter how brief, would draw attention to 'de dutty deejay's' death and that would not be good for business. He had made the right decision in letting his boys handle it over there.

And he would handle his wife from here. That he could do. He had found out were she was hiding quite by accident. He staked out her mother's place and other friends and relatives he knew of but the Saint had come up with nothing.

Then, one Friday evening, he had noticed Maude, the old woman who had cooked for them for years, taking some of Monique's personal effects with her as she left for a three week vacation in Hanover. He'd found that Monique was actually staying with the old woman, but when his men had moved in the bitch slipped away and disappeared in Montego Bay.

He had no appetite for his breakfast, and pushed it away in disgust. He stretched and yawned, just as one of the new staff he had employed 'whined' up to the table to place a perspiring jug of orange juice before him. He smiled up at the young dark-skinned woman, her heavy chest at eye level, and snaked a hand under her dress. He massaged her buttocks, releasing a giggle from her as she hurried off.

This was the only therapy that would calm him at the moment and he was making sure he got plenty of it, hiring and using the girls as he pleased.

He rose from his seat, not bothering to tie his gown, and idled along the corridor to the shower. Another day...and another opportunity to hear the news from New York that Simba Ranking was dead.

But he wasn't going to sit around doing nothing, waiting for the phone to ring. No, today he had plans — and today he would start to implement them. His gown fell to the floor in a heap as he stepped into the shower.

It would be a good day, he could feel it.

TWENTY-THREE

Hector phoned two weeks after their first fateful meeting.

Simba was more than pleasantly surprised.

He hadn't expected to hear from him. But it seemed as though Hector was a man of his word. They'd arranged to meet at Moses' apartment block at eleven o' clock that night. But instead of letting Hector take the stairs to the apartment and disturb the family by ringing the bell, Simba had taken 'a fresh', put on his clothes and went to stand outside waiting for him to turn up.

The night air was cool and relaxing. Simba looked around and saw lights blinking out in the apartment windows opposite as people turned in for the night.

But for him the night was only just beginning.

Cars were parked in disorderly lines along the pavement and the more decrepit wrecks, pock-marked with rust, perfumed the air with the smell of stale oil. Nearby, Simba could hear the baby-like scream of cats in heat prowling their urban jungle. A siren sounded in the distance and broke Simba out of his reverie. He lifted his sleeve and checked his watch. Hector was either going to be half an hour late or he wasn't coming at all.

The Ranking pushed one hand in his pocket and took four steps along the pavement as if he was about to leave, then decided against it.

Him coulda get hol' up inna traffic, he thought, *me ah go gi him a lickle more time, still.*

When Hector did arrive, five minutes later, his excuse was more interesting than Simba's traffic theory.

"Yuh waan see my girl, nevah want me come out tonight, star," he laughed excitedly as he beckoned Simba into the car. "But you know how it go, me ah de bedroom bully, she jus' haffe cool, boss."

Simba laughed too. Hector was just as 'bummy' as he remembered him and tonight looked like a real 'bad bwoy'.

The only jewellry Hector was wearing was a chunky gold chopperetta and a gold ring on his right hand. But the beige mesh suit he had on was a classic example of quality dancehall fashion. 'Traaaash!'

"So which dance we ah go, boss?" Simba asked, switching the cassette deck on. A tape by New York's champion sound, Addis, began playing.

"Domino International, rude bwoy ah Flatbush, Brooklyn."

The drive from St. Alban's to Flatbush Avenue was forty-five minutes. Simba saw a trickle of people heading to the dance as Hector turned off the main road into a driveway which led up to the hired hall. Hector parked the car and they walked up to a knot of people congregated outside the entrance. The sound of bass boomed through the walls.

"It cork, boss," Simba said, fed up at the prospect of boring through the crowd to get inside.

"Nuh worry, king man!" Hector grinned broadly, "You t'ink me woulda mek a don like you, get caught up inna crowd? You mad, man!" Hector drew his portable phone from inside his jacket and, with his head leant to one side like the 'artical don', he punched in some numbers, paused and started talking to someone. From what Simba could make out, someone was directing him to a line of fire doors situated at the side of the building.

"Come, rude bwoy," Hector said as they skirted the fringes of the crowd, ending up at the side of the building.

Hector knocked and the security door flew open; the heat enveloped them as they stepped inside quickly before any of the crowd could follow.

It was as if they had been transported into a different world.

Simba saw a small indoor sports hall that had been transformed into a prefabricated 'dancehall lawn', the open air spectacle of the stars in the sky replaced by low lights in the ceiling.

A dancehall alive and throbbing. He'd really missed this — he hadn't quite realised just how much, until now. For the first time since he had fled unwillingly to this city, Simba felt like he could conquer the world. The music seemed to be coursing through his veins, lifting him.

This was his element, his life.

"You nuh see not'n you like, boss?" Hector asked him, already stretching over to touch the hand of a young lady passing by. She frowned. Hector grinned, his attention focused on Simba coolly taking in the surroundings. Hector knew Simba had 'presence' the first time they met at the altercation at Vibesman studios. And even as they walked in here, female heads turned to watch him. Recognition, maybe, but Hector doubted it. Star quality. He reckoned the deejay could probably take his pick of the beauties milling around. Simba nodded towards a young fit-looking woman in the distance,

"Healt'y body," he said matter-of-factly. Hector laughed, steering them both over to the drinks room. And with Dragon stout and Heineken in hand they went and stood between two towering speaker boxes.

Hector lit up a cigarette.

"Cancer stick, don?" Simba declined.

"You nuh smoke?" Hector sounded surprised.

"Sensi, yeah man. But cigarette me nevah pick up, star. Too busy ah look gal."

Hector laughed heartily, sipping on his Dragon.

"Me know man. Cocks man fe years."

They stood silently for a while, enjoying the atmosphere. Simba focused on the turntables at the other end of the large hall, the focal point of everyone's attention. *In time these people will be rocking to my tunes,* he thought to himself.

Hector broke into his thoughts.

"So why yuh decide fe come ah New York now, Simba?"

Simba massaged his hairless chin. "To forget, boss!" he said. "But certain man nuh waan me forget."

Hector nodded.

"But de music business haffe gwan regardless, ah jus' me sabotage certain t'ings. Maybe ah fear me nuh sure." He looked uneasy.

Hector didn't understand what he meant, but in time he knew Simba would trust him enough to explain everything.

"Listen, man," Hector cut in, "any time you waan move ahead wid yuh career, don. Me ready."

"You ready?"

"Me ah go show you somet'ing, don. Come."

Hector set off, weaving through the dancing crowd towards the turntable. Simba followed closely.

The mixer was sifting through a case of records and tapes as they approached, oblivious to the pandemonium around him as some unknown deejay was assaulting the crowd with his X-rated lyrics. The selector's designer glasses were wet with sweat and his hands rotated wildly like propellers as he reacted to the deejay's hand signals.

Simba stood back and watched Hector go up to the mixer and start talking close to his ear. And after an animated discussion Hector came back to him, grinning as usual.

"Show de people wha' you can do, don," he said, gesturing towards the microphone. Before a stunned Simba could say a word, he added, "Contacts, my bwoy!"

Lyrics swirled in Simba's head. Impromptu 'chatting 'pon de mike' was a gift possessed by only a small number of talented deejays, and he had that gift. The operator nodded, tipping his headphones towards Simba. Delroy raised his fist in respect to him.

"Bonafide!" the D.J. answered, keeping his eyes on the blinking display units of his equalisers and digital output monitors, making sure there was no lapse in the music.

"You have dah new Salt fish riddim deh?" the Ranking asked. He knew the Mafia and Fluxy tune well and had already constructed lyrics around it. It had been used by two other artistes before, but neither had done it justice.

Now it was the Ranking's turn. He wouldn't fail.

"Yeah man," the operator said confidently. "How you want it lick?"

"Jus' fade out de vocals."

Before he could take another breath the twelve-inch was on the turntable and the 'riddim' ripped out from the surrounding speakers.

He gingerly lifted the microphone to his lips and let his 'rock stone tone-a-voice' take over.

De Ranking deh 'bout, man!
Simba Ranking to all bad bwoy,
Gal pickney, hol tight. Not'n fe fear.
Here me nuh!

Simba ah no outlaw, him ah no gangsta,
Will you remember me, when dem full me up ah copper?
Me is no rude bwoy, me is a chanter,
Bettah me cool an' praise de father...

Each word fell with precision, every expression delivered smoothly, and from his cramped space he began to control the crowd.

If there had been any doubt as to whether Simba was as talented as he was three years ago that doubt soon melted away. His performance now was even better.

Dis yout' yah hot property, thought Hector. At last he had found a champion deejay.

And when the music faded out the roar of voices was the only sound to be heard — bigging him up, and firing simulated gun shots as dancers flicked lighters to show their appreciation.

Simba's eyes glowed with a mixture of excitement and apprehension. His career could start again. But in no time his name and location would be whispered in the Saint's ears and then he would come for him.

He had to be prepared for that.

Somehow.

TWENTY-FOUR

Mavis!!!
No journey too great when a woman find whatever she seek,
She will swim de deepest sea an' climb de highest peak,
Is a certain climax, she waan reach,
Dis is Merciless, have got to practice what him preach,
Lawd ah mercy
Mavis, by Merciless

The smell of aftershave lingered on Simba's face in the warm air. Courtney kept pace with him as they took the last turning for home, his stomach growling with hunger.

Delroy was feeling quite content with himself, an emotion that he had not felt since coming to New York

"De grapevine, star," Hector had said describing his so called army of contacts. "Dat's how t'ing get done so quick, when me do t'ings."

And his boast hadn't been idle chat either. Less than two weeks since Simba's spontaneous re-introduction to the dancehall he had gone into the studio to do two specials for Addis and Dominoes sound systems.

Producers around town who'd heard about the new and improved Simba Ranking were asking questions about using his talents but Hector, who seemed to have taken on a managerial role, ignored all the offers.

"Harbour sharks." He dismissed them with a wave of his hand. "We ah run t'ings fe we way, yes?"

Simba's nod of agreement hadn't been the most positive of responses but Hector, caught up in his own excitement, hadn't noticed. If Simba wanted to get back into the music 'runnings' there was no other way.

Simba pushed the door to the apartment block, deep in thought. No retreat, no surrender, he decided.

To his uncle's displeasure, Simba had that Friday off work and he had used it to visit Courtney's barber shop and discuss business with Hector. He now wanted to just shower and eat and go meet Jessy — an American girl who had introduced herself to him at the Dominoes dance and with whom he had a very special date.

Inside the apartment Simba was about to head upstairs when Ms Gee came through into the hall.

"I glad you come, bwoy," she said a little breathlessly.

"Everyt'ing alright, aunt?"

"Me fine, son," she said. "I have a message fe you."

A sly smile crossed her lips.

"You girlfriend call…"

Simba groaned. *Which gal?* He'd met a trailerload of women since he'd been in New York and several had his number.

"Which girl dat you ah talk 'bout, aunt?"

"Monique."

Simba looked visibly shaken.

Monique?

"Which part ah yard she call from?"

"She nevah call from Jamaica. She call from New York."

Monique in New York. Simba felt elated and confused.

How did she find him? Was it a trap?

"Me tek dung an address she give me," said Miss Gee, handing him a piece of note paper. She was puzzled by her nephew's reaction.

"She need fe see you at this address five o'clock sharp."

Simba took the slip of paper and checked his watch. Ten minutes past four.

"It sound important, son."

Courtney came out of the kitchen with a sandwich, on his way up to his room. Simba snatched his plate and placed it in Miss Gee's open palms.

"We ah go out, star."

"But me jus'…"

Before he knew it, Courtney's coat and hat were rammed into his arms and he was being bundled through the front door. He slammed the paper into his cousin's hand:

"We need fe find this place yah, an' fast!"

Miss Gee didn't hear the stream of curses from

Courtney's mouth — the door had slammed shut and they were gone.

Simba bounded out of the car straight into Grand Central Station at five minutes to five. Courtney told him to head for the central information desk, then parked outside, his stomach rumbling with hunger.

"You cyan miss it, man. A four face clock deh 'pon top ah it, right inna de middle ah de main concourse."

Simba headed down the stairs at full tilt... but then began to slow his pace. He stepped down to the slick floor, feeling vulnerable in the vastness of the station.

Wha' de fuck me ah do? Until that moment he had ignored the doubts and fears that were screaming out in his head; but meeting her in the open could prove to be fatal. He wouldn't put anything past her scheming husband.

Why *was* he nervous? Because it might be a trap. Of course. But that wasn't all. Because it might *not* be a trap; it might be *her.*

A man in dark glasses not watching where he was going bumped into Simba's shoulder and spun away, losing his balance. He glared at the black man but Simba just kept walking. tried to pinpoint anything unusual but he was not sure what he was looking for. Then the information desk came into view. And there she was — Monique — turning around as if she had sensed him from a far. The Ranking stopped dead in his tracks, and looked around him suspiciously.

Her eyes seemed harder, less naive, but she was just as beautiful as the last time he'd seen her, even in the casual pink tracksuit and sneakers she now wore. The question was, could she be a threat to him without even knowing it?

They looked at each other for seconds that felt like hours. Simba remained tense.

She broke the silence as she walked over to him.

"Hi Delroy, you look...well?"

She was finding it difficult to control herself. But the

Ranking hid his true feelings, mumbling something incoherently. Now that he was face-to-face with her his relief turned to anger. He remembered their last conversation before he ran from JA.

Monique had decided to stay even when Simba had insisted she leave, he could not understand why, even now. It had haunted him, grieved him…he had tried to forget about her.

Now here she was.

"So…am I going to get the silent treatment, or are you going to blow up and tell me exactly what you think of me?"

"Me pass dem stage deh now, man." He rammed his hands in his pockets and screwed: "Wha' me want fe know is how you find me, an' why yuh decide fe find me."

She sighed heavily.

"I located your selector friend Pablo, who had heard a great deal about me…from you. He told me where your mom lived and Mama told me where you were."

Simba looked shocked.

"You go ah Rema ah look fe me? An' my people tell you how fe find me? Yuh did desperate fe find de Ranking."

"Weren't you desperate to see me, too?"

Simba's eyes seemed to answer 'yes', but he said nothing.

"Yuh know yuh husband coulda harm yuh, kill yuh?" He began; she held on to his hand and gripped it. "A dat me dida worry 'bout." Simba continued. "Then me just start seh cho! Me nah see Monique again. Either de bwoy hold her or she decide fe stay."

"Stay!" She sounded offended. "I know you were worried and I'm sorry I had to put you through that. It was hard for me too. But now I know where I want to be."

She paused.

"With you. I've had the time of my life and money just can't buy me that. I'm not going to keep denying how I feel about us. I need to be with you even if our lives are in danger."

What she said went for him too, and denying it was

pointless. Monique was able to look through his coarse exterior and see into his heart.

If it was meant to be, we will meet again.

He hadn't forgotten her parting words. Now it was clear that she meant it to be; Monique had searched for him in some of the most dangerous regions of Kingston, then travelled from Jamaica to New York to be with him. His anger drained away.

"Do you forgive me?" she asked, both hands outstretched and trembling slightly.

One inna million.

He took her soft hand in his and Monique pulled him closer, wrapping her arms around his neck. Simba held her and squeezed her tight. The smell of her perfume brought back a rush of good memories.

"Not too hard, lover man," she teased. "I'm pregnant and you're going to be a daddy."

The Ranking blinked rapidly and backed off to look down at her stomach. His nose flared. She looked up into his eyes.

"I'm only eight weeks gone. There's nothing to see..."

Me a baby father!

It was too good to be true.

Speechless, he lifted his head up, carrying the subtle smell of her perfume with him and it was then he saw them. Over her shoulder two men, wearing the type of clothes that made them indistinguishable from the majority of black youths in New York approached him. What became significant about them was the trickle of dialogue that caught Simba's ear. Jamaican! They were pointing at him excitedly. Simba tensed immediately as they kept coming.

De bumboclaat man dem mussa follow her from yard! Fuck!

His reflexes took over. He spun without a second thought, leaving Monique standing there wide-eyed.

"Simba Ranking!" one of the men called out.

To wait for the two men to dip into their sports bags was romancing suicide and Simba preferred to die on his feet. He moved...and charged the two approaching men at top speed.

He caught them by surprise, ramming both men to the ground. As the three of them skidded along the floor, one of the men's bags flew into the air, crashing to the tiles. The sound of glass shattering made Simba turn. The second man's bag dropped to the floor and slid away from him.

Simba knew he was going down, so was first back on his feet while the Jamaicans writhed on the floor like over-turned beetles in the midst of the streaming commuters. The Ranking lunged for the first bag. If he could just get their weapons…

Simba ripped it open, and the unmistakable smell of J Wray and Nephew rum wafted out. A bottle had smashed, saturating the inside of the bag. But there was no gun!

The taller of the two Jamaicans was back on his feet, still swaying from the impact.

"You come ah York an' ah tek coke Ranking, me t'ink you nevah touch de pipe." He turned around his voice rising a few decibels as if he wanted to make an announcement "De Bloodclaat man come yah an' tu'n crack head. Yuh haffe run 'way wid dat bwoy," he cursed.

Ah nuh bad bwoy dem man yah? thought Simba, but he had to be sure. He stuffed his hand quickly into the other bag and knew for sure he had fucked up when he came out with nothing more dangerous than a pack of condoms.

Simba was left feeling like an idiot. The two 'Yard man', who had swiftly become ex-fans, regained their composure and as the curses flew left and right. They were keen to find out if the Ranking could take as well as he gave.

He saw security men heading towards the commotion; it seemed as if every man wanted a piece of him. Well, they would have to catch him first.

He broke away and made tracks for the exit, grabbing Monique's hand on the way.

As he mounted the stairs, the only thing on his mind was the fact that he was going to be a baby father.

Fe real!

TWENTY-FIVE

Tuffy was under pressure, extreme pressure. His usual cool demeanour was melting away day by day. If the Saint lost faith in his abilities the word would get around.

He had been oh-so-close to trapping Simba, but 'de bwoy' had managed to slip through Vibesman's greedy fingers, disappearing into the bustling anonymity of the city. The only lead he had from that incident was the name of a freelance engineer the deejay had hooked up with.

He was betting his reputation on a hunch. If his gut feeling was right, and Simba wanted desperately to get back into the music business, that would be his downfall.

Picturing Ranking's head on a platter — very soon — his mood changed for the better. Tuffy manoeuvred his borrowed BMW through the busy streets of Brooklyn. A dancehall cassette blasted away, making Bounti Killa sound like he was 'chatting' from his back seat.

Turning the air conditioning unit to low, he shivered, and caught a whiff of cordite fumes on his clothes. He smiled as the images of the past three hours rewound in his head.

His 'bredrin' Rustler had problems with a gang of Colombians who were ripping off a Yardie prostitution ring with a sideline selling crack. Rustler, Tuffy and seven more 'born fe dead' Jungle man had reduced the car carrying the 'Colombian pussies' to a smoking lump of scrap metal.

Hot metal jackets spat out of the Uzis and fell like rain. The sound of it had been like music to his ears, and it brought back memories. Tuffy remembered his first killing in the shanties of Riverton city and the rush of power he felt.

Under the protection of Mr St. John he escaped punishment by the security forces and his reputation spread. He'd held a place on Jamaica's most wanted list for two years and then the powerful politician had spirited Tuffy away to the States to help run his US operation. Drugs!

The Jungle Ites Posse took their own large share of New York's 'crack' pie, of course, and made the man who had organised them into a multi-millionaire. Tuffy reckoned that, for the lifestyle the Saint had given him and many other poor 'juveniles' from Jamaica, he deserved it.

The carphone rang. He turned down the thumping bass and took the call, hands-free.

"Yush!" he said, sounding irritated.

"A me man!" Rustler's voice croaked through the earpiece. "You can talk."

"Me safe me breddah, what ah gwan?"

The don got straight to the point.

"We find out whe' your bwoy Simba ah go deh."

"Yuh sure, don?" His eagerness showed in his voice.

"Me always sure 'bout business, prento." There was a brief pause as the Jungle Ites don thought.

"You evah hear 'bout dis sound yah name Taurus?"

Tuffy had been to many sounds, but the name did not ring a bell. "It jus' build?" he asked.

"Before fe yuh time, man!" Rustler grunted a laugh. "Is a ole time sound dem ah bring back from de fifties ah yard, it ah do a tour ah de States an' your bwoy Simba Ranking an' a few other top ah de line deejay ah chat 'pon it ah York."

Tuffy laughed out loud. He would soon be getting back to what he did best.

"If ah so, then ah so." He sounded philosophical.

"You ah ramp wid dis yout' yah fe far too long, ah time now fe drop him. Yuh nuh t'ink so, prento?" Rustler said.

"Ah time, man." Tuffy sounded distant. "Overdue time."

TWENTY-SIX

A car horn outside woke Delroy from his disturbed sleep. He was spread-eagle on the bed with the sheets wrapped around him and pillows thrown to the carpeted floor on either side.

His eyes flickered open as he breathed deeply and lifted his head wearily from the mattress.

He blinked rapidly.

Was he dreaming or was Monique actually here in New York?

He frowned in the dimness. His throat hurt and his mouth was chalk-dry from hours of talking. As the seconds ticked by the fogginess clouding his head began to dissipate.

This is no dream, she's here.

He yawned and peered over to his clothes hanging in disorder on the chair. Then he remembered her news.

He was a 'baby father'.

He sat up in his bed and sucked stale air through his flared nose.

They had talked all night, any doubts he had harboured about her motives were now gone.

Monique didn't have to be here talking to him at all, with or without a baby. She was well-enough connected within Jamaica's high society; even without the Saint's dirty money she could live well and prosper. Men would queue up to be with her if that was what she wanted.

And it was that attraction he was struggling against. The

old fires were lighting and becoming hard to control. How could he make something like that be known. *Rude bwoy fe' years in love.*

He had come a far way by even admitting the truth to himself, but his instinct for self-preservation still tried to protect him from the dreaded commitment. If 'de yout' was his then he would protect it and his baby mother with his life.

If?

He had regretted it afterwards, but it had been one of his first questions.

"Wha' mek you so certain ah me do dat?" he had asked, pointing at Monique's stomach.

"Because Hugh is sterile."

His question had stung her but the answer had come back without a hint of emotion.

De fucker was firing blank.

Everything was making more sense. The Saint must want him dead more than ever now that Monique was pregnant with Simba's child. The Ranking had performed a task he would never be able to do himself.

He rose up on his elbows, and tried again for the fifth morning in a row to read the time on an old-fashioned alarm clock on the dressing table across the room. As usual no manner of squinting would help. He kissed his teeth, stepped out of the comfortable bed and stumbled over to the dressing table: 8:30 am. His stomach was grumbling, his mouth tasted like a cesspit and the room was dark and smelt of perspiration. He flung the window and curtains open, flooding the room with bright sunlight. He hadn't exercised properly since being in New York, and this morning he felt the need more than ever. He stood with his legs wide apart, back straight and head tilted back slightly, doing the deep-breathing exercises that Father Ho had drilled into his head. He remembered his priest and martial arts instructor's words as he relaxed: *This is the only type of breathing that cleanses the lungs and purifies the blood to build your scrawny body and to learn how to defend yourself.*

Simba moved smoothly into the Chinese horse position. He cleared his head of all thoughts and concentrated his mind on his task as he moved into the second phase of exercises.

Delroy sat in the kitchen, mouth watering as he took in all the delicious aromas of a culinary masterpiece in the making. He'd completed his Chinese exercises nearly an hour ago and he had quickly showered and changed as Aunt Gee shouted his name from the direction of the kitchen. She was humming a merry tune as he entered, flitting from frying pan to boiling pots swathed in steam, and the image of her as a mystic obeah woman frantically mixing her potions caused him to smile. He watched Miss Gee as she dipped into the pots and placed some green bananas, dumplings and sweet potatoes onto a waiting plate. His stomach rumbled uncontrollably as the fried plantain, ackee and saltfish were added and the plate was placed before him.

"Fe dem late night yuh keeping you need to keep yuh strength up." She looked down at him, amused by his look of surprise. "Eat up nuh!"

If this sumptuous meal is breakfast, then what will dinner be like? Delroy wondered. He tucked in heartily.

"Respect, aunt."

He didn't even hear when Miss Gee said goodbye and left for work — *de food was dat sweet!*

Later, with everyone away, Moses had given up trying to make Simba work with him, he stretched himself lazily on the sofa in the 'front room' and resisted the urge to switch the television on.

Instead his view shifted to the stacks of cassettes in the mahogany cabinet. He chose an audio marked 'Mixed Reggae' which was a few years old. The date alone brought back snatches of images he would always cherish. It was about then that he had made his first small mark in the music business, winning the Tastee Talent competition at

Half-Way Tree and setting his course.

There was nothing wrong with trying to relive it, and he placed the cassette into the deck, adjusted the volume and pressed play…

A sharp ringing brought him abruptly back.

Simba jumped in his seat, startled, and eased himself up from the sofa to answer the phone.

"Hello!" he said his mind clearing as the riddims played low.

"Hello, this is the international operator with a call from Mr Paul Gunther of Kingston, Jamaica. Will you accept the charges?"

Simba thought about the bill but decided he could cover the cost. He hastily agreed to accept the call.

"Kiss me mumma…Wha'ppen to you boss?" Pablo burst out before Simba could say a word, obviously glad to know that he was talking to his friend at last.

"Me deh yah super, wha' ah bruk man, how come ah jus' now you ah ding me bredrin?"

"Bwo-o-o-o-oy!" Pablo exclaimed. "Me haffe explain to you all de t'ings, wha' did ah gwan fe you understan', boss."

"So fill me in 'pon everyt'ing nuh rude bwoy, me need fe know man." Delroy prompted him.

"You is a big timer ah yard now, star," Pablo bellowed down the phone.

"Yuh know de yout' deh Squiggly Banton?"

"Yeah man!" He answered in recognition. "Him always deh 'bout ah Arrow Dub Studio ah Winward Road. Cool yout' still."

"Well, him do a tune 'bout dis whole t'ing yah, boss. Wid you Monique an' de Saint. A big news ah town. De single go inna de charts at number fifteen an' ah move up de line, 'pan rapid."

Simba shook his head. He wasn't really surprised — nothing remained confidential in Jamaica for long — but he never expected to be the subject of someone's tunes.

"Me talk to yuh ex t'ing Monique as well, don. She come all de way ah Tivoli ah look fe me. You believe dat. She want you bodily."

Simba sighed.

"She deh up yah a'ready star. She find me."

"Wha!"

Delroy filled him in quickly on her arrival in the Big Apple and her husband's threats.

"T'ings did ah hot after you chip, don man. Me just keep a low profile and listen to all de almshouse rumours ah go roun." He paused for a second, thinking. "De first t'ing me hear is dat you left town inna hurry wid de gate money. Me hear dat from Mikey D an' me immediately know a lie him ah tell, somet'ing else did ah gwan. Him admit you hold him up wid gun an' threaten fe kill him an' Talman an' from dat me jus' start t'ink it mus' have somet'ing to do wid you fucking Hugh St. John woman, then everyt'ing start fit into place."

"Yuh know," Simba agreed.

"From me see Talman me know it was vibes, man dat easy fe figure out," Pablo said.

"So de dread mask de money and seh me teef it," Simba shook his head. "De one Mikey D tek my warning as joke business, me promise him a'ready seh me ah go come back fe him raas, yuh nuh. Dig up me 'matic if him try bandulu I. Him ah go pay fe dat bumboclaat, you hear me?"

Pablo was silent.

"Not'n nuh do Mama, prento?" Delroy's voice was lined with panic.

"No man, she cool, seen? It's other t'ings yuh fe worry 'bout."

"Like wha?"

Pablo proceeded to tell him that Monique's husband had sent a hit man after him.

"De word ah go round seh is gun hawk from Olympic Gardens ah look fe yuh, Simba. Me nuh know if ah true, Ranking. But still me ah tell you fe watch yuh head back, me breddah, seen?"

Delroy was silent, wondering if there could be any truth in the rumours. The Saint was well connected, but the States was a big place. Delroy's mind refused to linger on that point; he had a job to do and if luck or God was on his side he would be the one attacking the Saint.

"Ranking! You still did deh super?"

"Yeah man," Delroy answered.

"Well me want you t'ink 'bout dis." Pablo's voice turned solemn. "Is 'bout yuh father, star."

"Wha' 'bout him?" Simba asked, the bitterness rising in the pit of his stomach again.

"You nah go believe dis, Ranking."

Pablo's voice lowered as he quickly relayed his story. Apparently the policeman who had been kidnapped and interrogated by some 'area man', had buckled under pressure. He was now a crazy man, roaming the Kingston Streets shit-stained and greasy asking everyone he met for forgiveness.

Simba sat up.

"Him did deh dung ah Coronation market," Pablo continued, "an' ah bawl out de man name who sen' him fe kill Missa George. Two days later dem fin him inna a gully, wid him cock inna him mout' an' a shot to him head."

"Who fe name?" Simba snapped harshly.

"De Saint!"

Deep down he knew. Simba felt his blood freeze and his heart shudder. He slammed his fist down on the soft padding of the easy chair and cursed loudly. Tears burned his eyes as he remembered the blood-drenched figure of his father. Gunned down needlessly because of Simba's relationship with another man's wife. Guilt flooded through him.

Guilt — and the overwhelming passion for revenge.

TWENTY-SEVEN

Hector's office was two sizes up from a broom cupboard, but what it lacked in size it made up for in its immaculate and ordered presentation. It was painted eggshell white and was tastefully decorated. On his polished wood desk lay a letter of refusal from the Apollo Theatre in Harlem.

This was the third time in as many months he had tried to book an act in the Apollo's talent contest, and had no success due to the long waiting list.

He decided to approach the problem from a different angle next time. His spar, a sound engineer at the theatre, would have some suggestions. A bottle of Southern Comfort could always get him in the mood for some ideas.

He would leave that for some other night. Tonight he needed to run a few things through his head and relax.

Hector's origins were humble. He hailed from the rainy but magnificently lush parish of Portland and had done very well for himself. He still felt the hunger for achievement that had warmed him as he stepped off the plane from Jamaica.

He had not done well in school, which he attributed to the back-breaking work he had to do on the farm with his father. His parents blamed his lack of academic achievement on his involvement in the parish's champion sound, Turbo Tone. Once he had been given the go-ahead to leave 'Yard', he promised himself that in the States things would be different. Instead of simply being a 'come around' helping the sound men to string up their boxes, he would be the man making the very music that was coming through those speakers.

He had wasted no time on arrival and enrolled in a sound engineering correspondence course, mastering the subject with hard work and becoming a qualified studio engineer. He worked with some of the top names in the reggae business. The nice apartment, his 'criss' car and this sideline business of promoting new talent had all come from a job he loved.

His office wasn't a 'big t'ing' but he felt proud to have it as his new base of operations. He had been working from home when he signed Bobby Checks. But that hadn't lasted. Vibesman saw to that.

When Vibesman secretly made him the offer of a five-single contract, Checks had seen immediate wealth. But the idiot didn't realise he had sold his soul to the devil.

Hector had imagined Simba would be more mature in the same situation. He had presumed that his efforts to promote Simba in New York would have been welcomed by the deejay. But they weren't; it had become a point of contention between them. It was as if the Ranking wanted to remain low-profile, with only two 'specials' under his belt.

A waste of talent.

Hector had already negotiated with Taurus Sound's road manager to include Simba on their New York bill two weeks from now. The posters were everywhere. Simba, for reasons best known to himself, wasn't pleased. The engineer-come-producer was becoming concerned about his attitude.

Why would a talent like Ranking sabotage himself on his way up? It sounded stupid, but Hector had witnessed it many times before. The fear of success.

Then Squiggly Banton's 12-inch import single 'Ghetto Man d'weet Sweet' hit the States. Hector heard the lyrics and immediately understood Simba's strange behaviour; he had made the wrong sort of enemies.

Armed with this information Hector had confronted Simba, who told him the whole sorry story. Hector sympathised with his predicament — even more so after he was introduced to Monique. He understood completely why her obsessive husband wanted him dead.

They sorted out their differences and began to focus on the business at hand. After all, Hector had said, it was pointless cowering from a threat that might never come.

Business haffe gwan said way.

Hector stuffed his last overdue cheque into an envelope and sealed it, plopping it irreverently in his out tray.

T'ings ah change.

With the Ranking back on track and set to bring in some dollars, Hector would at least be on time with the payment of his moderate outgoings. Two weeks seemed a long time to wait for the money, though. Maybe Simba could do a few PAs just before the gig to keep him sharp? He would see.

Hector checked his watch and then the clock on the wall for confirmation then kissed his teeth.

Late fe see me gal again.

On his way to the door, Hector paused. Maybe he should stop by and see Simba first before Marcia.

Nah!

For once his business wouldn't take priority, Marcia would see him 'up front'.

The man in the red Celica Supra blew ganja smoke out through his window, his attention wandering slightly as the prime indica made his senses swirl. Relaxation.

His contentment was brief. Through the haze of smoke he glimpsed Hector emerging from the building he had been watching for the last three hours. The yardie reached for his cellular phone as Hector crossed the road.

"De bwoy ah leave out, boss!"

"Follow him an' report back, seen?" Tuffy rasped from the other end of the line.

The 'Yard' man cut off the call.

Hector eased away from the curb, music playing low.

Seconds later the Celica followed.

TWENTY-EIGHT

Monique smiled to herself.

She could be stubborn when she wanted to be and in this case her obstinacy had paid dividends. She savoured the last morsel of food prepared by the chef, a man she didn't even realise could cook, and said a silent thank you for her pig-headedness.

She had never given up hope, and had kept on searching for Delroy even when there was no prospect of finding him. And now they were together, away from Jamaica, and finally coming to grips with the feelings they had for each other.

The 'wildest' of men could be calmed down by the right woman.

He had tried to hide his feelings in Jamaica, yet after all the denials they were together again. It was a love affair that was meant to be.

Delroy had his stubborn streak too, she thought, but in his case it was more of a problem than a virtue. He found it very difficult to open up to her, and seemed to feel he had to keep up the pretence of being on top of everything. There was nothing he couldn't handle, no problem he couldn't face…that was his attitude, but she knew he was angry and hurting inside.

Despite what he was feeling he had gone out of his way this evening to let Monique know that he did care, despite what he said. She appreciated it more than he could imagine.

"That was a beautiful meal, darling. Thank you."

Monique stood up from the table, licking her lips, and with a glass in her hand she walked over to the couch to sit down. The leather couch accepted her warmly. This apartment was beginning to feel like home to her already.

Home is where the heart is, they said. And the heart was here.

She had arranged the Greenwich Village apartment over the phone whilst she was still in Jamaica, through a commodities broker friend living in New York. It suited her fine. The interior was fully furnished with plush leather seats and many corner displays with plants or ceramic figures.

She had all the amenities she needed, and at night she relaxed with music and movies. The abstract paintings gave the place a feeling of pure relaxation. It was perfect.

Her days were fully occupied as well. When the Jamaican Tourist Board had wanted to send a consultant to help brainstorm with a local advertising company — on the start of a new advertising campaign for the island — Monique had planned to send someone else, but then decided to go herself.

She had covered her tracks well and made sure her superiors were warned against the things they might hear about her. She had lied about her reasons for leaving, but at least Hugh could spring no surprises on them in revenge. She was sure they would believe her version of events, until there was solid evidence to contradict it. That gave her time to play with.

The lights in the sitting room were low — the sound of R Kelly mellow in the background. Simba had called her out of the blue and decided to come over to keep her company and cook her a meal. A peace offering, she imagined, or was he just concerned about her welfare? Who cared? As long as they were together maybe they could thrash out in the open what had been worrying him.

Delroy entered and sat down at the other end of the sofa

in silence. He was not in a talkative mood, the memory of his father's death resting heavily on his mind. The fight had left him tonight — and instead of blaming Monique for what the Saint did, Simba had turned his simmering anger in on himself. She did not deserve it.

And so they talked, and he told Monique the truth about who killed his father and why. She tried to soothe him.

"I understand how you feel, Delroy."

Her voice lowered as she saw a new, horrific picture of Hugh, the murderer, in her mind's eye.

"Just the memory of the man sicks 'ma' stomach. Imagine — I had to sleep next to that animal. Do you know how that makes me feel?"

"Dat's why me want him first, baby," he said distantly. "Before anybody else find him. I waan see de fear inna him eye. I waan smell him ah shit himself when me pull de raas trigga at him head. Only then Missa George will res'."

Monique stared at him, wondering if Simba would really kill a man. She prayed that he would never need to.

"At least we're safe here," she said.

"As long as you stay right yahso ah New York," he agreed. "Close to me."

They changed the subject, away from their predicament to their opinions on family and children. The space on the sofa between them soon diminished, and by the time they started reminiscing about the good times they'd shared in Jamaica, Monique's head was in Simba's lap and his arms were around her waist.

She felt safe and protected. This togetherness made the tension she was feeling melt away. She sat up wondering why he had gone so quiet all of a sudden.

Simba had fallen asleep.

As his chest rose and fell steadily, she kissed him on the lips. After everything they had gone through she had thought that leaving him would solve her problems.

She wouldn't make that mistake again.

Smiling contentedly she closed her eyes and slept peacefully — something she had not done in a long time.

184

TWENTY-NINE

The Lounge nightclub in Jamaica, Queens, was one of the top reggae spots in New York. It had a good reputation for a relaxed atmosphere and rough reggae 'riddims'. It was the ideal place to be if you enjoyed the music and wanted to feel a 'Yard vibe' in the heart of the Big Apple.

Hector had suggested that they each take their lady, keeping them 'sweet' because of the neglect they were suffering from both men's busy schedules.

The Ranking liked the idea.

After reluctantly agreeing to do the many personal appearances that he was asked for as a result of Squiggly Banton's controversial lyrics, Hector and Simba had decided that any tunes they cut should be financed by themselves. That was costly, but the money they made from Simba's PAs would allow them to go into the studio, just barely. Simba refused to ask Monique for money, preferring to raise the funds himself. His attitude had changed after she told him she was pregnant.

The rumours surrounding Simba's exploits in Jamaica made the reggae fans more than eager to hear him on vinyl; record stores were flooded by requests for any recent tracks he had done. The demand was there — all they had to do was satisfy that demand with a wicked tune.

Taxis and limousines were pulling up to the entrance of the club, unloading passengers dressed in bright colours and shocking materials. The sheer and glittering fabrics spoke two words eloquently: sexiness and dancehall.

Inside the club the music played loudly and with little distortion. The dance floors were already full and an air-conditioning unit working at full capacity was fighting the heat issuing from the night-clubbers.

Simba's group occupied a table on the fringe of the dance floor, wine bottles and glasses set neatly on the table. Hector and Marcia sat at the table and Simba and Monique stood a few yards away overlooking the dance floor. Tony Rebel's old tune was 'bigging up' the beauty of Jamaica in his own inimitable fashion.

Jamaica is a nice place to live,
(Sweet Jamdung),
But de only t'ing is,
(Dollars nah run),
What a nice place to live,
(Sweet Jamdung…)

Delroy saw a drunken woman slip and stumble, knocking three other dancers to the floor. He snickered and sipped at his glass of brandy.

"That's the first time you've smiled all night," Monique pointed out. "Are you sure you're alright?"

She asked the question innocently but she already knew the answer. Simba was worrying about his mother, because he felt that the Saint would try and get at him through her. He knew she was safe so long as she stayed in Rema — and until the Saint had been dealt with he wouldn't rest easy.

"Ah nuh noting fe you worry 'bout baby," he lied. "Jus' my mind ah wander 'pon certain t'ings."

"What things?"

"Everyt'ing!" he snapped. Monique gave up trying to communicate with him. The Ranking reached out and touched her hand; that was as close as she would get to an apology.

"Try to relax, Delroy, you're too on edge." Her sexy Kingstonian tone was vibrant and warm. "If you're worried about Mama, don't be. She'll be okay."

"It will work out. You right." He said after a long pause.

"It all will work out."

"Ah fe yuh round now, you know don," Hector bawled out from the other side of the table. "Me throat dry like chipboard boss."

The engineer rubbed his neck and cleared his throat as if he were choking. Simba grinned and headed over to the bar for a bottle of champagne.

Sometime later Delroy was leaning back on his chair, taking a breather after his dance with Monique. He slowly turned his glass on the condensation that had pooled around the broad base and watched Monique's sexy walk as she made her way with Marcia and her friend Cathy to the 'ladies'.

On the other side of the dancefloor he saw Hector laughing loudly with a well-dressed women. Hector's antics always made him smile.

Major trouble if Marcia ketch you, boss, he thought.

Then the flow of music stopped and the club's resident deejay — who had been mute for most of the night — began to do what he did best.

"Yah man," he started off, his voice echoing over the speakers. "De vibes right tonight, man."

He paused.

"You know wha'…ah feel ah need to big up all the beautiful women in the only place to be, de Lounge nightclub. Respect due to all de man dem who come with dem own woman, bonafide. Heh, Heh, Heh!" he laughed. "Big up the Flatbush massive. Scorpion hold tight, big t'ings ah gwaning fe you. Ranking an' crew dah one ah fe *you!* All Jamaican, all African, all Caribbean man an' woman, hold tight, *seen!*" The turntable's needle hit the revolving vinyl and Shinehead's *'Jamaican in New York'* 'buss' from the massive speakers:

Don't drink coffee, I drink roots my dear
And I love my morning ride,
You can see it in my motions when I walk,
I'm a Jamaican in New York…

Monique, Marcia and her girlfriend were almost at the restroom when a unfamiliar voice, hard and menacing, broke into their chatter.

"How 'bout if you dance dis one yah wid Scorcher, Monique?"

He leant in the doorway to the ladies' washroom, blocking it completely with his frame.

How in hell does he know my name!

"Do I know you?" Monique asked brazenly, irritated by his smug smile.

"Me nuh waan you know me. But me know you."

The burly Jamaican returned her glare with a lecherous look. His patterned white silk shirt seemed alive in the disco lighting and a sharp-seamed pair of Twenty-Twenty trousers made him look smart but no more approachable.

"Me nuh tek no fe an answer y'know."

Monique sighed heavily.

"Look, whoever you are, I'd like to oblige you but my boyfriend wouldn't like the idea of me dancing with a strange man."

"Me nuh care wha' yuh boyfriend t'ink, him haffe cool if me ah dance wid you."

"But *I* care," Monique countered. "And the answer is still no!"

Marcia kissed her teeth and 'cut her eye' as they tried to shuffle past him. He ignored her and grabbed Monique's wrist viciously, wheeling her into him. She smashed into his solid chest and the smell of Old Spice cologne prickled her nose.

Monique's eyes shone panic.

She struggled desperately.

"Let go!" she barked.

"*Leggo!*"

The music drowned out her cries. The other women around her froze in their tracks, faces showing puzzlement and horror. He was grinning like a madman and, with no effort on his part, carried his captive into the men's toilet.

"We cyan dance proper out yah so baby, me need privacy

fe do de 'cool an' deadly'."

Monique could not believe this was happening. She screamed, thumping him as hard as she could and thrashing her legs violently, but to no avail. He just tightened his hold and laughed insanely.

"You ah go enjoy yuhself, just cool man."

Monique couldn't understand why nobody was making a move to help her. They surely couldn't think she was enjoying this.

Marcia and Cathy stood still for a few seconds, then Marcia finally backed away to get help.

Scorcher continued to pull Monique into the men's room. Monique kicked and scratched furiously. If no one was going to help her then she would have to help herself.

Then, without warning, there was movement behind her and the 'bad bwoy' turned quickly. His smug smile instantly changed to a look of contempt. He released his grip on Monique as if burnt by a hot iron, allowing the momentum to spin her into his attacker. She flopped into Simba's arms, tears gushing on impact.

She tried desperately to tell him everything in an instant.

"He was taking me...into the men's..." she sobbed in spurts. "I...I've never seen him before..."

"Jus' tense!" Delroy hissed, leading her by the arm to a safe distance behind him and never taking his eyes off the poised 'Yard man'.

Scorcher knew he was cornered, the ladies room behind him, the men's toilets to the left and a grim faced 'notch' standing in front. He dug into his waistband and whipped out a massive ratchet knife.

A killer fresh in from Yard, Delroy thought as Scorcher flashed the razor-sharp blade out of its wooden housing. He leaned forward marking the air with the blade and taunting the unmoving Simba.

"Hey, you big pussy Simba Ranking!" he called out. "You ready fe dead yet bwoy, eh? You gal never waan whine wid I, but me know you ah go dance to diss yah riddim yah. Scorcher seh so."

His raw sing-song patois branded him a 'town man'.

Scorcher lifted his blade upwards as if he was going through some martial arts preparation. Without warning he lunged forward, making wide sweeping thrusts. The knife flashed at Simba's throat but he side-stepped it smoothly, moving his upper body backwards and hearing the blade swish loudly as it passed him.

Scorcher timed his move; when he saw an opening, he faked an exaggerated swing to Delroy's left. The deejay reacted quick, dropped his weight and moved in the direction of his assassin's line of attack, readying himself to block the blade. As Scorcher switched direction the blade ripped across Delroy's line of defence, once and then twice. It slashed through his shirt at both places, lacerating the skin underneath.

First blood.

Monique screamed at the sight of Delroy's blood. Simba felt its warmth spurt across his chest. The smell of cloves perfumed the air and Delroy could feel only a dull numbing sensation and the slow trickle of blood. Then he realised what 'de yout' had done.

De fucker garlic de blade!

Some knife men in Jamaica would rub cloves of garlic over their blades, making cuts — even deep ones — go unnoticed by the victim until, in many cases, it was too late.

Scorcher shuffled in Simba's direction, passing the knife from his left hand to his right, and then suddenly kicked out towards the deejay's groin. But Simba saw it coming and thrust the knife man's big foot aside with the palm of his hand.

Scorcher lost his balance.

Death fe you now bwoy, was all the Ranking could think. He gripped his assailant's weapon hand with lightening speed, pulling him forward and trying to keep the blade at arm's length.

Scorcher's surprise turned to panic when Simba wrenched his wrist backwards with all his strength, the bone breaking with a sickening 'snap'. The knife dropped to the floor as his fingers sprang open and he grunted with pain, Simba followed through with a right hook that caught him on his jaw. His head snapped back with the force but he remained standing, uncertain on his feet.

Scorcher was in pain, his broken right hand swinging loosely at his side, but he ignored it as if he were high and came at the Ranking again. As he tried to punch at the deejay, Simba grabbed him tight round the neck like he was about to wrestle him to the ground; but instead delivered a skull-cracking head butt.

The yardie staggered backwards, a split in his forehead, blood trickling down his nose, pain spearing into his wrist, and crumpled heavily to the floor. His eyes rolled but he still tried to get to his feet, clawing his way up the door frame of the toilet behind him. Simba leered at him with disgust and decided to finish the job properly. He dropped low and delivered a horizontal snap kick, connecting with the knife man's solar plexus with such force that it sent him tumbling backwards into the men's lavatories. Scorcher's head smashed on a porcelain urinal with a crack of bone. His crisp shirt started to soak up the water and urine on the slick floor.

He was motionless. Blood dripped from the gashes on his head and his breathing was shallow.

"Pussy hole!" Simba said, with all the scorn he could muster.

A man laughed hollowly from inside the lavatories.

He walked casually out of the cubicle on the left and unzipped his fly, urinating in the bowl above Scorcher's head. He concentrated on the act for a few seconds and then turned his attention to Simba, who was eyeing him with curiosity and contempt.

Whe' me know dis man yah from? The Ranking was battling with his memory.

Then it clicked. It was the gunman from the airport that he'd seen on the news. A million questions crowded the deejay's mind.

Simba watched the shooter keenly, sizing him up. He

was thick chested and broad shouldered, but not as tall as he had looked on television. His face was rough with acne and his eyes were a startling nut-brown. Tuffy smirked grimly.

"So me finally meet de famous Simba Ranking inna person. An' him t'ink him is a ninja too, raasclaat."

"Yuh bwoy dung desso, nuh t'ink it funny." Simba added plainly, pointing to the motionless body on the floor. "Yuh brethren learn too late seh me nuh ramp wid certain yout."

"My brethren?"

Tuffy kissed his teeth laughing.

"Every day we have man from yard who wan run t'ings hot up yah, man who willing fe tek shot, willing fe go prison, sell rock and kill dem mumma if we request dat. Brethren?...Cho!"

"So you nuh, dawg heart, yuh nuh waan try finish de job?" Delroy taunted him. Tuffy stood his ground; he wouldn't make the same mistake his colleague had.

"Me nuh inna dem fist and foot t'ings deh, boss," he snickered. "Not when me have dis." He patted the large bulge under his sport jacket, his left hand not straying too far from the region. "Dis do de kicking fe me. You can skip bullet, ninja yout?"

Every nerve in Simba's body screamed *'get away'*, but as Simba's mind and body was locked in a struggle, time seemed to slow itself down. *Wha' fe do?*

Could he reach Tuffy before he reached for his tool?

Simba would die here and now if he couldn't.

Tuffy flung back his jacket with his right hand, exposing the black butt of his Sig Sauer automatic like a wild west gunslinger.

The gun came into view, his eager finger closing around the trigger, knuckles tightening, then his eyes left Simba's for a heartbeat. He looked back up but was immediately distracted. A wine bottle hit the wall above his head, shattering.

Hector ducked out of sight. But he had bought Simba a split-second of extra time to make his move.

Simba moved away from Monique, hurled himself

sideways as hard as he could, hit the carpeted floor hard and rolled behind one of the many partitions separating the tables, heart pounding.

Tuffy's rhino bullets sent the wood and padding above his head exploding into oblivion.

The crowd knew the sound of gun shots, and there was instant pandemonium.

Tuffy took aim again skipping around a group of scrambling women who had deserted their handbags trying to target his moving quarry.

It was not easy.

People were scattering everywhere, tripping and stumbling over each other as they all headed for cover.

The music played in the background, a surreal soundtrack for a real-life drama.

Tuffy wanted to see the deejay's blood splashed over the dance floor, he wanted to see people slipping over his brain fluid, then it would be a job finished and done with. But Simba was proving to be more skilled than he had expected.

Tuffy walked forward firing until the gun was empty and the slide locked back. There was a lull. He pulled a fresh clip from his pocket and slammed it in.

Simba scampered between two tables.

The shooting began again.

High-calibre slugs followed the Ranking's movements. There were screams as the shots shattered table tops, splintered chairs and sent fragments of masonry flying.

He was coming too close for comfort. *De bwoy mus' run out ah shot by now man,* he thought as he vaulted atop a table for a better view of his escape route. *Escape!*

Fuck, whe' Monique deh?!

Simba cursed himself and stared around him looking for her.

Tuffy couldn't believe his luck when he glimpsed Simba in the distance on the tabletop.

Easy shot.

He aimed and pulled the trigger.

Click-kik! Click-kik! His magazine was empty again.

Fuck!

Simba didn't even see him until too late. His would-be executioner's curses told him how lucky he had been.

Whe' Monique deh?

Simba was darting through the stampede when in the corner of his eye he saw a red haze against the far wall. Heading through the bottle-neck of people still pressing in the direction of the exit, he saw Monique being buffeted near the wall by a tidal wave of bodies. Simba charged towards her. Her relief was overwhelming. She hugged him close as Simba tried to shield her from the relentless pushing that threatened to crush the life out of them as they edged along the wall.

Suddenly the wall they were skirting sank into a depression that was actually a short corridor leading to a darkened set of double doors at the other end. A fire exit, maybe.

Simba immediately broke the bend, ignoring the flow of the herd in the other direction, and hauled Monique with him. He bounded down to the end of the corridor, slamming the exit door open and triggering the alarm.

The cool New York air hit them as they crossed the main road as cars honked their horns and drivers cursed. They went straight for a yellow cab waiting at the stop light, jumped in, and Simba barked his destination:

"De Village, boss."

Delroy's black Valentino shirt was soaked in blood.

"You're sure you don't need a doctor instead, bub?"

"Just drive, man," Simba snapped.

They sat in silence as the cab pulled away. They both knew their worst fear had just become a reality.

The Saint had tracked them down!

THIRTY

The bed was cool and comfortable.

The silk sheets were wrapped around Delroy's naked body like a second skin.

He lay silently, staring at the ceiling, trying to regulate his erratic heartbeat by deep breathing. That helped but the tension remained.

His muscles ached and there were small swellings on his knees and arms. He tried to ignore them, tried to clear his mind, questions about the consequences of tonight's shooting threatened to paralyse him into confusion. At least he had somewhere he could relax and and seek some answers.

Monique's apartment was the safest place he could think of.

Simba had made the driver take a round-the-houses route to Greenwich Village and the deejay had not taken his eyes away from the back windows throughout the entire journey.

If they were being tailed, he would have spotted it.

They had stopped the cab blocks away from their apartment and made the rest of the way home along looping avenues and back streets.

Simba bent forward and felt the sharp pains across his stomach and chest. Their close scrape with death had made them realise how much they wanted one another.

They had made their way to the bedroom, had a night

cap of rum spiked with cola and Monique had undressed. Then she started to handle him with kid gloves, stripping him bare. She had bathed his wounds which, luckily, were not deep and then, hesitantly at first, his entire body. She had sensuously sponged him down under the shower, the lukewarm water stung his skin into millions of tingling eruptions. Delroy had leaned on the plexiglass shower screen, his legs suddenly weak as he opened his eyes to see the mist of spray gently soaking the delicate chemise Monique was wearing while she bathed him. The silky coffee-coloured material clung to her skin, matching closely her light complexion. Her nipples protruded majestically — dark and firm, inviting to his eyes and tongue. His manhood responded with enthusiasm and he allowed the pleasurable feeling to overcome him.

He had no strength to resist or question it.

She completed pampering him and, weakly, he went to relax in her bed.

Now he was toppling on the brink of sleep and wakefulness in no time, the low humming in his eardrums continuing after a night of heavy bass sounds. Lyrics from the sexy queen of the pack, Patra, suddenly popped into his head and he chuckled.

Man is not a man if him ah nuh worker man,
Man is not a man if him cyan go ten furlong,
Man is not a man if him ah nuh worker man,
Me want a man wha' can tan 'pon me long

The sound of dripping water caused Delroy to look over to the bathroom door and his eyes met those of his baby mother. She stood in the door frame, steam from the shower behind her obscuring parts of her shoulders and neck. Glistening pearls of water trickled down her curvaceous form. He watched the progress of one of those droplets as it traced its way along her chest, merging with others that were running their own course. It continued down to her smooth slightly rounded stomach and into the glistening hair just above her navel. She moved over to the bed and looked into his eyes, communicating her desire for him as she slid between the sheets.

"I'm frightened, Delroy. How could they find us here so quickly. How?" She shivered with fear, squeezing her damp body against his.

"The man at the club," she hesitated, swallowing nervously, "he knew exactly what he wanted to do, and his smile…that bastard Hugh wants me to panic, to leave you. But I won't!"

Monique's resolve transformed into a whimper, her smooth shoulders jerking up and down with the emotion of her words.

Delroy didn't have all the answers, but he did know his father was killed because of what had happened between them. Now the Saint was after his flesh and blood and he would not stand by and let him harm his woman…or his child.

"I want you to hold me, Delroy, hold me close. Let's forget about tomorrow."

He was surprised at how helpless and insecure she sounded. But he could understand. He held her and she sobbed as the shock of the night's events finally set in. He gently kissed her neck and shoulders and thought about the pain the people he loved the most were constantly feeling.

As he gently stroked her stomach his hand brushed against her breast and he could feel a spontaneous surge as her nipple became rigid. Her hands clasped his with a sense of desperation and she guided his hands down, further down…he was becoming erect again as his hand massaged her velvety stomach, running his finger through the mat of soft pubic hair. A sigh of relief escaped her parted lips as she was firmly but delicately turned onto her side to face the man sharing her passion. He circled her dark aureola with the tip of his fingers, lightly rubbing her nipple and tantalising the uneven surface around it. Monique arched her body in response, low moans escaping her mouth without her conscious control.

Her hands were now exploring his testicles moving sensuously along the length of his penis, rubbing, squeezing, forcing his manhood to become even more steeled as its head throbbed, begging for release.

They kissed tenderly and Simba immediately lowered his lips to her full-bodied breasts again, sucking them in turn. She moaned and whimpered at the sudden electrifying sensation of two fingers caressing their way into her and she arched up to meet them.

"I need you inside me, I want to feel you fill me up, I can't wait for you—"

Delroy didn't hesitate any longer, lowering himself onto her, gently thrusting his lower body, following his own rhythm. She twisted under his hold, absorbing the pleasing stabs of his manhood. He was driving into her with crazy speed now. He moaned. She moaned. But Monique was the one to touch her pinnacle first and her body jerked with orgasm. Delroy came seconds later.

They remained still for some minutes, breathing heavily, eyes closed, savouring the ebbing sensations. In his pleasurable state, Simba pledged that Monique would never again be subjected to anything like the night's events.

He had seen too much bloodshed in his short life and wanted nobody close to him to suffer because of him ever again.

He hoped it was a promise he could keep.

THIRTY-ONE

Monique's first involvement in a shooting had left her numb. To Monique her life, her baby's life and her lover's life were on the line, and she could not sit back and do nothing.

She sat on the bed, naked but for a towel wrapped around her head, flicking through her big black Filofax eagerly.

She turned another page.

"H," she said aloud, opening up the divider and running her finger along the many entries. She stopped at the name Andrew Humphries and read his details.

Humphries was a former brigadier in the Jamaica Defence Force whom she had met quite by accident. She had been relaxing at her friend Elaine's home when the brigadier, who was married, had turned up to see her work mate.

It wasn't just a social call either. The affair had been going on for some time and was the sort of news that would tarnish the brigadier's exemplary military record if it ever got out.

At first Monique wasn't too keen on him; she made the effort to get on with him for the sake of her friend. But then she bumped into the brigadier at formal functions around town, and their relationship blossomed into friendship.

They had not spoken in many months, as Andrew had been appointed diplomatic envoy to the USA. He had invited her to the Consulate-General offices, where he managed a small department, but she had not taken up the offer.

Now she wished she had gone. He was the only person she knew in New York with political clout that extended to Jamaica.

The only person she could think of who might be able to end this madness.

Monique reached for the phone and punched out the digits that would connect her to his office. She sucked on her pen.

When the phone was picked up at the other end she was put through to Andrew's office.

"Hello," said a female voice.

"Can I speak to Mr Humphries?"

"Who should I say's calling?"

"Monique St. John."

A moment later she heard the familiar voice.

"Monique, goddamn it woman. Where have you been?"

"About," she said casually. "Trying to put Jamaica back on the map after that fiasco you called an election."

Andrew laughed.

"You nuh change girl, just as outspoken. How is Hugh?"

She said nothing for a moment, allowing the silence to take effect.

"He's trying to kill me, Andrew — and before you ask, I can't prove it."

It was his turn for silence.

"Monique, you know what you saying woman?"

She sighed.

"Listen, Andrew, I've known you long enough for you not to start patronising me now. I know you've heard that I've left him. The whole island knows. But what they *don't* know is the bastard wants me buried beside the man I left him for. I want him put away Andrew, the man's a maniac."

"Wait a minute, darling I know you must be confused and angry but what are you talking about? The man's still in Jamaica."

Monique wanted to scream at him.

"Hugh's not an idiot, Andrew. He has his hired hands here to do his work. He won't bloody himself when he has others to do the job for him. Wake up, man."

Andrew cleared his throat.

"You nuh t'ink you could be over-reacting just a little bit, Monique?"

"You have a short memory, Andrew. I'm the same woman who won Female Boss of the Year two times in a row, the same woman with a cool business head and the strength to take on the male chauvinist pigs with their boardroom games. Fucking *listen* to me, Andrew, I don't over-react. My life's in danger."

The Brigadier breathed deeply. Monique wondered what he could be thinking.

"What can I do, even if all what you telling me is true?"

"The man is a murderer..."

"Monique, you need proof—" Andrew interrupted. "And to get information on a man like de Saint after you an' him bruk up is going to be near impossible."

"So I need to be dead before anybody will lift a finger."

"I'm not saying that, Monique, is jus' dat...de man is connected."

"And so are you, Andrew. Please, I need your help. There's no one else I can turn to."

"I'm not sure what I can do, girl..."

"Talk to the Prime Minster, his deputy...somebody in the cabinet who's concerned with law an' order." She knew she was grasping now, desperately seeking help from anyone that she could.

"I need proof."

"That's what the Deputy Commissioner of Police told me after she laughed in my face. You owe me, Andrew."

There was a heavy silence at the other end.

"If it wasn't for me, your credibility wouldn't be worth shit."

She hadn't wanted to bring up his situation, but she had no choice.

"Monique, look..."

She cut him short.

"Do I need to remind you?"

"No," Andrew rasped. "You wouldn't do that to Elaine, she's your friend."

"I didn't want to, but I've got no choice. I'm calling in the debt, Andrew. I'm desperate."

Andrew grunted.

Static crackled in Monique's ears and she clearly heard the

'pang, panging' of his pen on the edge of his desk.

"I will see what I can do."

He hung up.

"Damn it!" Andrew Humphries cursed as he put the phone back in the cradle. Her timing could not be any worse.

He could not let her know the real reason he was posted to New York. He wanted to help Monique, but he couldn't. Not yet anyway. *An' de gal had de gall to blackmail him!*

He shook his head and grinned weakly.

He stood up, glancing briefly at the portrait of the Jamaican Prime Minister which hung opposite.

The 'main man' looked as concerned as he was.

He adjusted his tie and smoothed down his shirt over his ample stomach. His round, dark-skinned face looked tired.

He walked over to a safe in the corner of the room, turning the rotary combination and then cranking down the lever to open it. He took a folder out from among the computer disks, photographs and money and brought it back to his desk.

He sat back down and pulled out one of the files thumbing through the loose papers. He sighed. The recent election had been one of the bloodiest in Jamaica's history, and had highlighted the depth of corruption in politics. The new agenda was to root it out at all costs. The image of the island came first.

There had been a cabinet reshuffle. The Prime Minister was keen to see the problem resolved.

Andrew plucked out a few sheets of typed paper from the file and slid them neatly to a position in front of him. Hugh St. John's name was typed in bold print at the top of the first page.

The brigadier re-acquainted himself with the report the secret informants and police intelligence had pieced together. This time it read with a different feel; this time he knew how accurate their speculation had been. Hugh St. John was more sinister than his public image portrayed. To prove it, he'd have to keep Monique and her deejay boyfriend alive.

It was a good start for Operation Clean Sweep, although Monique and Simba Ranking would not share his optimism.

THIRTY-TWO

Jake leaned gingerly against the metal dumpster, his crisp leather jacket strategically placed over his broad shoulders. A well-built sixteen-year-old youth, his chest jutted out with meaty bulk and his well-fed stomach hung over his belt.

"Shit!" he cursed.

The stench welling up from the garbage container was becoming overbearing. He stepped away, peering down at his chunky Nikes and adjusted the waist of his Levi 501s.

"Why did them motherfuckers gots to leave that shit on my corner man? Hell, them City Hall cocksuckers are slowing up biz."

He moved away to a new position which was more comfortable and conducive to his commercial interests — where potential buyers walked directly past him instead of crossing the street to avoid the reeking dumpster.

Instinct made him look behind even though he knew that the alleyway was a dead end. There was a high meshed fence at the far end.

"Them niggers have got nothing bettah to do, man." He said to himself, eyeing the graffiti in the alley with disgust.

The avenue before him was getting busy and now in the increasing twilight it started to attract the type of people he could do business with. Sex, crime and drugs were the driving force for many of their needs and Jake was the man who could provide at least one of them.

"*Rock! rock! rock!*" he hissed as two lanky men idled up to him. Jake's eyes glinted with recognition as he tilted his head slightly. "Goddamnit, Birch what you want dude?"

The taller man smiled. "Me and my homeboy here came to see you, man. We were hoping…" he licked his lips hungrily "…and wondering if you could kinda see your way clear, homes, to trust me a shot brother, 'til the morrow, only 'til the morrow homes. You know I'm good for it, man…"

"What the fuck you talking 'bout, Birch? You tripping, motherfucker, or you just seen Jesus?"

"I need you man, I ain't got any other goddamn dealer to go to. Give me a break, homes. Chill out, man."

Birch was shouting now, desperation and paranoia spurring him on. His friend stood by, watching nervously.

Jake had been too easy on them, selling them crack at cut rates, even giving them cigarettes and liquor when he was in a good mood. And now they were repaying him by 'dissing' him on his patch.

"Get the fuck outta my face, Birch, before I have to kick your ass up and down this avenue."

But Birch was defiant.

"I need that fix man, I got to get that rock."

Jake jerked the .45 special from the back of his Levi's and jabbed the muzzle into Birch's bony chest without warning, once to his sternum and then to his ribs. Before Birch could react he brought his gun hand viciously upwards cracking the junky's chin and hurtling his body backwards. His arms windmilling, he groped for balance.

His doped-out friend dashed back into the housing project. Jake watched him scuttle away and shifted his attention back to Birch.

"You don't get my meaning, dude, so let me explain it slowly, so that your ragged ass can understand this shit."

He knelt beside him and pushed the .45 hard into his forehead.

"Yaow, listen up motherfucker. If I see so much as a glimpse of your shrivelled black ass cruisin' my surface, I'm gonna waste your ass. Believe!" Jake stepped back to a standing position and looked down in disgust at the tattered heap. He lashed out with his new Nikes, flush to the ribs, spinning the junkie into the street.

"You're breathing my air, sucker. Get the fuck outta here."

Birch got the message and limped away.

Jake couldn't help breaking into a smile.

Every posse must work, work harder,
Cause if your not working, yeah hey you gotta be loafting,
And if your not loafting, don dada you gotta be joking,
Yuh must work and don't be a jerk...

Barrington Levy crooned smoothly as Jigsy King's granite tone rode the melody. The sound from the speakers in the car played crisply as the Jungle Ites men took time to relax en route.

It had been a busy day for Tuffy and Rustler's boys, who had been visiting all the posses' dealers scattered around New York city — collecting cash, sorting out disputes and seeing to the general smooth runnings of the operation. Jake was the last man on their list for today. Tuffy's two sparring partners were slouching in their seats, eyes red and unfocused, sharing a coke-spiked spliff.

"Watch the bloodclaat leather, Tegat! Yah fool man," Tuffy barked without turning around.

Tegat flinched and brushed away some of the ash from the plush leather seats, smiling nervously as he blew out a stream of intoxicating smoke. He leaned back, stretching over to pass the spliff back to Yanks who was sprawled in the back seat.

Tuffy slowed the car to a crawl and gazed around cautiously before yelling "Yaow!" in the direction of a dark alleyway.

Jake boldly strolled out from the shadows into the artificial light of the street. Tuffy pulled up beside him.

"Wha' yuh ah seh, bad bwoy?"

Jake couldn't help a smile and boisterous chuckle as they connected fists in the usual yardman greeting.

"How's it sliding my man? Not seen your ass round here

in time." Jake's tone was inquisitive.

"Business ah yard man. You know de usual runnings, keeping t'ings under tight wraps, mek sure all me prento dem everywhere safe."

He looked at Jake closely searching for any change in his usual hard-ass attitude.

"It cool man, I'm doing my thang, just how you an' the Man likes it."

Tuffy nodded in agreement.

"Me can't screw how you run t'ings, my bwoy, you ah my top seller and most of all you respect de business and me love dat." A smile touched one corner of Tuffy's mouth. "But my contacts ah tell I some yout' from Miami ah try edge up 'pon yuh business."

Jake shrugged his shoulders.

"It's nothing man, nothing I can't handle myself, those cocksuckers are in for one big surprise if they fuck with me and my wage packet man." Tuffy had given him the chance to prove himself. Making him a dealer with his own turf. He wasn't about to let some "yout" come and spoil that. He leaned on the car door.

"If you cyan handle de Miami bwoy dem," Tuffy said "maybe me fe jus' move in a new man and me and de massive blow two bwoy brain. What you t'ink 'bout dat...?"

He left his question trailing.

"It's no prob, bro," Jake burst out. "It's all way past cool, you'll see..."

The yardie knew that response well and, yes, Jake could handle the situation easily; but he was leading him on to something bigger.

"Me waan yuh understan' me." He paused for effect. "Yuh an' everybody roun' me, can dead dis minute. But you see my business, me nuh want not'n jeopardise it. No little dibi dibi Miami bwoy. No seller who t'ink him rough but cyan keep him area under manners. No big pussy gal who t'ink she can come between you an' my runnings. Me waan fe clear dat dis is no problem and you and yuh bwoys dem can rectify de situation, immediately, seen?"

"I get your meaning man."

Jake was angry that Tuffy doubted his abilities.

"You clear 'pon wha' me ah seh?"

"Crystal."

Tuffy's mood changed.

"Yeah man, positive vibes. Me love dat. An' as a sign ah my faith inna yuh potential, me have a job fe you complete, an' a bonafide gift fe you."

He waved his hands at the pock-marked face of Tegat, behind him on the back seat.

"Me waan you treat dis like yuh gal, you hear?" Tegat slurred as he unwrapped layers of tightly bound chamois to reveal Jake's prize.

"Shi-i-i-i-i-it man, you mean motherfucking business!" Jake's eyes went wide at the sight of the cobalt-blue Uzi.

"Is it sanitary, man?" he asked, caressing the deadly little machine with his eyes.

"Clean as a whistle," Tuffy added. "An' totally untraceable."

"You t'ink we ramp, yout?" Tegat announced entering into the conversation. "Nuh mix dis up wid a Mac-10, my bwoy, dis is a Uzi. You can manoeuvre big man gun, rude bwoy?"

Tuffy grabbed the automatic from Tegat's lap impatiently and thrust it at Jake's chest.

"You gotta be kidding man. This is no problemo, I've got this sucker's ticket." Jake held the weapon up, tossing it into a more comfortable grip. He switched the selector to 'S' for safe and expertly rammed a magazine into the grip. The catch clicked sharply as it locked the load into place. He flicked the selector switch to rapid with his index finger and thumb.

"This mother is ready…to kick ass."

"Me know you is de right man fe de job, star," said Tuffy, staring at the youth. "Dat's why me have a job fe you."

"Anythang, man!" Jake smiled innocently.

"Me have a man me waan see dead, yuh can handle dat?"

The young man nodded.

"His ass is grass."

Tuffy smiled inwardly. Jake was one of the many young and impressionable youths in New York making a career in violence and drugs. The boys thought that they were in control of their lives, but nothing could have been further from the truth. Every dealer Tuffy dealt with knew him by another name — Packa, Riffa, Calas to name a few. The soldiers who he moved with were never called by name and so were unknowns and the structure of their activities was hidden from view. To them it was a small operation.

Jake and the others like him never saw that they were simply cannon fodder. Expendable players used to hide their game from the prying eyes of the FBI and DEA.

But now all Jake saw was an opportunity to prove himself and show his 'balls'. And that was what Tuffy was counting on.

"I dunno what to say," Jake beamed, placing the Uzi under his arm. "This shit is worth a thousand notes. You giving me this, man?"

"If you finish me job bonafide then ah fe you."

Jake lovingly wrapped the Uzi in the oil-stained cloth and placed it into the Seven-Eleven bag Tegat handed to him.

"By the way man, shit! Your dividends."

Jake reached into his leather jacket for the proceeds of a week's hard hustling. But before his hand got near the cash Tuffy had lifted an Auto-Magnum from the compartment at his feet and trained the 'iron' on Jake's head.

"Hey man!"

Jake's voice dropped to a gruff bass. He looked impassively into the barrel of the gun.

"What the fuck wrong with you niggers?" He asked coolly.

"Slo-o-o-owly," Tuffy demanded. And Jake obeyed, slowly bringing his hand out of his jacket with a bulging envelope.

He never took his eyes off the big Magnum.

A few dollars fell to the sidewalk.

"You haffe careful and alert in dem time yah, Jake. Trust no bwoy and never mek a man go inna him waist without you have a gun point to him head first. Learn dat."

Tuffy snatched the envelope from Jake's outstretched hand and gunned the engine into life, screeching away at high speed.

Jake watched the car pull away, heart hammering in his chest, the smell of burnt rubber spiking the air. He understood exactly what his mentor had said to him and was grateful for the advice. He had some serious business to attend to and he knew some boys from Miami would be picking shots out of their ass by this time next week. Nobody jeopardised his rep. No one.

Jake swung the plastic bag over his shoulder and decided that once he'd dealt with his little problem he'd be ready for Tuffy's hit.

And that time it would not be business, but pure pleasure.

THIRTY-THREE

Taurus sound system had ripped the New York dancehall circuit apart.

And if any 'drum pan sound who seh an Ole time system cyan tes', they had to withdraw their comments 'pon rapid' as the newly-refurbished warehouse facing Brooklyn Bridge played host to the hottest session of the year.

Cars had started to turn up as early in the evening as eight-thirty, the first in a continuous line of vehicles from all over New York.

The music world had begun to sit up and take note of the commercial value and quality of the music. Major record companies were spreading the gospel according to dancehall, keeping a green eye on any potential stars that could take the jaded pop world by storm. And tonight they were all clambering over themselves to hear Simba Ranking, Super Cat, Tumpa General, Shinehead, Shaggy and Heavy Dee on the venerated 'mike'.

In the car park, a white couple sat on the bonnet of their brown Chrysler convertible pumping out the hard sounds of Guns 'n' Roses and surrounded by masses and masses of 'staunch' dancehall fans. They had recently experienced and enjoyed the sights, sounds and ganja that Jamaica had had to offer, and had come here to try and re-live the experience. But Axl Rose's thrill voice was totally out of place in this setting.

A man two cars to the left was walking around a red

Toyota shaking his head in pure distress. After what seemed like an eternity of punishment the Yard man reached in his glove compartment, angrily grabbing a cassette and striding over to the annoying sounds.

"Yush!" he said looking neat in his dark brown silk shirt, matching lengths and Clarke boots.

"What dat you ah play star?" The white man grinned as he answered, "Mah man, this is some real legendary rock playing. You like it?"

"No boss, me no inna dem rock business deh. Look roun yuh." The young rocker did and wondered why faces were twisted in growls in his direction. The yard man lifted his head, adjusting his trilby.

"If you waan mek frien', star yuh bettah play dis." He handed the couple the cassette and turned back to his car. "You can keep it, general," he said, turning around.

"Give yuh a chance fe listen to some bonafide reggae music."

'Dem buss de gate' at about ten-thirty and the massive streamed forward to be met and frisked by Lion Security.

They were taking no chances.

Even the women — who, in other establishments, could usually get away with not being searched — stood still for the hand-held metal detectors; and just in case someone brought a Glock 17L, which was made mainly from high-tensile plastic, handbags were being searched too. 'Nuh gun baggage' could get through with their men's weapons stashed on their person for later use.

For such a momentous occasion security was paramount.

The sound test was completed on cue and Kanga 'the selector' grinned as he dropped a special from Toots and the Maytals. His opening play made the warehouse explode with 'Bow! Bow's!' and shouts of 'Wheel'.

Big it up sound man,
Taurus sound is number one!
Get yuh hands in the air sah,
Then you'll get no hurt mister.

No! No! No!
A say yeah! A say yeah!
Listen to what Taurus play
Everyone say yeah, yeah, when Taurus play

The selector was in full stride by this time, with three empty bottles of Red Stripe beside him, a full one in his hand and what looked suspiciously like a half-smoked spliff in his 'jawbone', he was 'nicing up de dance'. He threw down killer selection after killer selection, his mixing was fluid and his rapport with the excited ravers was like telepathy. He only had to call the artist's name and it was if they knew which 'riddim' he would drop before the needle touched the forty-five. Ratty, his 'second', made sure he had all the dub DATs and dub plates he needed in sequence, without hitch. But Kanga was still hard pressed for time, giving 'de crowd ah people' the dedications they wanted between the 'de haul and pull ups' and 'rewinds'. He jumped and pranced around the turntables as he released every 'fire hot track'.

His flamboyant antics were as necessary to the whole aura of the dance as his verbal gymnastics. Kanga thrilled the crowd with another selection.

"Sing out Buju! Sing out Beres!" He bawled "Listen dah one Yaaaah!"

Delroy stood in the shadow of a large speaker box, absorbing the electricity and passion that the music seemed to draw out of everyone. The music all around him thumped with such force that he could feel it vibrating in his chest, but that did not stop him from recalling the rapid progress of the last month.

Simba had finally gone into the studio with two of the tracks he had brought with him from Jamaica, and reworked them with Hector as engineer and producer, finishing up with a 12-inch single the Ranking was ecstatic about.

The record had hit the American streets soon after.

The Ranking had been glad that Hector was no novice in the business, as he handled the 'runnings' from mastering through to distribution.

Respec' was due.

'Love an' Gun Shot' was released using Squiggly Banton's *'Ghetto Man D'weet Sweet'* as a springboard for its success. It had been inspired by the Saint and Monique and that in itself made Hector decide to use it.

"Jus' how it go, from de horse's mout'," Hector had said.

The riddim track had also been totally overhauled using the new 'Spreadout riddim' as its backbone. It was timed just as the Banton's tune was sliding down the Jamaican, New York, Miami and UK charts after seven weeks of causing a storm.

Hector's ploy had worked. Simba's 'riddim' was steadily climbing the world's reggae charts. Now things were rolling Hector became even more concerned about Simba's safety and his own, especially after the close shave at the night club. He made sure security was dealt with in the form of some Bronx 'gangsta youts', he had given the responsibility to look after their welfare. Simba was never too far from their watchful gaze, and felt a bit more relaxed seeing them about.

But he was still careful.

An hour or so later, Simba was looking around the crammed warehouse. Dancing space was becoming a premium commodity. He had just finished performing two 'riddims' to flickering lighters and ecstatic shouts of appreciation. The 'ladies' were grabbing for him and screaming out his name and seemed to want to pull him off the stage.

Shaggy would have a hard act to follow.

The Ranking 'bigged him up' and left the stage with people shaking his hands 'pon rapid' and patting his back as he tunnelled his way through the hot and sweating bodies in the wings. They wanted more of him but he needed to relax.

Simba eventually found a dark area to 'chill out' and sip a Red Stripe while coming down from the high he was feeling. He was pleased with his performance, but he couldn't forget his other problems and the potential threat to his life. He couldn't allow his judgement to be dulled by alcohol, so the beer he had in his hand would be his only one for the night. He was taking no risks.

A young woman glided to a stop beside him in a gold sparkling, short legged, all-in-one jump suit. Her hair was gathered back tightly, black and glowing against her head, held into place by a matching gold band. A part of her face was in shadow but the remainder he could see was dark-skinned and stunning. Her eyelashes were long and jet black, and she fluttered them appealingly as she spoke.

"A great performance," she said with a clear English accent. "You've been hiding your talents in Jamaica for too long. I'm glad you decided to relaunch your career."

She looked around at the crushing crowd.

"They are too."

Her forward attitude had taken Simba quite unawares and left him searching for something to say.

"Me glad you respect me work…"

He paused, waiting for a name to fill the gap.

"Roxanne — Roxanne Lawrence."

Simba inspected her once again, trying to sort out whether she was just a well-wisher or even a groupie.

"De accent nuh sound like a yankee, whe' you come from Roxanne?"

She smiled knowingly.

"I'm English originally. But because of work I'm based here in New York. What about you, Delroy? You're far from Kingston — how is the Big Apple treating you?"

"You know how it go over yahso. Every man ah do dem own t'ing. No man nuh really care if you alive or dead. Yuh haffe jus' mek up yuh mind an' go for wha' you want. No ease up!"

"I have to agree with you. That's New York in a nutshell."

"But saying dat me nuh come yah fe skin-up. Ah New York de money can run smooth, an' ah dat me love, man. So wha' you t'ink 'bout de dance an' t'ing? You nuh look like de type ah lady who come ah dem place yah."

"You'd be surprised," she said in a sexy whisper. "This is not just pleasure, but business as well."

"Business?" Simba asked bluntly. Roxanne laughed.

"You have a healthy dose of cynicism but your manager Hector seems to think you're hot stuff."

"De best!" Simba quickly interjected.

She smiled teasingly as she turned Hector's business card over in her right hand.

"Okay then. Maybe I can help you."

Roxanne leaned forward, kissed Simba on the lips without warning, and left without another word.

Wha dat? He thought.

He was about to question her further but decided against it. He had the overwhelming feeling she would contact him again, and the next time she would not get away so easily. Either way, Hector would have the answers as usual.

Shrugging his shoulders dismissively, Simba returned to his beer which was warm and flat. He sipped it anyway and watched the crowd's growing excitement as Shaggy grabbed the microphone.

Elsewhere, in another part of the warehouse, Al's Video Production team were taping the dance in it's entirety and the two cameramen were making sure they chronicled the session in loving detail. They focused now on an area of the warehouse called bubblers' corner, where the dancehall girls congregated to show their whining prowess.The camera's attention was focused on a girl wearing see-through black shorts, her white thong panties showing right through. Her shiny black bolero jacket glistened as she whined slow and deep with her legs wide apart. Her fingers and hands mapped out the tune around her bulging 'pum-pum' and her face was sheer concentration. Her friend caught on after noticing the attention of the camera and she also bent over, her 'fit' backside wiggling in time to Mad Cobra and descending down into a helicopter landing.

Simba however, was preoccupied with another group of

young Jamaican women who were standing near the entrance. They were watching all the people coming and going, and commenting on what they were wearing and who they were with. Their hairdos were elaborate and sprinkled with gold or silver leaf and their outfits were skin tight, sheer and expensive looking. A much older woman, ill-shaped, black and coarse-looking came to join them and the women greeted her boisterously, offering her a Kool cigarette and making a place for her amongst them.

"Ah hope unuh ah go buy me a drink later on you know?" a gash on her right cheek wriggled like a centipede as she asked the question.

"Nuh mus' Muma Liza man," an eager young woman answered. "Ah you run t'ings, you nevah know?"

Liza broke into a grotesque smile looking intently at the long-legged light-skinned girl.

"How come you in yahso a'ready gal an' Barky deh outside ah line up?" Liza enquired. Sharon looked surprised and so did her friends.

"Him deh whe'?" She replied not quite believing what she heard.

"Outside, girl child. You nevah know him was coming to de dance?" The situation seemed to amuse the older woman, her eyes glinted wickedly and she could sense 'contention'.

"De bwoy tell me him sick and ah jus' becah Patsy call me why me come out, yah tonight." Patsy watched her sister's reaction. Sharon seemed composed but her anger was rising and she did not want to make rash conclusions until she saw with her own eyes Barky's lying intentions.

Patsy broke into her sister's thoughts. "If him come on yah, him better can explain how him recover so quick." The girls nodded and focused their eyes on the people entering.

Delroy was still hidden in the shadows of the speaker boxes, watching and listening intently. He had seen this act played out hundreds of time before but was still enthralled by the way in which Jamaican women handled these situations. He looked attentively at the women as they continued to talk between themselves.

"Nuh Barky dat over desso?" one of the women pointed, her voice excited.

"Whe'?" asked Patsy, her eyes looking in the direction of the pointing finger. "Me nuh see nobody."

"Look good man, him ah dance wid a big batty gal inna a blue mini skirt and white chiffon top."

The other women kept her finger pointing in the general direction unswaying. It was then the selector slowed down the tempo with Chaka Demus and Pliers and, nearly at the same time, Sharon caught sight of her man clinging to some other woman like 'how ticks cling to dog'.

"See the raasclaat bwoy Barky deh." Muma Liza said as Sharon strode towards him, friends in tow. She stopped a pace away, his back swaying to the music before her and she silently watched Barky's rhythmic hips and suggestive dipping in time to the slow tune. Anger welled up in her.

"Wha' you ah do yah so Barky?" She blurted.

He looked round, surprised, quickly pushing himself away from the woman and calming his shocked nerves. "When since me need yuh permission fe go nowhe'?"

Sharon ignored his question. "Ah who dat you ah rub up 'pon bwoy?" She asked acidly

"Listen, gal!" Barky's tone had grown more menacing. "Jus' go home because me no inna de mood fe play nuh husband and wife business wid you."

"Me nah lef yah until you tell me ah whe' you pick up… dah one deh from."

His dance partner had been silent, leaning protectively on Barky's side, but when she heard the insult she responded in kind.

"But see yah! Ah who you ah style 'dah one yah'?"

Barky stepped between the two women.

"Yuh ah hear me Sharon. You bettah go home, fass! Before you get a beatin' you nevah feget in fronta ah yuh friend dem, yah hear me?" Sharon stepped back but Muma Liza would stand for none of these threats to her niece. She pushed through the onlookers, grabbing Barky's 'matey' in her calloused paws, spinning her away into the shadows with a cracking 'box to the jaw'.

"You t'ink you can put yuh hands 'pon Sharon and no dead tonight bwoy?" Barky stared vacantly at Liza for a heartbeat, then his eyes filled with terrible malice as he clenched his fist and lunged at her.

The big woman was no stranger to fist fights; Barky would have to deal with this 'bitch' like a man. He kicked her in the side but it didn't even phase her as she fired a stinging 'box' with her ringed finger. He twisted his face as the ring dug into his flesh, a sheet of searing pain covered his cheek. He flung out his left fist as an afterthought but she was out of harm's way. Feigning to the right the woman purposely sent the wrong signals out to Barky and then dipped into her handbag, pulling out a corked phial.

"Bloodclaat! Monkey lotion!!" someone shouted.

The crowd scattered.

She pulled the cork off the container of acid. Muma Liza was now poised to fling the contents anywhere Barky tried to bolt to. And as Simba watched he knew that could mean burning innocent ravers.

Delroy struggled against the flow of bodies to reach the poised woman, who was shadowing Barky's every move. The Ranking ducked low and leaped into the air. His flying kick came unexpectedly, startling the poised woman. Her wrist snapped back, sending the bottle twisting upwards as she fell. Barky looked over at the broken phial as smoke lifted from the corroding fibres and residue and imagined being scarred for life. He left in a hurry, his credibility shattered and his night 'fucked'.

Delroy stood looking down at the sprawled woman, still angry that security had not thought to search handbags for anything other than guns and knives. He slowly turned to stare at her.

"What you tek dis place for, cridel, ah nuh Coronation market dis yuh nuh?" His words oozed out slow and ominous. "Me nuh defend dem almshouse business, deh ole gal. Me jus want yuh raas outta dis place yah, *now!*"

She looked up, jumping to her feet twisting her 'tough' features at Simba then she smiled.

"You know ah who you ah deal wid, little bwoy? You waan me jus mark up dat pretty bwoy face deh. An' mek sure you 'fraid fe look inna yuh mirror." Her eyes bulged and her broad flat nose flared. Simba was about to rush her, teach her some respect when two of Hector's bodyguard 'bredrins' came up to stand beside him.

"Is everythang okay, man?" one of them, a heavy-set youth with a red bandanna, asked Simba.

"You cool bro?" His colleague inquired.

"Me bonafide, boss. But dis gal yah mek me didgy. Show her de bloodclaat door." They didn't hesitate and began to drag the struggling and cursing woman out.

Then without warning someone called out to him from the crowd.

"Ninja Yout!"

Then there was laughter. Delroy spun quickly, the familiar voice ringing in his ears and he just managed to see the back of a light blue *Miami Vice*-style jacket burrowing through the crowd.

Tuffy's name sparked in his head like a neon light. That was him — he knew it.

The gunman was making sure Simba was within reach, trying to scare him. But the Ranking refused to be intimidated.

If Tuffy wanted to challenge him here, without his gun, that was fine. *Face him.*

No more hide and seek.

Pinchers replied instead and as his reworked 'Bandelero' erupted through the speakers, the earlier confusion was quickly forgotten.

Minutes later, there was still no sign of Tuffy. Nevertheless, Simba's bodyguards stayed very close.

Just in case.

THIRTY-FOUR

Tuffy kept his eyes on the only exit from the warehouse, his hand roving under Cutie's short skirt, massaging her backside.

The woman he had picked up in the dance sighed sexily and moved her body even closer to his, 'rubbing' him with such skill and sensuousness against the wall he was finding it hard to concentrate on his job.

'Dat's why a ghetto gal me haffe big up an' trust'.

He recalled Beenie Man's famous lyrics and smiled, but in seconds the humour had gone from his face as Simba and his 'Idren' walked up to the exit and stopped for a few minutes, talking to two men.

They then walked out. The men they had spoken to blended back with the people around, watching.

"Careless," he mumbled. Tuffy used his free hand to take the portable from his back pocket and his teeth to pull out the antenna, leaving Cutie to 'do her t'ing' as the music played. He punched the memory redial button and heard the line open.

"Ah fe yuh time now rude bwoy."

Tuffy thought nothing more of it, instead he was content with the surprises Cutie had in store.

Her eager hands grasped at his crutch.

The dance finally wound down in the early hours of Sunday morning. Delroy wanted to catch some fresh air and get away from the stale perfume, sweat and cigarette smoke.

He felt edgy among all these people and he wanted to leave.

The light inside was dull and the milling ravers provided cover for many a possible assailant.

Delroy and Hector walked out into the chilly morning air in search of some decent food. Simba had made sure the Bronx 'bad bwoys' kept an eye out for anyone suspicious trying to follow them — especially a man in a light blue suit. He was grateful for their protection and promised to 'big dem up' at a later date. The smell of the East River was raw and uninviting, a putrid mist lifted from its greenish surface and creeped towards the shore. But the stench did nothing to dissuade them from their search for food. They headed up Dover Street walking and chatting loudly to each other, checking out the deserted walkways and spotting fleeting images of vagrants awakened by their approach.

"If you walk up straight, an' then turn right," Hector said pointing, "we shoulda end up inna China Town. You waan risk it?"

"No problem," Delroy answered eagerly. "Me raw man an' if it mean fe walk clear ah Yard fe it, ah jus' so."

They took the right turn up St. James' Place and paced themselves to the street's end.

"Bwoy, tonight you hot up de venue, boss," Hector grinned, rubbing his hands together. "An' de amount ah contact me pick up tonight, is a shame. T'ings ah come together, star."

"A fe we time now, Hector."

Simba pushed both hands into his pockets, head lowered somewhat.

"Ah years me deh 'bout ah suffer still yuh nuh. An' you see how me jus' ah push up my nose inna de business now, propa. Not'n ah go stop me!"

Hector's face darkened.

"Together we mus' can work t'ings out, Simba, but you have a serious problem dat need deal wid."

"Right now me cyan help dat, Hector. What will be, mus' be. But if me can survive dis long, me can survive even longer."

Hector looked over to him trying to gauge his feelings; his face was impassive.

"I jus' waan you know seh, me deh wid you, seen?" The engineer shrugged his shoulders. "You nevah haffe put yuh life 'pon de line wid me an' de pussy Vibesman, but you do it. Me nah feget dat."

Simba dismissed his comments with a wave of his hand.

"So you owe me, an' me owe you. A nuh not'n, man. De Father bring we together fe a reason. If we can handle de raasclaat bwoy Saint how we handle de music business, we will live through dis."

Hector was taken aback. He'd never heard Simba refer to God before and hadn't expected him to do so now.

It was unexpected.

But he should have known better; Simba was full of surprises.

They reached East Broadway and spotted a chinese mobile diner — Chow Pong's — parked on the corner. The cream-coloured Chevy van was surrounded by hungry New Yorkers coming from the dance and the neighbouring night clubs.

"Can I help you, sir?" Mr Pong asked politely, looking at both men in turn.

Hector ordered for both of them and soon they were enjoying freshly made chicken in pineapple and prawn balls.

They were making their way down Dover Street, engrossed in discussions of future plans, when two high-intensity halogen lamps beamed from the avenue on the right. Delroy immediately moved closer to the inside of the sidewalk pulling Hector with him.

"Babylon!" he rasped.

"Somehow me nuh t'ink so." Hector answered unconcerned. "No siren a sound, ah jus' a man lost or him jus' ah fuck 'bout."

They picked up their pace anyway. The car edged out of

the side street and crawled onto the road, 50 metres behind them. When the car didn't overtake, their conversation stopped. Hector turned and stared at Delroy.

They could feel the light on the back of their heads. Trying to ignore it did not work either; the car kept its distance and paced them threateningly.

The Ranking tried to figure out what was happening as his eyes caught Hector's, he seemed unconcerned. Simba looked to the end of the street and tried to remember any potential hiding places or tight alleyways.

This did not feel right.

"You alright, Ranking?" Hector asked, as Simba looked from left to right nervously.

"Yeah man, safe."

His increased pace told another story.

Then Delroy spotted a low wall they had passed on their way down to the diner. Above the wall, a set of utility stairs wound its way up the side of a nearby building.

If he was wrong, the car would soon pick up speed and drive past them. If not, they had a chance to escape. The vehicle kept its distance, like a cat stalking its prey. Hector and Delroy quick-marched past the shops, their reflections forming weird broken images.

"You see dem stairs 'pon yuh left ahead ah we?" Delroy hissed.

"Why?" Hector heaved, creening his neck.

"Jus' trust me man. Look good boss, if you waan come outta dis alive."

Hector's mouth opened, shocked. He squinted as Simba asked again. "Yuh see de stairs, don. Just near de corner ah de jewellry shop, it ah run up de side ah dah black an' white building deh, you nuh see it?"

Hector nodded.

"Me see it boss, 'bout three hundred metres 'pon yuh left, yes."

"Yeah man, ah it dat."

He paused, not looking back but glancing fleetingly into the glass frontage of a passing jewellers. Their stalker's

Pontiac Trans-Am seemed to be picking up speed.

Simba's voice sounded tormented, his tone urgent.

"When me gi' de signal, me waan see yuh shirt back, seen! Nuh look back no matter what an' jus' keep moving. It harder fe hit a moving target."

Hector had missed something here. He swore Simba just said hit a moving target.

"Wha—"

"No questions don, just do it!"

Hector swallowed hard, nodding as if his head was on hinges. Nervous perspiration peppered his brow.

They hurried past a drunken wino huddled inside the doorway of a fashion boutique.

"So wha' you ah go do, Simba?" Hector gasped helplessly.

"Nuh worry 'bout me skipper, me deh right behind you."

Delroy strode ahead, determined not to show any fear or give away his plan of action. He counted off his steps.

1...2...3...4...5...

Simba stopped suddenly and whirled, turning to stare right into the windshield of the Trans-Am. The black car kept coming and the Ranking stepping back in response, slowly. Simba raised a defiant finger shaped into a gun and, forcing a smirk, pointing it in the car's direction.

His brazen action got an immediate response.

The engine revved, obliterating the sounds of angry voices from inside the car. Simba saw the dull glint of 'matics' being lifted from seats to eager hands.

"Run!!!" Delroy screamed.

His cry ripped through the tense silence and both men shot into action, sprinting in erratic zig zags past signposts and dodging fire hydrants, their arms pumping furiously.

The only thing on their minds was to reach the utility ladder and climb its rungs to hopeful safety above.

The Trans-Am's engine growled, its four tyres spinning in a desperate bid to gain traction on the tarmac. Smoke and the acrid smell of burning rubber accompanied the scream of tyres that drowned out the sounds of running feet.

The car made up the distance between it and the fleeing men in a heartbeat. As the driver throttled back, Delroy and Hector heard the menacing 'whirr' of the electric windows. The ugly snouts of Heckler and Koch automatics and Uzis poked in their direction, and they heard a magazine slam into its housing as the Trans-Am mounted the kerb and bore down on them.

They had almost no time to take cover. Then Simba realised that Hector was still running straight and upright, making himself an unmissable target — either he hadn't seen the guns, or blind panic was governing his actions.

He was two strides ahead of Simba.

A split-second before the guns opened up, the deejay lunged forward, stretching his right hand out and just hooking Hector's left leg. The engineer stumbled and hit the concrete hard, just managing to cushion his fall with his hands and rolling to a stop behind a newspaper stand.

The newspaper stand exploded — a spray of high-velocity bullets sending a cloud of shredded newspapers into the air. They hugged concrete, hoping the shooting would stop or the ground would open and swallow them. Neither seemed likely.

The car came up and passed them, spitting slugs into the concrete beside them, ricocheting off hydrants and sending shards of brick flying everywhere.

They were pinned down.

Delroy used this opportunity to act. He grabbed Hector by the arm and dragged him to his feet, hoping they could dash a few more metres to escape. The car's red brake lights flashed viciously as it fishtailed and spun a three-sixty degree turn, its wheels digging the concrete slabs of the side walk like a rotary saw.

There was a pause in the shooting while the gunmen regained their bearings and slotted in new magazines.

As the car caught them again, streams of bullets kicked up dust spouts on the pavement. Hector and Simba leapt to one side, straightening themselves on tiptoes as they slammed their backs against a metal shutter of an electronics store. They shuffled awkwardly around the corner to temporary safety.

But it was not quite what they wanted. An open plot of land lay between them and the waiting stairs. To cross it would mean becoming open targets, but they had no other choice. Simba pushed off first, propelling himself across the uneven surface. The orange flash of bullets making crisscross tracks of exploding concrete and soil with every step he took.

Hector was soon hot on his heels just as the Trans-Am screeched behind them for its fourth pass.

Remarkably, they reached the stairs in one piece.

They mounted the rungs in leaps, hearts pounding and breathing heavy. Alarms were wailing below. Delroy reached and looked down from the platform at the top of the ladder to monitor Hector's progress. He was just clambering over the last metal partition leading to the roof, a shattered and exhausted man.

Simba scanned the street below. The Trans-Am had stopped sharply and two men flew out of the car's passenger door. Both of them had their guns swaying loosely at their sides, one wearing a non-descript blue silk shirt and the other a distinctive baseball cap marked with black and white patchwork hexagons. He seemed angrier than the rest. He paced around in a small circle, blaming the others and pointing his Mac-10 at all of them threateningly. The other man did not fit the usual profile. Something about him signified the aura of a 'ghetto yout' but definitely not a Yardie, his gestures were different. He angrily kicked the tyres of the car.

Jake was fuming.

The cap man leaned into the car talking to the driver, then slapped the roof of the car angrily. Burglar alarms from the damaged shop fronts screamed out in protest, frustrating the men even more. But the fact that the police would be arriving on the scene in no time did not deter the 'cap man'. He kept looking up at Simba and the engineer, his gold wristband shimmering under the security lights.

"Next time!" he said, pointing the gun in their direction and cursing at the top of his voice.

Hector's eyes were wide with shock and he was trembling. Down below, the gunmen got back in the car and took off. The banshee wailing of the alarms continued and the distant sirens of approaching squad cars grew louder.

Simba spoke low to himself, his teeth bared.

"So de bwoy Tuffy mean business. Heh! Well, him ah go find out de Ranking is a hard man fe dead. Him bettah know dat. A hard raasclaat man fe dead."

THIRTY-FIVE

The Saint was teeing off at the Constant Spring Golf Club. He stared down on the solitary white plastic tee and gently placed his ball in the depression. He glared down the fairway, his number one wood club swung high and sweetly connected with the golf ball. The drive sent it hurtling 200 yards down the course. It was an expert shot that didn't even draw a smile from his lips. His angry scowl remained. His golf cart pulled up beside him, driven by a stiff-faced caddy, his security men following at a safe distance in a second electric cart. The young caddy looked nervously at the men shadowing them and sharply took the Saint's club. They silently pulled away to his next drive.

Five strokes later.

The Saint putted the ball, rolling it across the green straight towards the hole. It hugged the rim and followed the edge, threatening not to go in. It did eventually, and for the first time a genuine yet mercurial smile cut across the Saint's features. Then and only then did he explode. He slammed his putter down onto the moist green, adding a sharp bend to the design of the Wilson club.

"Tek me raas back to the club house, now!" he barked at the caddy.

Hugh St. John was not having a good morning; his efforts to relieve his tension with a round of golf had failed dismally.

His bodyguard had woken him early that morning to say

that Stumpy, the courier from New York, had arrived with the long-awaited report from his stalkers.

"Jus' how you want it boss, sign, seal an' deliver."

Stumpy held out his leather-clad prosthetic hand. His previous hand had been hacked off when he'd tried to pick the pocket of a local don.

St. John had flung the documents aside. All he wanted to know was whether it was true that his wife was with Simba Ranking in New York.

Stumpy nodded she was.

He was unable and unwilling to control the fire and fury burning deep inside. This bwoy had become familiar with his wife's body in the most intimate of ways. A ghetto 'yout' was making love to his wife, utilising all different types of sexual positions...inside her body...pleasuring her.

His wife, his woman.

He was gripped by a tremor of anxiety and hate. He shook his head to clear it. She had slipped out of the country and had run to her deejay man for comfort and protection. Deserting her husband, for worthless trash. He would show her running was pointless.

Simba had been lucky so far, but for how much longer? He would make a mistake sometime soon and, when he did, the Saint's men would be waiting.

As for Monique, he would prefer to have her back alive, but not if she insisted it should be otherwise.

The golf cart pulled up beside the pavilion and the Saint hopped out before it came to a standstill. His three security men were already there, hands close to their shoulder holsters, scanning the bushes lining the vast luxury course.

"Glad you're back from the course, sir," said the receptionist as Hugh walked past. "I've got an urgent message for you from a Mr. Walker. He left this number for you to return his call."

"Thanks, Trevor, I'll deal wid dis now."

He took the note and hurried down the hall. The cool air rejuvenating his dulled senses, and tingling the skin on the back of his neck as he breezed through to the private rooms reserved for VIP card members. His easy-care golf shoes clicked on the lino floor as he walked past the portraits of the club's glum old English founders set on the walls leading into the lounge.

It was already busy at 11:30 am as the diplomats, millionaires and politicians who frequented the club prepared for a day of golf, drinking and political dealing. So many deals and contacts were made here that it was known as the secondary parliament.

The Saint nodded at the Colombian attache Eduardo Gato, dressed in full golfing regalia. The poor ambassador would choke on his croissant if he knew that the Saint was on first-name terms with some of the top dogs in the Cali drugs cartel.

The Saint pushed his way through the swinging doors, still smiling, and headed into the luxury rest rooms. He pulled out his room key and entered number 15, closing the door behind him. He switched on the air-conditioning unit and relaxed behind the desk, pulling the blinds just a touch to let traces of sunlight through. He pulled his electronic voice modifier out of the desk drawer, plugged it in, reached for the phone and punched out his contact's untraceable number in New York.

His contact's stolen mobile had been altered electronically; the Saint was confident that the care he took to stay one step ahead of the authorities would defeat any surveillance operation mounted against him.

"Yaow!" came a voice on the other end.

"It's me," the Saint said, his voice digitally modified to sound like a woman. "How t'ings running?"

"Everyt'ing safe, boss. We have another million dollars being wired to de Bahamas bank. De shipment ah gun deh 'pon it way and all de papers Stumpy gi' you dem already."

The Saint growled. Tuffy was stalling.

Their was a long pause.

"De only t'ing is...de bwoy Simba still ah slip we."

The Saint clenched his fist.

"We nearly kill him an' him bredrin de other night, boss.

230

But we couldn't stay 'pon de scene, police fly dung 'pon de place. De two ah dem missin up from desso."

The Saint's silence was worrying Tuffy; he tried a reassuring note. "Him cyan run fi ever, don, de bwoy bound fe slip up an' when him do, yuh problem solve."

"I wish it was dat straightforward, my friend, but Simba Ranking ah mek me look bad. Him mus' be laughing now t'inking he's dealing with amateurs."

Lucky for Tuffy that he was on the other end of the phone and not in front of him.

"He's been raas lucky so far, but take no chances wid dis. Drop everyt'ing and show him you don't fuck wid what is mine an' get 'way."

He took up his letter opener and admired the inscriptions on its blade. The Saint continued:

"I want someone close to him dead!" He drove the point of the implement forcefully into the top of the desk.

It vibrated.

"I don't care how it done. If you can't find him nuh worry, cah me have big plans fe him. But give me something else, someone else inna him family. I want him fe *regret* de day him fuck wid me!" he raved. "An' in time I want to piss on his whole family's grave, yuh hear me?"

He was shouting now.

"I want this dealt wid *now*. Not tomorrow or next week but *now. Now!*"

Tense silence.

"It's done boss."

"This ghetto bwoy intends to play wid fire an' nuh get burn. Not'n nuh work so."

A crackle came from the receiver and it seemed as if the distance between both speakers suddenly increased without warning. Tuffy's low distant voice came through the earpiece like a message from hell.

"Him ah go bawl eye water fe one ah him family, trust me 'pon dat."

"I will, me friend, I will." The connection clicked twice as if someone else had just been disconnected and hummed into silence. The politician listened carefully — his suspicious nature telling him the sound could have been remotely human — but he heard only a distant electronic wheeze. He replaced the handset with a feeling of satisfaction.

The note with Mr. Walker's number on it had drifted to the floor. This was one of the many business calls he should have returned but never did. He was losing touch; but as far as he was concerned everything could wait, including this. He opened his wallet and a picture of his wife smiled up at him.

He would enjoy the look on the bitch's face at her baby father's slow, painful death. She had a choice. Her life or the life of her unborn child. Then the better man would have won.

THIRTY-SIX

The yellow cab slowed to a standstill as the light turned to red on Fifth Avenue. It was a late Wednesday afternoon as the Bajan driver twisted the dial of his portable radio to WRKS. The sound of the top forty charts blurted from the speaker and the driver nodded his head in time with Kris Kross' new single, his face a mock show of pain. Delroy closed the glass shutters between himself and the driver, he wanted to enjoy the music without the mad antics of the driver.

He leaned back into the newly-upholstered seats and peered up at the Trump Tower, his thoughts settling on the past few days.

Moses had heard from one of his spars in the music business that the Ranking was causing massive waves in the reggae music scene. One evening, when Simba had gone round to see them, the dread had been forced to admit he'd been wrong. The things he had heard and seen his nephew achieve left him with nothing to say but to congratulate him. Simba had done something that in his own time he had refused even to attempt. His nephew was just a bitter reminder of his own shortcomings.

The atmosphere had been tense at his uncle's apartment. Miss Gee was upset that Delroy had left their home — he was now living with Monique — and she blamed Moses and the increasing friction between her husband and Simba, despite all Simba's reassurances to the contrary.

Delroy couldn't tell them that his main reason for moving out was to save their lives. He didn't want the Saint's men harming them because they were close to him. No more blood on his account.

Delroy was concerned that Monique's work with the advertising agency was nearly at an end. And what then? She couldn't go back to Jamaica, not yet, not with the Saint still on the warpath. And with the baby due in a few months, he didn't want her out of his sight for any long periods of time. The Saint was capable of anything.

He gazed through the window and tried to focus on his more immediate problem. Time!

Hector sat beside him in silence; he was angry too but tried not to show it.

He had been planning tonight's gig at the Apollo for some time, getting Simba's name on the list for amateur night. The new lyrics had been prepared and they had bought the backing track and some other electronic equipment they would use on stage. Now it seemed his efforts would be wasted. Marcia had written off his car at the last minute and left them almost no time to reach the theatre. The massive tailback did not help either.

The anguished expression on his face said it all.

"Dis show yah important, don," Hector said. "Not fe de money, cah we nah go mek none, but fe de exposure."

But now it seemed as though they'd miss the very strict registration time. They were both silent for most of the trip then, without warning, Hector snapped into life. "We ah go perform tonight, don."

Simba shot a look of surprise his way.

"You willing fe tek a chance tonight, Ranking?"

Hector's eyes twinkled slyly.

"Dem coulda fling we raas out, but…"

"But wha'?"

"You will have yuh name fe sure inna de papers an' ah nuh just ghetto people ah go hear 'bout you."

That got Simba interested, and he listened intently as Hector revealed his plan.

"You sure dem cyan lock we up fe dat, star?"

"Nuh worry, man, de only t'ing dem can do we is escort we out. An' by then is too late."

"So everyt'ing we need fe your plan we have available?" Delroy asked, looking down at the satchel beside Hector's feet.

The engineer dug his hands into the leather bag and brought out a modified cordless microphone.

"Dis piece ah equipment yah can bruk inna any audio sound system, widout drowning out de backing instrumentals or de original vocals," he boasted.

"Dis?" Simba asked, amazed.

"A miracle inna micro-electronics, my boss. Dis—" he handed Delroy the wireless microphone with a small unit the size of a matchbox attached to its side, "—is de answer to our prayers!"

The cab pulled into Lennox Avenue, passing three guys singing acappella to a wide-eyed congregation of young girls.

The driver slowed the cab down to a crawl.

"You'll be there in a tick, boys."

He turned directly into West 125th Street and stopped directly in front of the Apollo Theatre; the Bajan looked pleased with himself. Delroy paid him, adding a tip as reward for being the only cab man brave enough to take them through Harlem.

The driver pulled away grinning from ear to ear.

"Me ah go talk to my spar inna de sound booth an' try set t'ings up. Me will meet yuh later."

"Little more."

Delroy walked away to join the excited throng of people as Hector idly trotted behind him.

A few moments later he was standing in the Apollo Theatre foyer looking at the photographic montage of Motown giants and other black stars. He shrugged off his nervousness at Hector's wild plan and paid the ten dollar entrance to the stalls.

Inside the main auditorium, he could feel the hum of

excitement resonating all around. People were standing and sitting, boisterously laughing, chatting and generally making merry. They were all excitedly waiting for the MC to stride on stage and announce the show's commencement. Delroy sat in the last row, first seat in the far left-hand corner. The circle protruded over him, throwing shadow over the few rows underneath.

Wicked!

He'd have all the privacy he needed.

Delroy was surprised to see video technicians walking around the stage. Then he realised how perfectly Hector's plan fit in with what was taking place now. It seemed that tonight's show was to be a taped special, *'Showtime at the Apollo'* and would be aired a week from today on prime time television.

Butterflies fluttered about in Simba's stomach.

Then the lights dimmed and the MC walked to centre stage to get the show under way.

The smartly-dressed master of ceremonies outlined the night's performers and performances, and promised a feast of new talent.

Delroy's stomach knotted.

The amateurs took to the stage first and fared dismally as the audience booed and cheered at the same time. The Apollo's own Sandman popped up on stage with funny costumes and appropriate props to dispatch the really bad ones. The dancers mostly flopped and the singers mostly croaked, but laughter and the sound of people enjoying themselves filled the theatre.

During the interval Simba shuffled out of his seat and walked casually down the aisle, eyeing the stalls on both sides. He stopped suddenly when he heard Hector's telltale loud mouth, and saw him chatting up some woman who was comfortably seated in her chair as he perched on the arm rest.

Simba smiled.

He hated to break Hector's chirping in mid-sentence, but his friend had something he needed.

236

The MC dashed back on stage after the interval, making a well-timed entrance just as people were settling back into their seats. He released his usual smooth talk of welcome, and played up to the cameras as he introduced the next segment of the evening's entertainment, and with a hungry audience yearning for action he brought on the sweet haunting voice of Jamaica's Austen Flex. The Jamaicans present immediately burst into applause, whistles and cheers as the Americans calmly took their time to assess the giant of cultural reggae music. The dreadlocks floated on stage in a shimmering black and gold outfit, his locks flowing to his shoulders.

"HOW YA DOIN', APOLLO?" Austen's voice boomed across the hall to a positive response from the onlookers. "I want to bring to you tonight a taste ah wha' you Yankees missing here in de States." Pockets of laughter were heard around. "Respect to all the girls inna de place, we love you all to the max. This one is fe you, you and God knows who. Now roll dis one yah, Mr Music!"

The sampled instrumental track eased through the speakers and Austen Flex's honeyed voice floated powerfully over the tune causing immediate recognition from the fans. Hands shot skyward and the 'Bow! Bow!' of simulated gunshots peppered the air from Flex's already hyped-up Jamaican followers. He performed smoothly and effortlessly, working all sides of the audience. He completed his first song and stood triumphant, looking over the ocean of faces applauding wildly.

"You all love dat?" he asked, drawing high-pitched screams of 'Yeah!' in reply.

"Yeah man, New York posse hot tonight. Still I waan to give you this next and last one from my new album with Motown called 'Pan Rapid', I hope you'll all enjoy it Apollo, respect."

He slowly raised his hands and the music came to life in response. And when he'd finished, the audience were warmed up and yearning for a third set. The MC calmed the crowd down and started a teasing preamble to the next star appearance. But the crowd was already chanting his name impatiently — *'Wynn! Wynn! Wynn!'*

MC Jackson retreated to the wings as the spotlight hit centre stage.

Suddenly the def beat 'busted' from the audio, surrounding everyone in sound, as only Terence Wynn's voice could be heard harmonising with the upbeat tempo. A flood of dancers ran into position and on the once-empty stage a sort of expectant electricity crackled. The dancers took their positions, all moving stylishly on the spot with only the sweet voice of the Motown star in the background. The lighting technicians focused fleeting coloured circles around Terence Wynn's dancers, their skin glistening red, blue and yellow as sweat slicked across flexing muscles.

The host of screaming female voices sensed that their idol would soon be strutting on stage. Voices lowered slightly and the atmosphere filled with a hum of anticipation. Then the man himself strode into view.

A white beam of light arrowed into forestage were he stood. The screams were deafening.

"We're gonna lift the roof off the Apollo tonight!" his voice echoed, and was answered by the audience's ecstatic roar.

"Are you all ready to party?" he asked. The crowd shrieked they were. Terence looked unimpressed, cocking his head as if he wasn't sure what they had said.

"I said are you ready to pa-a-art-a-ay?" he asked again, calling for even more rapturous 'yeahs'.

He paused.

"Then let's *pump it up.*"

Delroy's heart was thumping hard as Terence Wynn came on stage for the second time, working his audience to a frenzy. Simba knew it would be now or never. If the man performed his hit single — *'In The Mood For Some Action'* — he had to be ready to break in. He prayed there would be no hitches.

He cradled the magic microphone in his hand. He'd taken it from Hector during the interval and was simply waiting for his cue.

Under severe duress from Hector, his 'Idrin' in the sound booth had adjusted his equipment so the microphone would easily cut into the Apollo's audio network. But still Simba wasn't sure it would work.

The Ranking stood up and paced in small circles, listening to the finishing guitar chops of the star's second number.

He tensed, sitting down again, along with hundreds of others as the Motown star prepared for the next song. Wynn stood on the stage like an obsidian statue, his head bowed and his breathing heavy from an exhausting dance routine.

Seconds passed — maybe even minutes — and suddenly Wynn and the dancers broke into spontaneous movement again. The swing beat king sounded off 'In the Mood for Some Action' and the screams and shouts of the Apollo Theatre rose up with him. Unnoticed by anyone, Simba Ranking came out of his seat and backed into the shadows. He switched the microphone on, felt a powerful hum in his hands and waited in anticipation. He breathed deeply as the first guitar riff came right on queue and then Delroy tensed ready, as he forced his 'gravel pit' tones through the microphone.

Man of action,
Woman you meet yuh redemption.
Se-e-e-e-arching for gold,
An nuh gold yuh find,
Simba nuh goldmine.
…One time!

His voice mellowed with the music, leaving Terence wondering what the hell was happening.

"Come dung Missa Wynn, cah you know we ah de action pack."

Terence — the true professional that he was — began singing on his usual queue, sparking his dancers into action. He wasn't sure where the interference was coming from, but he continued regardless. Simba nodded his head, timing the beat as the instrumental chorus came up. He came in again, bleeding into the audio and chatting in superbly-timed short spurts of incisive lyrics.

The hardcore reggae fans raved at the novel approach taken by the R&B singer. They swayed with his die-hard fans and lapped up the fusion of dancehall and funk.

Terence was still wondering who was bleeding into his song as he stomped the floorboards with his dancers. But whoever it was, he couldn't deny it was a good mix.

Simba Ranking looked out over the sea of bopping and surging bodies. He could have the crowd eating out of his hands if they only knew he was doing the 'chatting', but he wasn't sure of how the performer or the audience would react to his presence.

Fuck wha' dem t'ink, me nah back dung now!

Terence Wynn would have to either accept him or not.

If the photographers needed a picture to place with the articles they were bound to write, he would provide them with 'nuff shots.

Simba held the microphone between his index finger and thumb and marched down the aisle 'chatting' with perfect timing over the music.

He saw astonishment and surprise on the faces of the audience and heard whoops of delight accompanying every step he made — and soon even some shouts of *'Simba Ranking!'* began to pierce the air. As Simba reached the front of the auditorium, Wynn shuffled his lithe body to the stage's edge and looked down at him. His dancers froze and so did the music, and Simba crooned the final word to a wave of outstretched arms and screams.

Terence Wynn's gaze was unwavering; he glared at Simba and Simba glared back at him. Then, slowly, Wynn's passive expression changed.

He smiled.

"Respect concrete and *grill up!*" Simba boomed through the mike as the roof lifted with applause and shrill whistles.

THIRTY-SEVEN

If this was a dream, the Ranking did not want to wake from it.

He had never signed so many photographs and record sleeves in his life. And *'Love an' Gunshot'* was at the number one spot in New York and London.

Dancehall 'riddims' played low in the background and the second floor of the Riddim Nation record outlet was jam-packed with boisterous and screaming fans.

Hector looked on from behind his 'prento' with pride, arms folded and beaming as people clambered over themselves for autographed copies of his latest hit single.

Simba tried to stifle a yawn but couldn't. He was looking weary but still on form as his coarse voice 'lyriced' the girls into giggles and squeals.

A large contingent of American girls were there, raving with the rest of the groupies.

They knew the 'runnings'.

Some young women who had not been influenced by the culture had taken the time to penetrate the wall of Jamaican patois in order to appreciate what was being said. For the ones who hadn't, the infectious rhythms were the attraction.

The Ranking was breaking down barriers.

After two hours of constant scribbling and posing he needed some rest.

Hector 'braced up his chest' as he made the announcement and, as he expected, was met by rowdy boos and jeers.

"Respect!" Simba growled, standing up and giving the peace sign to all his fans before being escorted away to the back of building.

He left an uproar behind him.

His first taste of 'farrin popularity' left him with a tingle of satisfaction and made him feel light and powerful. The royalties from his record were trickling in, and money was becoming less and less of a problem.

He felt almost unstoppable.

Almost, but not quite.

He was thriving, but although there had as yet been no further attempts on his life, he was still painfully aware of the Saint's obsessive bloodlust. He went nowhere without his 'Bronx bwoy' bodyguards.

Delroy walked into a large storage area flanked by his bodyguards with Hector trailing behind. They turned right, walking on red carpet past staff toilets towards the emergency exit doors at the back of the building.

There was no escape for him there.

The persistent groupies milling about outside recognised him as soon as he stepped into the cool evening air and immediately flocked him for autographs.

Dis ah de beginning, Delroy thought, frantically signing. Reporters lurked on the outskirts of the crowd, waiting for interviews; it seemed they would have a long wait.

An authoritative female voice unexpectedly spoke out.

"Ladies and gentlemen, my client is quite tired from the evening's proceedings, he will do signing and interviews with his fans and the press at a later date, now if you'll excuse us…"

Delroy looked up, surprised to see the dark skin and long elegant eyelashes of Roxanne Lawrence again.

She snaked her arms through his and led him away to a chauffeur-driven limo and leaving Hector with a bemused look on his face.

The uniformed driver ushered them into the back. Simba slid onto the leather seats as the door was slammed behind

242

him. Roxanne sat opposite. She was wearing a black miniskirt and his gaze followed her legs down the coffee sheer tights and black designer shoes.

"So what ah gwan Roxanne? We buck again, man. Wha' deh 'pon yuh mind?"

She smiled a mischievous smile.

"I have a proposal for you."

Simba crinkled his eyebrows, still puzzled.

"Wha' kinda proposal?"

"Something I know you won't be able to say no to."

Delroy leaned back in his seat and crossed his legs.

"Me ah listen."

"I've done my homework on you, and your manager was right. You do have potential. Number one hit singles and a positive write up from the R&B magazines on that Apollo performance. You're hot property. It's not just your talent that's saleable, Simba, but your profile too. Being involved in some scandal in Jamaica sells more than just papers, you know."

He nodded.

"If you want to have a solid worldwide following — and I know you can, in time — you're going to need major league backing. I think I can give it to you."

"You have somet'ing fe offer me girl, then stop play games wid I and put yuh proof up-front."

Delroy leaned forward, becoming more interested now; his eyes twinkled in the sparse light.

She sighed.

"I'm an A&R scout for Pony Records and they've been showing a great deal of interest in this new generation of dancehall stars. Because my parents are Jamaican and I've grown up with the music, I volunteered to find out who was who."

Delroy listened carefully. It seemed the 'break' he had prayed for all his life had come. Roxanne's voice had locked into professional mode.

"My proposal is to expose you to the wider reggae world," she explained. "My company's sponsoring the annual Reggae Awards in England, and I want to invite you along — all expenses paid. What do you say?"

It took less than a second for Simba to weigh up his reasons for leaving New York. This could be the only time he had to breathe easy. He could actually be away from the Saint's assasins. Safety.

"When we ah leave? Name de date, baby."

"Good!" she said "Then the only problem is your visa, which could take some time to process. In the meantime just sit tight."

"Wha' 'bout my spar, Hector?" Delroy asked. "Him is de man who open up certain way fe me still. Any t'ing dat ah go gwan, him haffe get a piece ah de action."

"No problem. You and your manager are on your way to London. But just remember that I haven't totally sold you to my boss yet. I like your style, but the final decision doesn't rest with me. No contracts or anything legal until the man at the top gives the go-ahead. Personally, I think you will be signed. I can be very persuasive when I want to be..."

Simba didn't doubt that for a moment, but his thoughts had already started running away with him.

With money and influence I would be a dangerous man. An equal to the Saint.

But that was for later. Right now he was nervous and expecting more attempts on his life.

So how could he say no to an offer like this?

Roxanne leaned back in the leather seats after Simba had left and stretched over to the drinks cabinet. She poured herself a brandy.

"We can go home now, Peter," she said to the driver. "I think I've done enough for one night." The chauffeur nodded curtly and pulled the limousine slowly into the stream of traffic.

The car phone rang.

Roxanne took a sip of her drink and gingerly picked up the receiver. She smiled when she recognised the voice.

"Now this is what I call good timing," she said. "I've just finished talking to the man himself and his future looks good from where I'm standing."

She paused listening to the caller's comments.

"You're too modest," she said. "If you give me the opportunity, I'd like to thank you personally sometime." Her voice lowered seductively. "Without your tip I wouldn't be trying to sign him up to our label. I really do owe you."

Roxanne had said those words many a time, but this time she said them with real meaning…to the handsome Jamaican businessman she had met a year ago at a charity function in Kingston.

Until three weeks earlier she hadn't spoken to the man since their first meeting. But then he'd called out of the blue and personally recommended the talents of Simba Ranking.

He was doing the deejay a favour, he said.

He owed him.

It was the best piece of advice she had been given in a long time.

"As I promised," she continued, "I'll fax you the details of the gig in London, so you can surprise him in person when he performs."

The voice on the other end answered.

"No! No!" Roxanne said. "Don't thank me, take me to dinner when we meet up in London."

She paused waiting for the reply, her smile broadening.

"It's a date!"

She laughed out loud, anticipating their next meeting.

"And don't worry — he won't suspect a thing."

Night-time New York shimmered like a fairy tale city in the distance as Courtney fired up a spliff and settled his back into the driver's seat of the Ford Mercury.

He wound down the window slightly and directed a smoke ring towards it. The tension in his shoulders and arms drained away under the influence of the cannabis and a dull lump of a headache was slowly dislodging itself from the crown of his skull with every pull of the relaxing smoke. He needed something to bring him down from the rigours of a hectic day, and what a day it was.

He had just concluded a meeting to organise a talent contest for the neighbourhood he worked in as a youth leader; it had collapsed into an uproarious argument over the most trivial of things. Courtney himself had to forcefully step in and gently nudge the direction of the meeting to a positive end.

This had sapped his strength, but thankfully it had ended with a decision. Minutes after the adjournment of the meeting he was heading for home. Every mile he drove his bed seemed to be calling to him with a more insistent voice. He pressed hard on the accelerator and the Mercury responded by lurching forward just as a white BMW rocketed beside him from nowhere. Courtney looked over to his left as the car kept in line with him, its tinted glass revealing nothing.

The driver behind thumped angrily on the horn to get past the encroaching BM, but the driver ignored it. The other cars in the left lane joined in the frustrated chorus, and it was only then that the BMW slowed up, its indicator flashing red, making space for the other cars to drive by.

Instead of following the irate drivers up the highway, the BMW nudged in directly behind the Mercury. Courtney slowed the Mercury down and moved with caution over to the other lane, but the BMW kept it's distance, the driver preferring to shadow his movements from under Courtney's rear bumper.

Dis bwoy yah mussi luv me, Courtney thought. Then questions started to crowd his mind. He wondered if the terrible twins from the Stuyvestant housing complex where he worked were playing a practical joke. But those dudes didn't have two nickels to rub together.

A BMW was out of the question.

His mind stopped churning as he veered off the expressway. He was hoping the BMW wouldn't follow.

But it did.

If it came down to a high speed chase he would stand no chance. His American ride was no match for the cream of

German engineering.

What the fuck is their game?

The BM' edged up beside him again, effortlessly, making Courtney steady his grip on the wheel and gaze intently at the road ahead. He was struggling to keep his eyes focused on some distant point, trying to ignore what the car pulling up beside him was doing, but his curiosity was stronger.

He turned his head around stiffly, just in time to see the tinted glass of the BM slide down. The man at the wheel was a black man, his dark glasses edged near the tip of his nose. He was leaning back in his seat with one hand nimbly manoeuvring the power steering. The man indicated for Courtney to pull over. Instead Courtney pressed the accelerator pedal to the floor with all his weight. The car surged forward, but the BMW easily matched it.

Panicking now, Courtney kept making fleeting glances at his pursuer.

Wha' de fuck ah gwan, man?

Then multiple orange flashes erupted from the interior of the BM. His question was answered. There was an unnerving lapse of time in Courtney's head as the *Budda! Budda!* of automatic fire shredded the Mercury's rear door and window. He knew it was a warning, they could have so easily sprayed the length of the car. In his confusion and fright he slammed the brakes and slowed the car to a crawl. The BM shot past and immediately braked in response, reversing in haste. They came level to the damaged Ford, all barrels blazing, and Courtney instinctively dropped below the level of the dashboard as the windscreen buckled inwards with flying shards of glass. He released his seatbelt and awkwardly rolled out onto the warm tarmac on all fours.

"Shit!" Courtney cursed as the BMW screeched to a stop. Car doors opened and slammed. It was then that Courtney became aware that he could do nothing to save himself. He was about to die and didn't even understand why.

The footsteps came closer. There was no urgency in their rhythm — they knew their man had nowhere to go.

Courtney stood up from behind the car feeling it was better to show himself like a man than grovel like a dog. The men looked at him with his hands raised skyward and levelled their weapons on his head and chest. Courtney closed his eyes, his lips trembling a prayer when the men opened fire.

Courtney tensed — expecting death to come quickly — but instead:

The surface of the road in front of the three approaching men suddenly erupted in an explosion of bullets and flying masonry.

"Who the bloodclaat dat!" one of the men screamed, swinging his MP5 submachine gun away from Courtney and into the direction of fire. But he would never know the answer to the question as his slow trigger reaction condemned him to death. Bullets tore into his chest, exiting through a shattered spinal column and throwing him backwards. His finger spasmed around the trigger and his dying body shook helplessly as he pumped bullets harmlessly into the air before collapsing. An extra magazine clattered out of his pocket and his body stiffened, then went still.

The other two men were totally exposed, one was crouched staring intently into the darkness and the other was spinning wildly, having no idea where the sniper shots rang out from.

"PLACE YOUR WEAPONS ON THE GROUND BEFORE YOU." The booming voice echoed from a loudhailer. "LOWER YOURSELF TO YOUR KNEES AND PLACE YOUR HANDS BEHIND YOUR HEAD."

With no cover and obviously out-gunned the yardies knew it would be stupid to attempt to shoot their way out. They threw down a Mac-10 and an SP89 pistol and stood arrogantly with their arms across their chests.

"I SAID ON YOUR KNEES, MOTHERFUCKERS."

They went to their knees.

It was then that Courtney saw the men emerging from the shadows, approaching the two 'bad bwoys' with extreme caution.

There were DEA men and a group of black agents with A.C.I.D. marked in bold white letters across their backs. They were all dressed in dark blue uniforms with shells of bullet proof armour on their chest and backs. Helmeted in stark black, they barked orders to the two sprawled men. The ACID men came over to the spread eagle Jamaicans, their silhouettes dark against the shop fronts as they aimed their weapons on the prostrate men at point blank range, expertly frisking them.

Courtney's heart was pounding in his chest and his head was racing. His eyes shot from left to right as police vehicles came on the scene.

What the fuck was going on, man?

"Mr Mackay!"

The voice startled Courtney as he spun around to face a young white man.

"I think we need to talk, Mr Mackay." The man was in his early twenties, freckled and obviously Ivy League material.

"I'm agent Richardson of the DEA." He flashed his ID badge. "I know you're upset, sir, and need answers to your questions, but if you'll bear with me all will be made clear."

He took Courtney's elbow and led him over to a limousine that was parked carelessly on the pavement. The man opened the door and waved him inside, where he was met with an outstretched hand.

"I'm sorry we had to meet like dis, son," the man said, sitting with his legs crossed. "You don't know me, but what I haffe show you in a minute will explain who I am and what dis is all about. Right now what I can tell you is that yuh cousin is in serious danger an' only you can help him."

Courtney slumped back in his seat, attentive but frightened.

Brigadier Andrew Humphries watched Courtney's nervous shuffling and hoped he would keep his composure. He needed him to be focused. For if Courtney was to be the key that would end the corrupt reign of the Saint, there was no room for error.

THIRTY-EIGHT

Delroy folded the letter he had just finished writing to Mama Christy. The British Airways flight was about to land at Heathrow; he could just imagine the expression on his mother's face when she heard where he was and what he was doing.

Moses and Miss Gee had seen him off at JFK hours earlier, wishing him luck, but Courtney had been tense. He'd simply hugged Simba emotionally and told him to be careful. Simba had been baffled by his behaviour but had had no time to question him.

Monique was fast asleep in the seat, even as the aircraft jolted downwards towards the runway.

What a gal can sleep, man.

Simba stretched over and gently secured her seat belt. How she was able to sleep through a landing was beyond him.

Hector was also asleep in the seat behind, his 'darkas' hung precariously on the tip of his nose and his lip hanging down. The stewardess walked past and accidently nudged him awake.

Across the aisle Roxanne was engrossed in discussion with the other members of her management team. They were full of enthusiasm at the prospect of enlisting new reggae acts, and made it very clear that they felt Delroy was the right man to spearhead that initiative.

And as if that hadn't been enough, Terence Wynn's agent

had contacted Hector after their performance at the Apollo. They wanted Simba to record a re-work 'In the Mood For Some Action' just as he did it that night in Harlem.

Two weeks later the remixed single featuring Simba Ranking had shot into the number nine position on the US charts.

It seemed the Ranking could do no wrong.

"Weh you deh pon, don?"

Hector popped his head around the seat, pushing his 'darkas' back into position. "Me tell you already seh you t'ink too much, star. Leave dat to me."

"Me still ah try to tek it all in boss."

"Believe it man!" Hector answered. "Ah dis we did ah work hard for, ah tek risk for, an' see it yah. A high profile dat ah get better, day in day out. An' a week away from York an' de mix up. No more skipping gun shot, rude bwoy."

"Freedom," Delroy added.

"Nuh dat me ah show yuh, man."

They had a smooth passage through immigration and as Delroy and the others made their way past the lines of customs officers they were immediately met by a British Airways Special Services agent.

Roxanne rushed forward to hug her.

"Its been a long time, Susan."

"Too long," the agent replied, taking Roxanne's hand in hers. "I hope you won't be too busy and we'll have time to catch up on some gossip."

"Of course we will," she chuckled. "But not before I introduce you to my associates."

The airport was hectic but Susan bustled them through the baggage hall and customs and led them to where their two chauffeurs awaited. She said goodbye there with a promise to meet up at some later date.

"Come and meet the guys," beamed Roxanne excitedly, introducing Devon, her long-time driver. The other chauffeur she was not familiar with. "You're new to the team," Roxanne said. "Sorry, I don't know your name."

"Michael," the black driver answered with a smile.

"Glad you're on board, Michael."

He nodded and shook her hand warmly.

"Respect!" Delroy said shaking both men's hands in turn. "I hope de man dem know London, star, becah I waan see everyt'ing."

"That's no problem, boss," Michael promised. "You won't miss a thing."

"Me ah go hol you 'pon dat."

Delroy was excited by the prospect of freedom as he shouldered his way through the crowds to the coolness of outdoors. He and Monique could relax, if only for a week, knowing that the Saint couldn't possibly have learned that they were in England. He'd asked Roxanne not to leak anything to the press about his appearance at the Reggae Awards, and only Moses and his family knew they were going. Now, in London for the first time, he would let nothing upset him. As he walked his eyes scanned the surroundings, and suddenly Simba blinked in shock. He'd seen someone to his right that should not be here...

His heart skipped a beat.

Through the crowd he could just make out a man wearing a baseball cap with black and white hexagonal patterns.

De man who try lick me inna de Trans-Am!

His mind warped back to the attempt on their lives in New York as his frenzied thoughts tried to compare the figure in the crowd with the vivid memory of his would-be assassin.

Coincidence, surely!

He tried to rationalise it.

Caps like that must be owned by thousands of people all over the place. Cool it, Ranking.

He tried to relax his still-taut muscles but as soon as he convinced himself of how stupid he was being, he glimpsed the shimmer of gold from either a chopperetta or wrist band.

The shooter had the self-same gold band around his wrist.

252

He tried to follow the man's progress through the flux of bodies, but he simply disappeared from view.

"Is everything all right?" Monique enquired. He had let go of her hand in his panic, and she reached for it again.

"It safe baby, jus' a man me t'ink me know." He smiled weakly, trying to reassure her and himself that everything was alright…but now he wasn't so sure.

Harlesden was last on their list of places to see after two days of discovering the city. Simba had wanted the name of a good barber and Michael had mentioned a place on Church Road. He had phoned up the shop in advance to make an appointment.

They had dropped Monique and Roxanne off in Oxford Street then Michael, their driver, had woven his way from the West End to north west London. Despite the light November drizzle it was still a bustling Saturday afternoon.

"This is it, boss!" Michael said proudly as Hector and Delroy stepped out of the Lexus.

"This place is like a second home to me bredrins," he explained. "Even though I live in Kilburn, I'm here regularly buying food or gambling at my spar's place or…"

"Raasclaat!" echoed across from the market stall on the other side of the road, followed by raucous laughter.

"My kinda place, man," Delroy said, grinning. "It look like a black man run t'ings yahso."

"Yah man," Michael laughed. "Most of the business people are black and this area is controlled by Indians and black people. Things come a far way from when my parents came here in the fifties. But we still have a far way to go."

"Me nevah really t'ink seh place ah England look like dis," said Hector, his hands rammed deeply into his pockets. "It remind me ah parts ah Brooklyn or even Jamaica, Queens. Me love de vibes, man, but de weather nah seh not'n."

"That's England for you boss, get used to it."

A traffic warden broke into their conversation, politely asking Michael to move along.

"Bloodfire," Delroy burst out laughing. "Dem English

people have manners' fe kill, eh man. De Yankee dem nah deal with you dem way deh, yuh know."

"Face card," Michael answered. "Don't let them fool you, them people yah can be vicious with a smile." The engine whispered to life as Michael pulled away from the curb.

"Pick you up an hour from now, alright," he called back.

"Safe," said Hector, looking over at Delroy.

"Yeah man," Delroy nodded in agreement. "Dat safe, Mikey."

Michael was more relieved to leave than he could have admitted to them. He had a rendezvous to make in south London and his present boss didn't like it when he was late. In fact he would get really pissed off, with his heated Jamaican temperament if Michael waltzed in even ten minutes past their meeting time.

Fuck it!

The best thing for him to do was to relax and try not stress himself, but the traffic would make him tense and irritable by the time he arrived. He would have enough to cope with as it was dealing with Simba Ranking.

Michael opened his jacket and released the strap on his shoulder holster. Keeping his eyes on the road he pulled out his shiny Smith and Wesson and placed it on the seat beside him.

That's better, he thought and turned his radio to Choice FM.

Delroy met Hector in the fast food restaurant after 'reasoning' with some of the local tradespeople. He had just left the Avantgarde clothes shop, promising George the proprietor he'd be back for a 'murda' suit he saw, and then he'd bought a large cup of beef and pumpkin soup from the Scandal Takeaway. Hector chewed on a fry as Delroy sat down.

"Any idea ah how we ah go deal wid de Saint, when we get back a New York?" he asked.

Delroy sipped at his broth and chewed a piece of salted

beef. He slowly looked up at his friend.

"De only plan me have is fe tek out dis gun bwoy before him tek me out."

"Yuh ah go risk yuh career an' life. It nuh worth it, don."

"But me nuh have no other choice. Yuh have a bettah solution?"

Hector was silent.

"Me nah run up and dung fe de rest ah me life, rude bwoy," Simba continued. "Music come first, don, but me haffe get de bwoy St. John off me back. An' fe do dat badness haffe gwan."

"It can turn out worst fe you Simba. T'ink good 'bout it."

Delroy was adamant.

"De Saint haffe go dung, nuh matter what risks me tek. I man want to be alive when my yout' born. But if me haffe dead, then me ah tek him an' nuff ah him bwoy dem wid me."

The last of his soup was slurped down in tense silence. He stood up soon afterwards, changing the subject.

"So whe' dis Barber Plaza place deh, Hector?"

He shrugged.

"Jus' round de corner, Michael seh. We can find it, man."

"De barber brother name...Chips," Simba said finally, after struggling to remember.

"An we appointment is about...now," replied Hector consulting his watch.

"So mek we see if dem England yout' yah bad like de New York head man dem nuh."

They walked outside thinking only of progress and headed for their appointment.

THIRTY-NINE

Delroy lay on his back and stared at the elaborate design on the ceiling. Their suite at the Marble Arch Hilton was opulent, to say the least, and when he'd first entered it he had thought there'd been some mistake. Monique had introduced him to some of the top hotels in Kingston, but he had never been in a suite before.

The large sitting room had recently been decorated and the brilliant white walls blended coolly with a white leather sofa. The bedroom housed a king-size bed covered with silk sheets, and the adjoining bathroom boasted a seashell-shaped jacuzzi.

Ah fe me time now, thought Simba as he lay thinking about how far he had come in so little time. Monique lay beside him with her head on his chest, stroking his erection.

"How are you feeling, loverman?" she whispered.

"Me safe, man," he answered. "A long time me ah wait fe dis."

He turned to face her, the scent of her body spiced with a mild perfume that never failed to arouse him.

Grudgingly, he was starting to realise just how lucky he was.

Monique already knew.

She leaned over him and read his facial expressions briefly, then kissed him full on the lips.

"This is like old times," she said, a slight smile on her lips. "But without the fear of him. I'm enjoying being with you more now than ever."

The Ranking laughed out loud, wrapping his arms around her shoulders.

"You an' a hundred other gal," he snickered.

"Don't get carried away now." She smiled. "You know exactly what I'm trying to say."

"Jus' cool man, me know wha you a deal wid." He paused, becoming serious. "I man respect you even more fe it. One ah dem day yah, no more running. But fe now, mek we just tek one day at a time, seen?"

Monique's expression changed as the enormity of their problem presented itself again. She was dreading going back to New York after this; she had spoken to Andrew Humphries twice since their first phone call, but he was proving to be of little help. He told her his enquires had been fruitless, but her underlying feeling was that he was hiding something from her.

But what?

Simba noticed the change in her and playfully nibbled around her exposed nipples. Her despondency was gone in seconds, and like children they play-fought, Monique giggling hysterically as Simba tickled her.

They left the Hilton at six in the evening in a three-car convoy, Michael's Lexus in front and tailed by two Jaguars, their occupants excited and expectant.

Delroy sat up straight on the back seat of the Lexus, he was calm but bursting with energy as he joked with Michael. Monique sat close to him; her hair glistened in the passing car lights, a solitary curl falling over her forehead; her elegant black dress shimmered when she moved, highlighting her breasts and hips.

The deejay shifted his backside in his seat; he felt glad she was with him but couldn't miss the concern in her eyes. He knew she was tense not only because of their dilemma but also because this was an important night for him. Hector was excited but kept telling Simba to keep calm.

The Ranking had no worries, though. He was relaxed and confident. Everything was running smoothly. Michael was keeping a respectable distance from the lead black Jaguar which contained Roxanne and two more passengers.

Simba looked back through the rear window to the third car in the convoy, which was transporting Hector and a girl from Pony marketing department.

Tonight, he would really make a mark. He wouldn't disappoint.

He watched cars and buildings flashing by. His fingers drummed in time to Ini Kamoze's *Here Comes the Hotstepper*, and he wondered what his first meeting with 'kernel' David Rodigan would be like.

The Kiss FM studios was their first stop-off for his interview with 'Roddy'. Then it was straight on to the Hackney Empire for his PA at the British Reggae Awards. The timing would be tight but his manager was leaving nothing to chance; Simba was very impressed with Roxanne's professionalism.

He heard a rumble from under the car that he couldn't ignore any longer.

"Shit, a flat," said Michael. "I'll have to pull in a petrol station to change it. Just give me 'bout ten minutes."

Michael pulled the car into the Texaco station. Roxanne's car had driven on out of sight, her driver not knowing they had stopped. When she realised she'd lost them, Roxanne called him on the mobile. Hector's driver had followed the Lexus into the gas station and parked up on the other side of the gas pumps.

It had begun to rain lightly; Michael was cursing, vexed at the fact that he had to change the tyre. Monique was suspicious. Simba tried to relax her.

"Relax," he said. "De man ah work 'pon it. We will be outta dis place yah inna no time."

Two cars pulled in behind Hector's Jaguar; he was wondering whether to brave the rain and go into the station's shop. He looked over at the newcomers, admiring the sleek European bodywork.

A 9000 CS Saab, ah it dat, he decided after some deliberating. The other car was unfamiliar to him, and he gave up trying to guess the make and model.

The Pony girl was engrossed in her book and the driver had pulled his cap over his eyes for a quick nap. The engineer decided to stretch his legs. He was about to make a dash to Delroy in the Lexus; despite the cold and rain, it was better than being couped up in the car.

Before he could open his door, four men got out of the cars behind them.

The 'youts' walked casually over to where Michael was crouched; too casual for black people in the rain.

Hector began to feel very nervous. He wiped the condensation from the window and watched the men very keenly.

They headed across the slick tarmac looking over their shoulders and eyeing the open-all-hours shop with the Asian attendant standing inside. One of the men had a red bandana tied around his head and was hunched in an oversize Click jacket. The one leading the group seemed unaware of the freezing rain. His furry Kangol hat was twisted to the back and his Karl Kani suit absorbed the light flurry.

They passed the gas pumps, breaking into two groups of two as they approached the bent-over figure of Michael.

He looked up as he heard the splashing of their feet behind him. Half-expecting Hector, he was surprised to find two men looming over him and another one a step behind.

"Safe!" he said, looking at both men in turn. "You alright, boss?"

The huge man in front, Big Bout Yah, reached down, grabbed Michael by his jacket collar, and hauled the driver up to his feet without showing any sign of effort.

Natty, the smaller of the pair, grinned through his thick lips and explained:

"We want de Ranking, driver. You ah go bring him out? Or you want me draw him out?"

His furry Kangol glistened with rain. He waited.

This doesn't make sense, Hector thought as he looked on. *For crying out loud, why is Michael grinning?*

The driver looked innocently bemused, as if he was unsure of what was happening. They didn't expect that, and the big man took just an instant — an instant too long — to react. Michael suddenly spun his body around back-stepped, leaving his jacket dangling limply in the man's hands.

Shit, he thought. His cover was blown. He'd fucked up.

If he could only get to the gun in the car...

His move had aced them, but they recovered quickly. Natty looked at his 'sparring partner' in disgust, pulled his Browning GP35 with his right hand and completed a low sweeping turn, then placed his shot and fired.

Michael had slid across the bonnet of the Lexus and tumbled over the other side, heading for the car door.

Natty's pistol kicked his hand and wrist back as his shot burst through the windscreen and the driver's door. The slug tore through Michael's shoulder.

His body jackknifed backwards in a spray of shattered clavicle and blood.

The single discharge thundered through the Ranking's head, jerking him away from his conversation with Monique. That was the first they knew about it.

"Raasclaat!"

He looked desperately around. The windshield shattered, spraying them with chunks of glass; Monique screamed; shock froze Simba to the seat momentarily.

Wha' de bumboclaat ah gwan?

He kicked the back door of the Lexus open. It hit solid flesh and bone and stopped, as a massive shadow loomed over him. The big man gripped the door firmly, his fingers making a grotesque squeaking sound on the inside of the window.

The Ranking rolled back and kicked again, aiming his heel at the huge fingers. He was rewarded with a muffled grunt of pain as the giant let go.

Here was their chance — maybe their only one.

Turning to grab Monique's wrist, he saw her leaving through the far door. He twisted and bounced over the back seat across the width of the car and shot out into the open air after her...following her into the arms of the second team.

Simba didn't see the massive fist coming at him; but his reflexes were operating independently — and fast. He side-stepped the wheeling blow, but there was no space to avoid it completely and he stumbled against the side of the car, hitting his head. The gash that opened up on his forehead immediately spurted blood.

Simba was disoriented. Big Bout Yah grabbed Simba's shoulders and slammed the deejay's head twice against the bodywork of the Lexus.

Simba's world turned topsy-turvy and fell into his assailant's ugly face, distorted into an even more horrific mask as everything around him slowed down. Voices boomed, echoing through his head like a hollow canyon. He struggled weakly against the sheet of darkness overcoming him but it was pointless.

His muscles relaxed and his will to remain conscious disappeared.

He sunk deep into darkness.

Hector saw Michael forced backwards in a spray of blood.

He watched helplessly as the man in the Karl Kani suit lowered the gun and signalled his two men, who brought Monique kicking and screaming over to him.

Why the fuck, of all the limousines in the entire world, did I end up in the only one without a phone!?

Michael was down on the cold wet concrete writhing in agony, his teeth clenched, trying to stem the flow of blood with his left hand, but Delroy was nowhere to be seen.

It seemed like hours before Hector's leg muscles would unlock and allow him to leave the car and duck behind the perspex siding of a car-wash.

No use rushing into this, he had to think fast and hope Simba was managing to stay alive.

He peered through the siding of the car wash at the man with the gun slapping Monique viciously in the face. His voice boomed across the forecourt.

"Wha' you ah do gal, a dis yah dis me."

The two men holding her laughed out loud. The fourth man — six feet plus and built like a brick outhouse — emerged with Delroy slung over his broad shoulders like an old carpet.

He looked like he was in a bad way, but he didn't look dead. Hector was trying to wish the Jaguar away into thin air when he saw that Devon, their driver, had woken up with the gunshot; Hector gestured frantically for him to stay put.

Simba's limp body was dumped in the back of the Saab. Monique was pushed into the other car.

Has the attendant phoned the police, or decided not to get involved? Either way there was no sign of him.

The men were in their cars and preparing to pull away when Hector took a chance and sprinted through the drizzle to Michael. He dived behind the shattered door of the Lexus and looked through the gaping hole where the window had been; the gunmen hadn't seen him, and hadn't connected the parked Jaguar with Delroy.

Michael wasn't moving, and didn't seem to be breathing. Hector picked up his wrist and checked. He was still alive. Michael moaned and turned over on his back; his eyes flickered open.

The engineer sighed his relief.

"You alright, boss?" Hector rasped.

Michael nodded and attempted a smile, but winced with pain at his effort.

"Never felt better."

"Yah joke at a time like dis man, you ah lose blood, star, an' you need a hospital an' quick."

He cradled the driver's head on his knees. Michael coughed and twisted his head slightly to look into Hector's eyes gulping out his words in agonising spurts.

"There's no time for that, Hector. Dem man deh are members of the Jungle Ites Posse. Simba is a dead man...if them leave an' we lose them...you must...leave me if you

262

want see you bredrin alive."

"How—?"

"Me know all this," the driver gulped hard, "because I'm...involved in a police operation. We've been following your movements and theirs...from Jamaica across the States and now...here..."

Michael's eyes flickered and then closed with pain.

"...Simba made the man, de Jamaican government ah investigate, make a serious mistake...fuck it..."

Michael fumbled a small radio out of his pants pocket and pushed it into Hector's wet hands. The sound of the two cars moving off seemed to boost the injured driver from his weakened state. Hector popped his head up again to see the Saab turning right into the traffic. The red eye of its roof-mounted brake light glared through the rain at him.

"Me alright!" Michael wheezed. "Just follow dem an' call me. I need to know where they end up!"

Hector nodded.

"Then for fuck sake, get going nuh."

Michael coughed blood as Hector scurried back to the Jaguar. He dragged the driver and the girl out of the car and told them to call the police.

They looked at him blankly as he drove off.

Hector pulled his Jaguar smoothly out into the flowing traffic and accelerated until the Saab and the second car were about four cars ahead of him. He thought it over and decided that things wouldn't get any worse while they were driving. At least he had some time to come up with a plan of action.

So the Saint had tracked Delroy and Monique to England; the man was insane. And all the police in the world were tracking the bastard themselves.

What the fuck had Simba got himself involved in?

A red light came up before the Jaguar. If he stopped, he would lose them for sure. Hector pressed the gas pedal and yanked the wheel right. The Jag responded immediately its back end sliding slightly to the left, its underbelly sparking as it hit the edge of a pedestrian island, but Hector soon had the car back under control.

He checked his speedo. He was clocking a steady fifty as he moved into position two cars behind them. No ideas had come to him yet and he was becoming desperate. What would he do when the cars stopped? How could he deal with armed killers?

Moments later the engineer was startled by a high pitched siren close behind him.

Shit!

He glimpsed the white helmet of an English motorcycle cop in the rear-view mirror. He couldn't stop now. Simba and Monique's life depended on it. Hector ignored the policeman and kept his speed up.

The cycle cop's K-100 moved forward to nudge wickedly close to the Jaguar's fender. Hector slowed the luxury car down. Then when the car was almost at a crawl the engineer suddenly swung the car left, clipping the bike's front wheel and sending it careening onto the pavement.

It was a moment of madness, but right then he didn't care one way or the other what had happened to the cop. His eyes were fixed on the two cars just ahead of him. His only concern now was saving his 'spar' and his 'spar's' woman.

His only problem was, he had not figured out how yet.

FORTY

The tenth floor Special Branch incident room at New Scotland Yard was a hive of activity.

Andrew Humphries was proud to be a part of such a ground-breaking collaboration.

The Brigadier was standing amid the organised confusion, leaning over a table with a large scale map of north London spread over it. He wrinkled his nose in the smoky atmosphere and looked over at the young Met officer drawing a ring around part of Hackney with a blue marker.

The Brigadier shook his head. A grey-jacketed man raised his left hand to them and prominently showed his five fingers then swiftly refocused on the communication equipment.

The freckle-faced Met Officer responded by rubbing off the circle on the perspex digital map table and cleared his throat in the direction of the Brigadier.

"Sir," he said, "the man from ME5 has just indicated to me he has five minutes to triangulate the exact position of Michael's car. And I'm estimating we should be able to deploy your men and the Force Firearms Unit in armed response vehicles in under fifteen minutes. It's a pity that American bloke didn't call in the exact details of his whereabouts…"

"Let's be t'ankful fe small mercies, young man," the Brigadier added. "If Hector hadn't run the motorcycle cop off de road then we wouldn't have been able to narrow things down to this part of London."

"All we can hope for now, sir, is that the Air Support Unit spots the Jaguar before we do. Commander Higgles wasn't able to spare more than one helicopter from Lippits Hill — but we'll keep our fingers crossed, eh?"

The Brigadier nodded his agreement just as another circle of light appeared on the map table. The officer marked the impression as the blinking light went out.

"Any time now, Brigadier," the officer said, forcing a smile.

Humphries turned away from him and walked over to his temporary workstation on the far end of the room. He flicked through some files and took up his diary of engagements. A stocky Jamaican in bulging blue fatigues came over to him.

"Ah wha', Danny!" the ambassador said, looking up at the man.

"We start get in some ah de faxes boss, from Yard and New York…"

He handed them over and Humphries viewed the streaky photo representations of the suspected Jungle Ites posse members who were now in London with the Saint.

Their profiles read like chronicles from the wild west; murder, attempted murder, robbery, rape and drug trafficking featured prominently.

The Saint would have come over with four personal bodyguards, then there was Tuffy…God knows how many men would accompany him.

He leaned back in his chair and called over a glum-faced detective from the 'Yardie Unit', SO11, then passed on his informed guess at the number of armed gangsters present at the scene.

Two years of painstaking surveillance, undercover work and information gathering was coming together, and it seemed that the Saint — one of the 'big six' suspected by the government on corruption charges — was about to be trapped because he'd broken his own cardinal rule: 'let the garbage men take the garbage out'.

The Saint was getting sloppy.

A steaming cup of coffee was pushed in front of him and he immediately took a sip from it. The bitter liquid coursed through him and the caffeine went to work on a tired body and mind. But then...

Beep! Beep! Beep!

The map table's high-pitched sound bursts stirred him from his trance and he scurried over to join the other officers around the table.

"What de raas is happening, sergeant?" asked the Brigadier in a breathless whisper.

A middle-aged white man turned to face him; a personal comm link was attached to his ear and weaved its way to a protruding mike bobbing near his lips.

"The triangulation process used by ME5 to locate the car has come up trumps, sir. We've mobilised all units and should be able to move you and Commander Higgles to the scene as soon as our blokes are in position."

Men were throwing on jackets and darting through the doors.

The Brigadier wiped a film of sweat from his forehead and looked at his own administrative staff busily helping their English counterparts.

It was good to know he'd be right there when Operation 'Clean Sweep' ended, one way or the other.

He strapped on his pistol and headed for the transport.

Unfamiliar pain...a throbbing headache and stiffened limbs...the vague hammering of his heart. And then...the veil of darkness lifted.

Delroy opened his eyes, dazed.

He blinked, triggering a pounding earthquake inside his skull. He felt nauseous and his nose and the side of his head throbbed with a dull pain.

A picture of the night's events was returning to his mind. He licked his dry lips and his tongue dislodged flakes of blood that dropped down onto his grubby shirt. He tried to raise his hand to examine the gash above his lip, but he was held fast by ropes that bound him hand and foot.

Delroy could feel the cold steel of a car bumper against the back of his leg as he rose up from a lying position on a rusty bonnet, his face pointing to the ceiling; his head swirled. Simba was strapped across the front end of an old yellow Datsun, his back facing its cracked windscreen. Both his hands were outstretched and his feet together. He could stand up but his movement was restricted. The ropes tied around his wrists were anchored to the steering wheel, the ropes at his feet were tied securely to the axle underneath.

He braced himself against the ropes and heaved, but it was pointless. He was trussed up like a 'prize fowl', ready for a modern-day crucifixion...in a damn car park, of all places.

All his senses seemed to be realigning themselves; his vision was fighting the glare of headlights to make out the silent silhouettes in the distance. Then, as two of them approached him, their features became clear. When they were about five paces away his heart sank; it couldn't be worse than this.

Monique... an' de bwoy Saint standing by her!

All his efforts to out-smart Hugh St. John had come to nothing. Now the man stood before him gloating, gripping Monique's wrist and glaring at him.

Two gunmen came to his side, their eyes flickering with intense hatred. The Saint released Monique from his grip and adjusted his grey pinstripe suit.

"How it feel to be a man who ah go experience a slow and painful death, Simba Ranking? You nuh, I find it hard to believe dat you, an uneducated 'ghetto yout', was fucking my wife, dragging my name through de shit and then running around New York with my property, my woman."

He paused, drawing Monique close to him again.

"Did you t'ink you could run from me forever, boy? Nobody who fuck wid me an' my family can escape me."

"What family are you talking about, Hugh?" Monique spat. "You haven't got a fucking family."

He laughed hollowly. Delroy watched him with disgust as he ranted. He hawked and spit. A globule of blood and saliva shot in the Saint's direction, splattering his newly-acquired Savile Row suit.

The Saint flinched, looking down at his soiled breast pocket and then back at Simba. He strode up to him his eyes ablaze and lashed out with the back of his ringed hands, twice. Monique squealed and tried to rush to Simba's side but one of the gunmen held her back.

"Please don't hurt him, Hugh! Please!" The Saint came back to her and grabbed her by the lower jaw, forcefully shutting her mouth, smearing her lipstick clown-like over her cheeks and nose.

"Shut de fuck up gal, you should be begging for your own life, not for this miserable piece of shit. Him is a raas animal, yuh nuh see dat?" he shouted. "An' I should have expected a dog like you to react like a fucking dog. No matter what."

He stared at Simba and shook his head. He took out a white handkerchief from his jacket pocket and wiped the spit from the terylene and wool jacket.

"But me will forgive you, I will gain my pleasure watching you squirm and then die with the knowledge dat dis whore ah go lose her pickney an' be treated to the pleasures of dis…"

He grabbed his crotch and leered. Delroy bucked against the ropes, trying fruitlessly to get at 'de high colour raas' throat, but he knew the ropes would not give way to his weakened effort.

He screamed curses at him

"Why you nuh let me go then, batty bwoy? An' mek we deal wid de case, man to man. Or is jus woman yuh have de strength for? You nuh seh yuh a rude bwoy, wha' happen!" Simba's shouts came out as streams of vapour from his mouth.

Some of the men around snickered.

"So de puss hasn't got your tongue after all, Mr Deejay man, maybe you can compose a lyrics in hell 'bout dis. It would definitely become a number one, don't you t'ink?"

"You nah get weh wid dis, pussy hole, if you harm her. Some weh, some how you ah go pay fe dat. Yah hear me!!!"

The Ranking's tone became measured this time, uncannily cool and deadly serious.

"If you dida tek care a business, me wouldn't inna business. You ah de one who fuck up an' then you waan blame her. Let her go man, you know she pregnant. Fe once inna you bloodclaat life show some mercy."

Simba's voice cracked with emotion.

"A dungtown man with a conscience."

The Saint applauded, his hand claps echoing sharply off the concrete walls. "But it's too late for dat, just like it is too late fe compromises. Nobody can cross me and live to tell de tale."

He massaged Monique's breasts with the palm of his hand. She tried to fight it, but she was held fast.

"How you manage to hol' onto a woman like this bwoy, Obeah?"

He flung back his brown hair and cackled hideously.

"THEN I AM THE WITCH DOCTOR."

His laughter trailed away and he was serious again.

Simba looked upon the madman pacing. Excited. What Simba would give to be free.

He was good as dead.

It was said that dying men become more aware of everything happening around them, and Simba believed this. His fear-heightened senses picked up the sounds of droning cars, distant music, the dripping of water on concrete and even a far-away helicopter.

Then he thought of Mama.

She would know nothing of his whereabouts, she would just hear that her one son had disappeared off the face of the earth. He breathed deeply as panic threatened to overcome him.

Hugh St. John came a step closer, pulling Monique with him, moving his roving hand from her breasts to her stomach.

To the left of Simba's view two men stepped out from the shadows to stand beside St. John.

Tuffy smiled broadly and so did his 'sparring' partner. He was still wearing his trademark hexagonal-patterned black and white cap.

Tuffy was decked out in a crisp designer shirt especially for the occasion and arrogantly had his gun slung under his arm in open view.

"This is de man," Saint said, patting Tuffy on his shoulder and motioning to the man beside him, "who you should thank for a job well done. Then wid my brilliant scheme, I brought you here." He paused, the elaborate trap he had set still amusing him. "You nevah know dat me get yuh first major break in the music business, bwoy. I created you. It was a recommendation from me dat set you up wid Pony Records."

Simba stared at him blankly, surprise sapping his emotions.

"Yes, even yuh manager help trap you too. You wouldn't believe what a woman will tell you after a good fuck," he snickered. "But she nevah know 'bout dis surprise party me plan fe you. Dat was my secret."

Delroy kissed his teeth loudly but did not give him the pleasure of a reply. The Saint continued to edge closer to him, his ice-cold, blue eyes piercing.

"So you t'ink I'm a animal like you, eh?"

He laughed his annoying cackle again.

"Even though you were fucking my wife behind me back — and maybe even in my bed — I'm going to show you dat the Saint is not like you. Him nuh hide. Him do him t'ings up front. Like a man. But a bwoy like you wouldn't understand dat."

St. John stopped a breath away from the searing gaze of his captive. "Say goodbye to de whore; I'm in a good mood."

Monique stood in front of Simba. Her eyes were wet with tears as she flung her arms around him and held him close.

"I love you," she whispered, and before he could

respond, the Saint brutally wheeled her away from him leaving only the smell of her sweet perfume.

St. John sunk back into the gloom with his soldiers. He was tiring of the game now, and anticipating a celebratory gambling binge at The Ritz. His many sleepless nights were about to be over, and The Saint was now eager for the process to proceed without further ado.

He'd had his fun, now it was showtime.

He nodded to a man who was leaning idly against the wreck of an old Escort a few feet behind him. The man stood straight.

"It was an invigorating chase," he shouted back at Simba. "But me 'fraid I have more pressing t'ings on me agenda. We will meet in hell, lover man."

"Dat cool!" Simba growled. "Me ah wait 'pon you, batty bwoy."

St. John's hand fell to his side as if he was starting a Grand Prix race and the man inside the Escort gunned its rattling engine to life.

With a hacking gear change and the grating clutch of oil-free bearings the car shot off.

Its front end lifted and its tail swung on the slippery concrete.

The wheels spun, issuing oil-tainted smoke before it gained a grip on its course towards a helpless Simba Ranking and certain death.

Simba was rooted to the spot, his muscles numb and locked rigid. As the Escort bore down on him he glared into the headlamps that would bring the end of his life. Simba was sure he could hear the goading of St. John in the distance wishing, willing the car to move faster, to end it.

Simba's eyes were wide with terror.

This is not how it should end.

The sound of two shots from a high-powered weapon exploded through the air at the same moment as the windshield of the oncoming car shattered. The driver's head jerked backwards and the car swerved, finally crashing into a wall.

It took a split-second for Simba to realise what had happened. *Someone up there wants me alive.*

'Raases' and 'bloodclaats' erupted from the watching gun men.

IT WAS A STING.

Simba looked up. The helicopter he had heard in the distance was hovering above. He rejoiced as he stared into the smiling face of a police pilot. An armed policeman rushed towards him and cut him free, even as bullets tore around them.

Where was Monique? Simba looked to his left to see armed police loping forward. Suddenly there was an ear-splitting discharge as a sawn-off double barrelled shotgun flashed from his far right, mangling the chest of the policeman who had freed him. The buckshot burst through his Kevlar vest and showered the wall behind him in an explosive gush of blood and fabric.

The thought of the dying policeman's family flashed through Simba's head. He remembered his father.

But he had to *move* — get to Monique before the Saint.

Simba crawled closer to the fatally wounded policeman and picked up the Heckler and Koch MP5 that lay beside him, then made his way forward.

He kept low, close to the wall, moving as quickly as possible under the continuing hail of bullets. He was more alert than he'd ever been, despite the pounding in his head, and when a figure way ahead of him ducked into a car shielded by two other cars he recognised it as Monique.

He made to move but was forced back by two bullets whizzing past his ear. Their closeness made him roll to his right, slamming hard against one of the car park's pillars and thrusting his MP5 forward in the direction of the fire.

The man trying to pin him down was the giant who had knocked him unconscious at the gas station. Bigga's gun hand was tilted at an angle as he weaved his way through the crossfire towards Simba. The man's tactics were suicidal; he was standing up straight amidst ricocheting bullets, heading towards the deejay with weapon raised. Simba fell to his stomach, pushing himself to his right and rolled desperately.

A round of bullets dug into the ground where the Ranking had been laying seconds before, but as Big Bout Yah swung around and aimed again, Simba fired his submachine gun. The MP5 bucked in his hand. The bullets sprayed across the yardie's path just as he ducked behind a column, and most of the rounds tore into the masonry. But one bullet sneaked by, nicking the big man's thigh, ripping his trouser leg and sending him spinning sideways in a flurry of arms and legs. With two massive strides Simba was at the injured man's side, just as he reached for the 'matic that had been knocked from his hand.

The Ranking kicked the pistol away and quickly dropped to his knees to ram the gun butt into the man's neck.

Big Bout Yah was quicker and stronger than he expected.

He raised his massive hand and fired a scorching fist to the side of the Ranking's head, sending him reeling backwards. Big Bout Yah jumped to his feet, blood oozing down his thigh. Simba was knocked hard to the floor, his senses tumbling for just a moment, but he quickly clambered back to his unsteady feet and tried to aim his MP5.

As he raised his weapon the man reached for the gun slung around Simba's neck and lifted him off his feet. It was so quick and unexpected that Simba wasn't able to take a breath before the leather gun strap was around his neck and he was being choked.

Simba thrashed desperately, but the big man's strength was too much for him.

He couldn't take a breath.

Me nuh dead yet, bwoy.

He dug his fingers into the giant's ramrod-stiff arms, his nails drawing blood like talons and making Big Bout Yah throw back his head and grunt. Simba was blacking out. He lifted his body up off the ground with the little strength he had left, the big man's arms buckling under the added pressure and his grip loosening. Simba shook his head groggily, gasping for air and with one unbroken movement he drop-kicked the killer in his groin.

Big Bout Yah let out a bellowing shriek, swayed and then his legs buckled. He fell forward, releasing the hold on the Ranking's throat.

But he was trying again to regain it.

Simba wasn't going to be caught out twice. He swung the butt of his weapon hard against the back of the yardie's neck.

A dull whack sounded on impact as Big Bout Yah, swayed like a big Guango tree and slumped forward on his knees. His eyes rolled in their sockets and fell in an untidy heap.

Badda bloodclaat man.

The gunfire had now died down, to sporadic well-placed shots. Delroy looked behind him and glimpsed the police shackling some surviving yardies with plastic cuffs.

Further away, on the other side of the car park he could just make out the figure of Monique, being dragged by St. John towards the stairs to the ground floor.

Simba's relief that she was uninjured gave him added strength. *"Saint!"* he screamed out. "Me want *YOU*, bwoy!"

The Saint stopped and turned around slowly, gripping Monique by the waist and forcing a small Beretta against her temple.

"Wha' you ah try do, ghetto bwoy?" the Saint shouted. "Frighten me? You cyan take me widout harming dis—"

He jammed the gun with more force into Monique's stomach.

"Do you want to risk me splattering your yout' all over de floor. You ah idiot."

Simba met his stare as plumes of smoke obscured their view of each other for seconds at a time. Simba's face twisted and his eyes narrowed.

"As long as yuh dead, batty bwoy, me nuh give a fuck how me do it." Simba paused and continued that unconvincing line.

The Saint laughed out again.

"Don't bullshit me, young yout. I know you wouldn't do anyt'ing to hurt her, now would you?"

Tuffy moved from the doorway leading to the flight of stairs like a ghost and spoke impatiently.

"Drop de raasclaat gun, Missa Ranking, yah waste yuh time 'pon dis. Jus' slowly kick it over to me an' I man promise yuh death will be quick."

Simba obeyed, dropping the H&K with a heavy clank in front of him and pushing it forward with his foot.

"I have to give it to you, Simba. You is a hard man fe dead," the Saint leered, "but you are out of your league here."

St. John raised the Beretta, training it on Delroy's unprotected forehead, and forced his hand up Monique's soiled dress to massage the inside of her thigh. Monique spat in his face.

Gunshots still exploded in the background.

"You will die seeing de whore screaming for more of the Saint."

St. John ripped Monique's knickers off and flung them in Simba's direction.

"Smell dat fe de last time, ghetto bwoy."

Inside Monique, something snapped.

Shame, anger, hatred, at that moment she didn't care.

Her eyes seemed to glow with fire as something that had been seething deep inside her throughout this whole ordeal finally surfaced — and it came up bringing with it all the rage and hatred that only a black woman could muster.

She lashed out viciously, not caring whether she lived or died, knocking the small gun out of the Saint's grip. Her long false nails raked a bloody highway straight across his face. He screamed and clawed at his wound, and Monique in shock collapsed at his feet.

Simba acted quickly.

In what felt like a heartbeat, the Ranking was diving towards him.

The man who had stuck by Tuffy's side throughout the whole affair suddenly came to life as Simba headed towards the Saint. He fired his Wildey Auto, dipping low and rapidly pulling the trigger. It thundered its discharge as the slug whizzed by Simba's shoulder and slammed into the ceiling. Tuffy slunk back near the stairway door and took aim but it was much too late.

Simba came at St John with one intention, 'to kill, cramp an' paralyse'.

He reached the politician in seconds, seeing the image of his dead father before him.

His anger rose beyond his control.

St. John heard him, felt his presence but his own blood was trickling into his eyes and his wild swinging fists connected with the air as the Ranking fired his right foot downwards and grabbed the older man by the shoulders, forcing him onto his knees. The air left his lungs violently as one of the Saint's ribs cracked. Simba delivered a vicious snap kick to his side, then another blow shattered the politician's knee joint.

A splinter of white bone shot outwards through flesh, like a hollow piece of wood.

His screams could be heard over the crackling flames. But Simba was past caring as he yanked him up to eye level and drove his forehead into the curve of his nose. There was a crack of heads and the Saint's body slumped forward, a low moan coming from his bleeding lips.

And, as the smoke cleared a little, he heard metal against metal as the weapons behind him 'went 'pon cock'.

In his eagerness to reach his father's killer, his momentum had left his back towards the staircase. The same staircase which was covered by Tuffy and his cohorts.

Simba spun round…heaving the unconscious body of the politician around in front of him.

The night exploded again with the chatter of guns as the gun men spewed hot metal indiscriminately. The force of the bullets hammered St. John's body and slammed Simba backward as his human shield popped open like a wet teabag.

Tuffy's ears rang and the smell of cordite tickled his nostrils. *Now the job was done.* But then, as the smoke cleared, again his joy turned to anger. St John's lifeless body was sprawled on top of the bloodied deejay's.

Multiple shots dug into the doorframe beside Tuffy and

the remainder of his men…

"*PUT YOU HAND INNA DE AIR, BWOY!*"

Two Jamaican ACID men trained their sights on him.

It was time to retreat and regroup with however many of his men had escaped. Tuffy shot one last look of hatred at the approaching lawmen.

"Me job done, star," he cried out. "De deejay bwoy dead an' unuh can do not'n 'bout it."

And at that he disappeared into the choking fumes.

Hard man fe dead.

Delroy pushed the dead body of Hugh St. John off him. Soaked in crimson, he crawled on his belly towards a wide-eyed Monique. He was aware of footsteps approaching them from behind, but he just didn't care anymore whether it was friend or foe. He had had enough.

"Get over here now," the voice boomed. "I want de medics here." The smoke-shrouded man was pointing agitatedly in Simba's direction. As he came closer, Delroy opened his eyes.

"You did well, me friend."

Simba stared into the sombre face of Andrew Humphries.

"Monique was right, you is one hell of a raas fighter."

Simba nodded.

Whoever this man is, he's on our side.

He struggled to keep his eyes from closing.

"Whe' de medic dem deh man?" Humphries shouted, leaving Delroy to take Monique in his arms. The Ranking was in a dream state, balancing on the brink of exhaustion as he tried to figure out where the men in green overalls were taking his woman. He couldn't have stopped them if he wanted to. He slumped down against the wall sucking in air. He felt so tired…

He fell from his seated position onto his shoulder and a spear of searing pain shot from his arm to what felt like his spine.

It was only then that he realised it was coming from a gaping bullet wound.

He blacked out.

EPILOGUE

Two week's later, Simba Ranking was seated before the award-winning radio deejay he had longed to meet ever since the heady days of Barry Gordon's Boogey Down Show on JBC.

The Ranking was still recovering from the traumatic events in north London.

The Saint was dead, he could now breath easy.

He owed Andrew Humphries his life.

Monique had been the one who had caused him the most concern but after she had been examined by the hospital doctors, and treated for shock, it was clear that both she and the baby were well.

As far as Simba was concerned that was all that mattered. His family was intact, after all they had gone through.

My family.

He had never been able to picture himself saying that.

But 'Jah know' it feel good.

Mr George would have been proud of him.

Ironically his career had rocketed ahead because of the threat the Saint had posed to his life. He had paid his price many times over and he had a gunshot wound to the shoulder and arm, with multiple lacerations and burns all over his body, to show for it.

His top ten single with Terence Wynn was in the British pop charts and the US R&B charts, and already arrangements were being made for a second collaboration.

He was a lucky man. He looked over at Hector, his bandaged head bobbing to Rodigan's expert mixing. He was just glad to be alive. And his 'baby' sat beside him; his hands constantly rubbed Monique's stomach.

Fate had thrown Simba Ranking into a position that he may not otherwise have reached with years of hard graft and sweat.

It did haffe go so.

And now, with his signing to Pony just around the corner, Roxanne and the management team had assured him that the name Simba Ranking would soon be on everyone's lips.

He sank back with a content smile on his face and looked around the cramped studio. He watched the flickering displays and the equipment that was sending out the wicked sounds of the deceased deejays of Pan Head, Early B, Dirts Man, Tenor Saw and the other dancehall dons who met their end in violent ways.

Once David had wrapped up the memorial section, he broke for adverts and keyed up the Ranking for his slot with a knowing nod.

Night time finds me…
Tuning in to Kiss FM…
With Rodigan on your radio

Freddy Macgregor's jingle introduced David's preamble into Simba's beginnings, with the radio deejay reeling off a detailed history of where Delroy first started as a deejay, the releases he had not known had spread overseas and his subsequent chilling out to promote Nubian Hi-Power dances and then his own…then to the present, and his ground-breaking collaboration with the soul star Terence Wynn.

The background music that was interspersing the preview of his life was his first ever release. Hearing it, the bad memory of Mikey Dread boiled to the surface again. It lasted only seconds.

Rodders continued.

"After about three years of silence two new singles have been released to rave reviews. One is *'In the Mood for Action'* and the other *'Love an' Gunshot'*. He's joined us here live on Kiss 100 FM. We were expecting him over three weeks ago then, unfortunately, he broke his arm — but he's with us now, sling and all. Simba Ranking welcome to London, and congratulations on your startling new singles."

"Glad to be here, Roddy," Simba replied. "Respect, boss."

"I must ask you—" Rodigan pursed his lips with a glint in his eyes, "—you just reappeared from nowhere after years of being in the wilderness…what happened and what caused this incredible move back to the top?"

Simba looked at his bredrin Hector and squeezed Monique's hand. Both men burst into laughter and tried to keep a straight face while Roddy was trying to figure out what they found so amusing.

"Rodigan…" the Ranking smiled broadly, "…dat is a long, long story star, you sure you want fe hear it?"

David nodded and smiled back.

Freedom!
I wanna be free from all chains and all bangles an' rope,
Free from all bars an' all borders an' dope,
Free to praise de lord because me nah praise de Pope,
So mind how yuh wash yuh face inna Babylon soap,
I was born to be free, cause me a ole gangalee, gangalee,
And who have eyes they will see
***Gangalee*, by Louie Culture**

END…for now

BESTSELLING FICTION

I wish to order the following X Press title(s)

❏ Single Black Female	Yvette Richards	£5.99
❏ When A Man Loves A Woman	Patrick Augustus	£5.99
❏ Wicked In Bed	Sheri Campbell	£5.99
❏ Rude Gal	Sheri Campbell	£5.99
❏ Yardie	Victor Headley	£4.99
❏ Excess	Victor Headley	£4.99
❏ Yush!	Victor Headley	£5.99
❏ Fetish	Victor Headley	£5.99
❏ Here Comes the Bride	Victor Headley	£5.99
❏ In Search of Satisfaction	J. California Cooper	£7.99
❏ Sistas On a Vibe	Ijeoma Inyama	£6.99
❏ Flex	Marcia Williams	£6.99
❏ Baby Mother	Andrea Taylor	£6.99
❏ Uptown Heads	R.K. Byers	£5.99
❏ Jamaica Inc.	Tony Sewell	£5.99
❏ Lick Shot	Peter Kalu	£5.99
❏ Professor X	Peter Kalu	£5.99
❏ Obeah	Colin Moone	£5.99
❏ Cop Killer	Donald Gorgon	£4.99
❏ The Harder They Come	Michael Thelwell	£7.99
❏ Baby Father	Patrick Augustus	£6.99
❏ Baby Father 2	Patrick Augustus	£6.99
❏ OPP	Naomi King	£6.99

I enclose a cheque/postal order (Made payable to 'The X Press') for

£ _____

(add 50p P&P per book for orders under £10. All other orders P&P free.)

NAME _____

ADDRESS _____

_____

Cut out or photocopy and send to:
X PRESS, 6 Hoxton Square, London N1 6NU
 Alternatively, call the X PRESS hotline: 0171 729 1199 and place your order.

X Press Black Classics

The masterpieces of black fiction writing await your discovery

❏ The Blacker the Berry   Wallace Thurman   £6.99
*'Born **too** black, Emma Lou suffers her own community's intra-racial venom.'*

❏ The Autobiography of an Ex-Colored Man   James Weldon Johnson   £5.99
'One of the most thought-provoking novels ever published.'

❏ The Conjure Man Dies   Rudolph Fisher   £5.99
'The world's FIRST black detective thriller!'

❏ The Walls of Jericho   Rudolph Fisher   £5.99
*'When a buppie moves into a white neighbourhood, all hell breaks loose. **Hilarious!**'*

❏ Joy and Pain   Rudolph Fisher   £6.99
'Jazz age Harlem stories by a master of black humour writing.'

❏ Iola   Frances E.W. Harper   £6.99
'A woman's long search for her mother from whom she was separated on the slave block.'

❏ The House Behind the Cedars   Charles W. Chesnutt   £5.99
'Can true love transcend racial barriers?'

❏ A Love Supreme   Pauline E. Hopkins   £5.99
'One of the greatest love stories ever told.'

❏ One Blood   Pauline E. Hopkins   £6.99
'Raiders of lost African treasures discover their roots and culture.'

❏ The President's Daughter   William Wells Brown   £5.99
'The true story of the daughter of the United States president, sold into slavery.'

❏ The Soul of a Woman   Zora Neale Hurston, etc   £6.99
'Stories by the great black women writers'

I enclose a cheque/postal order (Made payable to '*The X Press*') for

£ _____

(add 50p P&P per book for orders under £10. All other orders P&P free.)

NAME _____

ADDRESS _____

✂   **Cut out or photocopy and send to: X PRESS, 6 Hoxton Square, London N1 6NU**
Alternatively, call the X PRESS hotline: 0171 729 1199 and place your order.